Arthur Paul Harper

**Pioneer Work in the Alps of New Zealand**

A record of the first exploration of the chief glaciers and ranges of the Southern Alps

Arthur Paul Harper

**Pioneer Work in the Alps of New Zealand**
*A record of the first exploration of the chief glaciers and ranges of the Southern Alps*

ISBN/EAN: 9783743414563

Manufactured in Europe, USA, Canada, Australia, Japa

Cover: Foto ©ninafisch / pixelio.de

Manufactured and distributed by brebook publishing software (www.brebook.com)

Arthur Paul Harper

**Pioneer Work in the Alps of New Zealand**

# PIONEER WORK IN THE ALPS OF NEW ZEALAND

# PIONEER WORK IN THE ALPS OF NEW ZEALAND

A RECORD OF THE FIRST EXPLORATION OF THE CHIEF GLACIERS AND RANGES OF THE SOUTHERN ALPS

By Arthur P. Harper, B.A.

Member of the Alpine Club, Vice-President of the New Zealand Alpine Club

*With Maps and Illustrations*

London

T. FISHER UNWIN

PATERNOSTER SQUARE

MDCCCXCVI

" The works of the Lord are great,
   Sought out of all them that have pleasure therein."

𝔗𝔥𝔦𝔰 𝔅𝔬𝔬𝔨 𝔦𝔰 𝔇𝔢𝔡𝔦𝔠𝔞𝔱𝔢𝔡

TO

## MY MOTHER,

WHOSE INTEREST IN THE EXPLORATION OF THE SOUTHERN ALPS HAS ENCOURAGED ME THROUGH MANY HARDSHIPS,

AND TO

## MY FATHER,

WHOSE EXAMPLE IN EARLY EXPLORATION I HAVE ENDEAVOURED TO FOLLOW.

# PREFACE.

In the years 1889, 1890, 1891, 1892, I made holiday expeditions to the Tasman District of the Southern Alps, and in 1893, 1894, 1895 was employed by the New Zealand Government to explore the valleys and glaciers of the West Coast of the South Island. I do not pretend to have made many high ascents, but base my claim to be considered an authority on the Alps of New Zealand on the fact that I have shared in the first exploration of nearly every glacier in the central position of these mountains. It is not right, in my opinion, for one who has special knowledge on a subject of general interest to keep that knowledge to himself; and for this reason—as well as with the object of recording our work, and helping others by our experiences—I have ventured to write the following pages.

The work of map-making and topographical exploration is sometimes undervalued, and a man's capabilities and exploits too often estimated by the number of high ascents made and new routes discovered by him, without considering the usefulness of the results. It is impossible to map the country without a vast deal of hard, and more or less monotonous work, and those who, in after years, make use of the maps are apt to forget this. We too frequently find climbers ignoring those who have preceded them, and whose work has materially helped them; some even attempt to add to their own exploits by omitting to acknowledge their predecessor's work. This is especially the case in the opening up of a country that is little known, and it is therefore right that a record of the first explorations should be made. I have, in the following pages, recorded all the pioneer work which has materially contributed to the present topographical knowledge of the central portion of the Southern Alps.

Not having studied any of the standard books on glacier science, my theories and conclusions are the results of the observations of several years, and I may have dwelt unnecessarily on points which are well known to those who are authorities on the subject.

Of adventures we had, of course, enough to satisfy any ordinary human beings, but they were so bound up with the work that we were apt to take them as a matter of course. I have, however, in recording our progress, described a sufficient number to convey an idea of the conditions under which the work had to be carried out. If the life was rough, I fear my account of it is rougher, but hope that the facts here set down may be none the less interesting because they appear in somewhat crude language.

Should any fellow member of the Alpine Club decide to come and climb our peaks, I shall be only too glad to give him all the information in my power, and trust that he will take this offer seriously, and write to me should he need advice.

The Map published in this volume has already appeared—excepting a few additional details which I have since added—in Mr. E. A. Fitzgerald's publication.

Before leaving the Survey Office in Hokitika, I helped the draughtsman to record the results of Mr. Douglas's and my work on the map at Mr. Fitzgerald's request, in order that the tracing which was sent to him might be "up-to-date." For, though the last of the unexplored country had been mapped by us before his arrival in New Zealand, it had not been transferred to the Standard Map.

ARTHUR P. HARPER.

*January,* 1896.

---

It is considered desirable to state that the letter announcing the transmission of the manuscript of Mr. Harper's book is dated "Christ Church, New Zealand, March 18, 1896." The manuscript was received in England on May 18th.

T. FISHER UNWIN.

# CONTENTS.

### CHAPTER I.

PAGE

Introductory Remarks on the Southern Alps and Climbing in New Zealand . . . . . . . . . . . 1—10

### CHAPTER II.
#### TASMAN DISTRICT.

Mount Cook—First Exploration of Murchison Glacier—First Ascent of Harper's Saddle—Other Climbs—Necessary Conditions . . 11—28

### CHAPTER III.
#### WESTLAND.

The West Coast of New Zealand—The Forest and its Plants—Birds . 29—44

### CHAPTER IV.
#### WAIHO RIVER—FRANZ JOSEF GLACIER.

Journey Southwards—Waiho River—Lake Maporika—Terminal Face—Camp I.—Attempts on Glacier—Hot Springs—Camp II.—Camp III.—Ice-fall—Baffled—Return . . . . . 45—63

CONTENTS.

## CHAPTER V.

### WAIHO RIVER—THE HIGH COUNTRY.

PAGE

Track Cutting—Dry Camp (No. V.)—Wekas—Another Failure—Maporika—Mount Moltke Spur—Camp VI.—Camp VII.—Gale and Shipwreck—Return—Callery River—Heavy Flood—Marching Orders . . . . . . . . . . . 64—79

## CHAPTER VI.

### COOK RIVER—BALFOUR GLACIER.

Old Moraines—Beach Travelling and Digging—Gillespies—Ryan's Range—Balfour Glacier—A Race with the Clouds—"Topsy" . 80—97

## CHAPTER VII.

### COOK RIVER—FOX GLACIER.

Slight Mishap—Douglas—The Chancellor Ridge—Victoria Glacier—Keas—Fogged again . . . . . . . . . 98—112

## CHAPTER VIII.

### FOX GLACIER (*continued*).

Return to Camp—Unpleasant Surprise—Result—Wekas—Back to Ryan's—Remarks on the Glacier. . . . . . . 113—125

## CHAPTER IX.

### COOK RIVER—MAIN BRANCH.

Rough Work—Large Boulders—Castle Rock—Rata Trees—Shelf Camp—Bad Weather—Short Commons—Cave Camp . . . 126—140

## CHAPTER X.

### COOK RIVER (*concluded*) AND ANCIENT GLACIERS.

Snow-storm—Tony's Rock—Head of the River—Return Journey—Check-Shirt Bird—Back to Civilisation—Topography—Ancient Glaciers . . . . . . . . . . . 141—158

## CHAPTER XI.

### THE FRANZ JOSEF GLACIER.

Second Visit—Winter Snow—Successful Ascent to *Névé*—Ice Formation—Moraine Formation—Old Moraines and Glaciers—Advance and Retreat . . . . . . . . . . . 159—177

## CHAPTER XII.

### KARANGARUA RIVER.

With Douglas again—Topography—"Futtah" Camp—Floods—Cassell's Flat—Bark Camp—Twain Gorge—Alone—Regina Creek 178—196

## CHAPTER XIII.

### KARANGARUA RIVER (*continued*).

Bad Weather—Twain Gorge—A Maori arrives—Douglas Returns—Karangarua Gorge—Lame Duck Camp—Douglas again Ill—Head of the River—A Lonely Christmas . . . . . 197—213

## CHAPTER XIV.

### LANDSBOROUGH RIVER.

Into Landsborough Valley—New Year's Day—No Birds—Starvation Rations—A Forced March—Haast Pass Track—Return up River—Brodrick's Pass—Back at Christmas Flat . . . . 214—233

## CHAPTER XV.

### TWAIN RIVER (KARANGARUA).

Douglas Pass—Head Basin of Twain River—Douglas Glacier—Camp—Horace Walker Glacier—Moraines—Lower Valley—Hasty Retreat—Bivouac—A Night with the "Taipo"—Return to Habitation . . . . . . . . . . . 234—251

## CHAPTER XVI.

### KARANGARUA DISTRICT.

Pleasures of Habitation—My New Companion—A Climb on Scott's Hill—General Features of the Country—Ancient Glaciers—Roto te Koeti—Alpine Vegetation—Insect Life at High Altitudes . 252—269

## CHAPTER XVII.

### A PASS TO THE HERMITAGE.

Instructions to go to Hermitage—Forestalled—Meet Fitzgerald and Zurbriggen—Saltwater Creek—Pass to Tasman Glacier—A Memorable Meeting at the Hermitage—Solitary Journey back to Copland River—West Coast Work discussed — Complete the Exploration of Copland River . . . . . . . 270—285

## CHAPTER XVIII.

### COPLAND RIVER AND GENERAL WORK.

Welcome Flats—Douglas River—Ruareka—Stranchon Glacier—Decrease of Native Birds—First Ascent of Ryan's Peak—Return to Hokitika—Conditions of our Work—Topographical Knowledge . 286—300

## CHAPTER XIX.

### GLACIER OBSERVATION.

The Number and Area of the Chief Glaciers—Relations of Névé to Trunk—Are the Glaciers Advancing or Retreating?—Rates of Motion—The Tasman Compared with the Franz Josef—The Future of the Southern Alps . . . . . . . 301—316

## APPENDIX.

|  | PAGE |
|---|---|
| Note I.—Meteorological Conditions of the Southern Alps | 317 |
| ,, II.—Altitudes | 319 |
| ,, III.—Black Swans | 321 |
| ,, IV.—Mount Egmont | 322 |
| ,, V.—Fitzgerald's Pass and C. E. Douglas | 324 |
| ,, VI.—Early Explorations | 327 |
| ,, VII.—Measurement Cairns and Photographs for Reference | 328 |
| INDEX | 333 |

# LIST OF ILLUSTRATIONS.

| | | |
|---|---|---|
| The Franz Josef Glacier from Camp VI. | *Frontispiece* | |
| Overlooking Murchison Glacier from Malte Brun Range | To face page | 21 |
| Mount Tasman from Malte Brun Range | ,, | 26 |
| Mounts Haidinger and De la Bêche from the Tasman Glacier | ,, | 28 |
| Batwing Camp | ,, | 51 |
| Terminal Face, Franz Josef Glacier, from Camp I. | ,, | 52 |
| View from Camp II., Franz Josef Glacier | ,, | 57 |
| The Unser Fritz Fall, 1,209 Feet, from Camp III. | ,, | 61 |
| Franz Josef Glacier from Spur of Mount Moltke | ,, | 75 |
| Mouth of Cook River and South Bluff | ,, | 81 |
| From Ryan's Spur overlooking Cook River | ,, | 85 |
| A Bivouac on Craig's Spur | ,, | 87 |
| Overlooking the Balfour Glacier from Craig's Spur | ,, | 88 |
| Fox Glacier from the Cone Rock | ,, | 101 |
| Looking down Fox Glacier from One Mile up | ,, | 104 |
| View from Cook River Flats | ,, | 126 |
| Rough Ice, Head of Franz Josef Ice-Fall (Winter) | ,, | 162 |
| Surface Ice of Franz Josef Glacier | ,, | 167 |
| Overlooking Cassell's Flat from near Mount McDonald | ,, | 180 |
| C. E. Douglas—A. P. Harper—Betsy | ,, | 183 |
| Mount McGloin and Gordon Falls from Cassell's Flat | ,, | 188 |

## LIST OF ILLUSTRATIONS.

| | |
|---|---|
| Mount McGloin from Regina Creek . . . . *To face page* | 192 |
| Gorge above Cataracts, Karangarua River . . . ,, | 198 |
| Looking up Karangarua River from Rat-Trap Camp ,, | 199 |
| Dovetail Gorge . . . . . . . . ,, | 203 |
| "Old Man" Falls, 250 Feet, Karangarua River . . ,, | 206 |
| A Lonely Christmas . . . . . . ,, | 208 |
| The Head of the Landsborough River . . . ,, | 212 |
| Looking for "Tucker" . . . . . . ,, | 218 |
| Mount Sefton—Thompson and Fitzgerald Glacier from Douglas Pass . . . . . . . ,, | 235 |
| Mount Sefton and Névé of Douglas Glacier from the Trunk . . . . . . . . ,, | 248 |
| A Welcome Clip . . . . . . . ,, | 253 |
| Small Ice Fall on Fox Glacier . . . . ,, | 274 |
| Near the Forks of the Copland River . . . ,, | 283 |
| Reduced to a Petticoat ! . . . . . ,, | 285 |
| The Douglas River and the Footstool . . . ,, | 286 |
| Mount Sefton from Marchant Glacier . . . ,, | 289 |
| "The Spike," Ryan's Spur . . . . . ,, | 292 |
| Ryan's Peak from the Lower Peak . . . ,, | 293 |
| From Ryan's Peak looking N.E. . . . . ,, | 295 |

MAP. *To face page* 1.

# PIONEER WORK

IN THE

# ALPS OF NEW ZEALAND.

## CHAPTER I.

INTRODUCTORY REMARKS ON THE SOUTHERN ALPS AND CLIMBING IN NEW ZEALAND.

THE main features of the mountain system of the South Island of New Zealand are tolerably well known, and need only be generally referred to here. Beginning at the north end of the South Island, we find, in Nelson and Marlborough Provinces, numerous ranges spreading from coast to coast and reaching in some instances an altitude of 9,000 ft. Amongst these hills very little flat land is to be found, though there is a vast area of low undulating grass and forest country well fitted for pastoral purposes. Though no glaciers exist in this part of the island, there are many grand peaks on which snow is found during most of the year, while the lower spurs are often clothed with luxuriant forest, of which a considerable area has been "cleared" and opened up for settlement. Further south these ranges draw together till, in the Southern Alps, they form a great mountain wall running from N.E. to S.W., which sends off a number of spurs rising into bold ice-clad peaks, and for upwards of one hundred miles presents a snowy barrier between the West and East Coast districts. To the eastward the Southern Alps send out great buttresses or offshoots, terminating suddenly in the broad Canterbury and Mackenzie Plains, which form, by their absolute flatness and vast extent, a striking contrast to the peaks behind; to the westward they slope rapidly, and in many cases fall in sheer precipices for some thousands of feet to the coast, leaving about ten miles of comparatively level country between them and the sea, until the Sounds of Otago are reached. Here, in the province of Otago, the chain spreads out again from coast to coast in lower hills, amongst which are flourishing farms and sheep stations on the eastern side of the island, while on the western side the mountains rise abruptly out of the sea to a great height. Amongst the Otago hills lie the beautiful lakes of Wakitipu, Te Anau, Wanaka, &c., which are backed by Mounts Aspiring, Earnslaw, and other fine Alpine peaks, reaching in some instances over 9,000 ft.

As the subject matter of this book is confined to the central portion of the Southern Alps, amongst the larger glaciers and highest peaks, a short description of the general topography of the mountains to the north and south of that district will be sufficient.

Between Christchurch on the east coast and Hokitika on the west coast a coach road, unsurpassed by any I have seen elsewhere, runs over Arthur's Pass at an altitude of a little over 3,000 ft. A railway presenting some formidable engineering difficulties, is now in course of construction by this route. For some distance south of Arthur's Pass the Southern Alps only rise above the snow line in the peaks, there being many passes free from snow in the summer. Many fine glaciers exist, however, at the head of the Waimakariri River, which rises near the pass and flows eastwards.

South of this river is the Rakaia, which takes its rise from glaciers on the main range and those of Mount Arrowsmith and the surrounding peaks, the chief sources being the Ramsay and Lyall glaciers, both of considerable size; the latter at present is practically unexplored. The peaks in this locality are very fine, the chief one, Mount Arrowsmith, 9,171 ft., being an offshoot of the main range and forming a splendid group of rock peaks. Comparatively little beyond general information is known of this locality from an Alpine point of view. Only one or two parties have been there for short visits,* but it is easily accessible, as there are sheep-stations and homesteads within easy reach of the chief points of interest. Alpine passes ought to be found over the Dividing Range without difficulty at this point, and no doubt before long we shall have more accurate and detailed knowledge of what ought to prove a very interesting district. The only record of a trans-Alpine pass in this district is that made by Mr. G. J. Roberts and his survey party in the seventies, when he ascended a branch of the Wanganui River on the west coast and reached the watershed. Afterwards the same party, having come round by coach to Canterbury, carried their triangulation up the Rakaia River, and joined the West and East Coast Surveys, ascending to the same point on the Divide, thus proving a pass practicable.

South of the Rakaia, the Rangitata River flows from two or three glaciers of more or less second-rate importance, as com-

* "New Zealand Alpine Journal," vol. i., p. 112.

pared with other Alpine districts.* Here again we find some fine peaks lying on spurs of the main range. The highest peak in this district is Mount Tyndall, on the "Divide" itself, but practically unknown, as, indeed, is the whole of this district above the snow-line.

The next and last river flowing to the east coast which need be mentioned is the Waitaki River, one of the largest in the South Island. Its two main branches take their rise from the chief glaciers on the eastern slopes of the main range. The northern branch comes from the Classen and Godley glaciers, under the name of the Godley River, flowing into Lake Tekapo, and leaves it as the Tekapo River, till it unites with the Pukaki River. The main or central branch comes from the four great glaciers, the Murchison, Tasman, Hooker, and Mueller, and flows for thirty miles under the name of Tasman River into Lake Pukaki, and thence continues as the Pukaki River until it is joined by the Tekapo River, the two forming, with other more southerly tributaries, the great Waitaki River.

My personal explorations on the eastern slopes of the Southern Alps have been confined to the head waters and glaciers of the central branch of this river, and I shall give more detailed information of that district in a later chapter.

The western slopes and offshoots of the main range are very precipitous, and the rivers, though of considerable size, are comparatively short, and, descending very rapidly, have cut deep impassable gorges through the mountains. Unlike the eastern slopes which are nearly all open, tussocky, grass-covered country, the west coast ranges are covered with dense forest to a height of 3,500 ft. to 4,000 ft.

* "New Zealand Alpine Journal," vol. i., p. 22.

Beginning at Arthur's Pass on the western side, the first river south is the Hokitika, which takes its rise from small glaciers on the dividing range, and corresponds to the Rakaia and Waimakariri on the east. Some thirty miles further south is the Wanganui River, which drains a large part of the main range and has four or five large branches, at the head of which are glaciers of second-rate size. This river has never been explored, except the one branch up which Mr. Roberts went in the seventies, and I believe that it heads the southern tributaries of the Rakaia River and part of the Rangitata. About twenty miles further down the coast is the Wataroa, another large river, draining the main range at the head of the Rangitata, Godley, and Murchison glaciers. It also has many large branches in the mountains, up which, no doubt, there are considerable snow-fields and some fair-sized glaciers, but except the tributary coming from the Sealy Pass at the head of the Godley Glacier, it may be said to be *terra incognita*. Some fifteen miles below the Wataroa is the Waiho, which takes its rise from some magnificent glaciers, namely, the Burton, Spencer, and Franz Josef, from the head of which saddles lead into the upper portion of the Tasman glacier.

Still travelling south along the beach we come to Cook River, some twenty miles below the Waiho. This river has three branches, and draws its supplies from the Fox, the Balfour, and La Perouse glaciers, all of first-class importance. Though these streams flow into the sea some distance apart, they are all closely connected in the ranges, separated only by narrow ridges, over which passes could easily be made. Below Cook River the Karangarua flows into the sea at a distance of some six miles. It also takes its rise from large glaciers, and has three branches—the Copland River, from the Strauchon and Marchant glaciers, the Twain River, from the Horace Walker, Douglas, and Fitz-Gerald glaciers, and the main branch from no particular ice-field, but draining the northern end of the Hooker range. These last three rivers—the Waiho, Cook, and Karangarua—draw their supplies from the highest and most important part of the Southern Alps, and correspond with the Tasman River on the eastern side.

At the head of the Karangarua a saddle leads into the Landsborough River, which takes its rise from four or five first-class glaciers, and flows southwards along the foot of the main range for 40 miles. On its right bank the Hooker range—a large and important offshoot of the main range—prevents it from finding a direct course to the sea. After flowing for 40 miles between these two mountain chains, the river takes a sweep round to the west and finds its way to the Tasman ocean at a point 65 miles from the McKerrow Glacier at its head. It is joined at the bend, 40 miles below the McKerrow Glacier, by the Haast, a small, unimportant stream, coming from the pass of that name, and for some unexplained reason giving its name to the main river from the junction to the sea.

From the Rakaia River to a point twenty miles down the Landsborough valley, the main chain practically rises above the snow-line the whole way, sending off long spurs or ranges on the east, and more precipitous ones on the west. The peaks themselves gradually become higher, till in Mount Tasman, 11,475 ft., the Divide reaches its highest point; Mount Cook, 12,349 ft., being an offshoot of the main range, and sending down all its drainage eastwards into the Waitaki.

South of Mount Tasman the peaks gradually become lower, and the range assumes a rocky saw-tooth form, sending up high rock-peaks with low saddles between them which, as the Haast Pass is approached, are uncovered by snow in the summer. The Haast Pass itself is the best trans-insular route, being only 1,800 ft. above sea-level. Below this pass there are again fine mountain groups rising to nearly 10,000 ft., containing many magnificent ice-clad summits and glaciers of no small size. The principal of these are Aspiring, Lydia, Robinson, Earnslaw, The Ark, Castor and Pollux, &c., all untouched from an Alpine point of view, with the exception of Earnslaw, a fairly easy peak, from all accounts, near Lake Wakatipu.

A few miles south of Mount Sefton, which lies at the head of the Twain River, the Hooker range branches off from the main Divide and continues some forty or fifty miles south. This range is higher and carries far more perpetual snow and ice on it than the Dividing range which runs parallel with it. For though the latter has many peaks rising to a considerable altitude, which would be covered with perpetual snow if situated a little north or south of their position, yet it is a noteworthy fact that here they are almost devoid of ice. The only reason I can give for this state of things is that the Hooker range, being higher, cuts off the moist sea winds from the main range, thus causing a smaller annual snow-fall.

The principal glaciers and ice-clad peaks of the Southern Alps lie between lat. 43° and 45° S., and in spite of the fact that this is nearer the Equator than the Alps in Switzerland, the snow-line is much lower here than in Europe, and our glaciers descend to lower altitudes. Taken as a whole, I consider that the perpetual snow-line in these mountains lies between 6,000 and 6,500 ft., or nearly 3,000 ft. lower than in Switzerland. I have seen one or two peaks off the main Divide which have snow on them all the summer from 5,000 ft. upwards, but these are exceptions caused by their shape and position. The glaciers descend to an extraordinarily low level. On the eastern side the terminal face of the Tasman is only 2,354 ft. above the sea, and the Mueller and Hooker, 2,500 and 2,882 ft. respectively. On the western side this peculiarity is still more marked. The Franz Josef Glacier, on the Waiho River, has its terminal face in lat. S. 43° 25′ 30″, and though it is within fourteen miles of the sea, it lies only 692 ft. above sea level. The Fox glacier, a few miles further south, descends to within ten miles of the beach and to 670 ft. of sea-level; the Balfour Glacier, at the head of the central branch of Cook River, has its terminal face at an altitude of 2,300 ft.

These facts at first sight appear to be extraordinary, but I think they may be accounted for by the peculiar climatic conditions prevailing in New Zealand. The northerly and westerly winds which so frequently come over the Tasman Sea carry an immense amount of moisture, and within a few miles of the coast they meet with the great wall of the Southern Alps; the consequence is a very heavy rainfall, in some parts of the ranges amounting probably to 140 ins. in the year. Even at Hokitika on the sea-beach the fall reaches 126 ins., and it is far heavier in the mountains. This great rainfall, combined with the height of the mountain wall which the wind meets, and which forces the moisture to a great altitude, no doubt produces a correspondingly heavy snow-fall and consequently low snow-line.

## INTRODUCTORY REMARKS.

When the map* of the Fox and Franz Josef glaciers is examined, it is not difficult to account for the low altitude to which these two glaciers descend. They have immense *névé* basins and only a narrow outlet for the iceflow, which being forced out in considerable bulk down narrow and steep valleys, descends to a far lower altitude than those of the eastern side. The Franz Josef, for instance, descends over 8,000 ft. in $8\frac{1}{2}$ miles, a fall of more than 941 ft. a mile on an average, and from the lower *névé* to the terminal face the fall is still greater.

For scientific men there are several most interesting problems to solve, and a great deal remains to be done by geologists, botanists and others. Up to the present only those who do not mind roughing it considerably have gone far afield. It is true that the main glaciers on the eastern side have been thoroughly explored, and parties have for some years made annual expeditions to the Tasman district, climbing a few peaks and making a pass here and there. But even on the eastern side of the Southern Alps, especially north and south of the Tasman district, there is an immense amount of work to be done by Alpine climbers. The details and general topography, however, of the eastern slopes of the central district are well known. On the western side it is only during the last three years that the ranges in this locality have been explored and mapped, so far as minor detail and topography are concerned. The higher peaks, however, have for some years past been trigonometrically fixed by the Survey Department from the West Coast low country, and it has fallen to the lot of Mr. C. E. Douglas and myself to be the first to push up the rivers and glaciers and determine the details of the topography.

* See Appendix, Note I.

Those districts lying at the head of the Wataroa and Wanganui Rivers on the west, and Rakaia and Rangitata on the east, have practically been left alone by Alpine men, and, as already stated, the first two rivers named are almost wholly unknown in their upper valleys. In the south there is work for years above the snow-line on the virgin peaks of the Aspiring group and also of the Hooker range, and unless more parties take up this most fascinating of all sports, the completion of the work must be left to the next generation.

All the larger glaciers, except those up the Rakaia River, have now been mapped and explored—I know from personal experience every one of importance in the central portion of the Southern Alps, with the exception of the Spencer up the Callery River—but many points of the greatest interest have still to be settled concerning their movement, advance or retreat, and also respecting the positions and effect of the large ancient glaciers on the formation of the ranges and valleys.

## CHAPTER II.

### TASMAN DISTRICT.

Mount Cook—First Exploration of Murchison Glacier—First Ascent of Harper's Saddle—Other Climbs—Necessary Conditions.

THE only locality in the Southern Alps which has been in any way opened up for tourists is the Tasman or Mount Cook district, which includes the four large glaciers at the head of the Tasman River and nearly all the finest peaks in the Alps. The leading features of this district have already been so ably and thoroughly described by the Rev. W. S. Green, Dr. Von Lendenfeldt, and Mr. G. E. Mannering,* that I shall not dwell on the description of the scenery, but shall only give a short record of my own and others' work here, which has materially added to our topographical knowledge of the district since Von Lendenfeldt made his exploration of the Tasman Glacier.

The chief point of interest is Mount Cook, 12,349 ft. For some years past an attempt has been made amongst those who climb in New Zealand to change the name of this peak to "Aorangi," a Maori word. Some of those who write articles on their climbs are fond of saying "Mount Cook, or, to be correct, Aorangi," or some such expression, inferring that

* "The High Alps of New Zealand," by the Rev. W. S. Green (Macmillan); "Der Tasman Gletscher und seine Umgeberg," by Von Lendenfeldt; "With Axe and Rope in the N. Z. Alps," by G. E. Mannering (Longmans).

"Mount Cook" is not the correct name. I have always objected to the innovation, and have made inquiries in all directions, but can find no proof whatever that "Aorangi" was applied to the peak, or that it ever had a distinctive name amongst the Maoris.

So far as I could learn from the Maoris of the West Coast, who could see Mount Cook and the other great peaks towering up within twenty miles, they had no name for any peak or range except those lower hills on which they ventured. Again, the Maoris had a wholesome and deeply-rooted fear of the mountains, none of the old West Coast natives ever went far from the low country, so it can hardly have been necessary for them to have individual names for the great snowy range. On the East Coast the Maoris could have had little knowledge of this district, as it is so far inland, and most of the South Island natives lived near the sea-beach, from which Mount Cook is only in one or two places visible, and can only be distinguished by persons well acquainted with the peak. It therefore appears that if any Maori name existed it would be known amongst the West Coast natives, who could see Mount Cook every clear day within twenty miles of the sea at the mouth of Cook (or Weheka) River, while those natives who lived on the Grey River, and those settled at Jackson's Bay in the far south, would be able to see it from nearly every part of the sea-coast, standing out in the most unmistakable manner.

In 1865 I had a Maori (of whom more will be said) with me for two months, and a very good, intelligent fellow he was. I asked him one day, "What does 'Aorangi' mean, Bill?" to which he answered—

"It mean de big, white cloud."

I said, "I suppose that is why you call Mount Cook Aorangi?"

"Oh, no; Aorangi not mountain, Aorangi a big, white cloud, here—there—" said Bill, pointing out sundry large, fleecy clouds.

I then pressed him more on the point, and told him he knew nothing about it, and that Aorangi was the name they had for Mount Cook. But he waxed quite indignant, saying—

"De Maori, he no name de mountains, only where he go, de white man he name 'em."

I afterwards made inquiries from other Maoris, and always had the same reply, that they had no name for the high mountains. It is not a matter of much importance, but it will be a pity to have the older name of Mount Cook superseded by a Maori word which has only been applied to the peak during the present generation. The name "Aorangi" is no doubt a good one, and if it is considered advisable there is no reason why it should not be adopted officially; but it is wrong to state that it is the proper name for the peak.

Mount Cook is not on the main range, but lies on a ridge which branches off in a southerly direction from a point a little south of Mount Tasman (11,475 ft.).* This offshoot is about twelve miles long, and includes some lower peaks of 6,000 and 7,000 ft., besides the three peaks of Mount Cook itself. On the western side, between it and the main chain, which here, after bending away to the west, turns again and runs parallel to Mount Cook for a short distance, the Hooker Glacier lies, and on the eastern side the great Tasman

* See Appendix, Note II.

Glacier passes along the foot, receiving supplies from the peak. The Hooker Glacier gives rise to a river of the same name which runs in a south-eastern direction along the foot of the Mount Cook spur to join the Tasman River some four or five miles below. A mile from the outflow of the glacier, the Hooker stream passes, sometimes along, and sometimes under, the terminal face of the Mueller Glacier, which winds in a northerly direction under Mount Sefton and the other peaks of the main range. Near the terminal face of the latter glacier, the Hermitage Hotel was built in 1885, and from it parties of climbers are able to make a comfortable start on numerous expeditions.

To the north of Mount Tasman the main range continues in a north-easterly direction to Mount Elie de Beaumont (10,200 ft.), a distance of eleven or twelve miles, after which it takes an abrupt turn to the east, to the Hochstetter Dome (9,258 ft.), and thence, again, it gradually assumes a north-easterly direction past the Godley district to the head of the Rangitata, and so on. From a point a little east of the last-named peak, the magnificent Malte Brun Range of rocky peaks branches off to the south, running nearly parallel to the main range and Mount Cook, and with them enclosing the great Tasman Glacier, which takes its rise from the peaks of Elie de Beaumont and Hochstetter Dome. Still further eastwards another and longer divergent ridge—the Liebig Range—branches from the main chain, running for a few miles in a due easterly direction, and then, sweeping sharply round, continues for twenty miles or more in a south-westerly direction.

Between this range and the Malte Brun, the Murchison

Glacier flows, having a saddle at its head leading into the Tasman Glacier north of Mount Darwin (9,715 ft.), another saddle over the main range into the Whymper Glacier on the West Coast, and a third, in near proximity, over the Liebig Range to the Classen Glacier, which lies at the head of the Godley River. The Murchison Glacier is the third in size of the New Zealand icefields, and draws supplies chiefly from the Malte Brun Range. Between the latter range and the main range, the Tasman Glacier, eighteen miles in length, flows, receiving several large tributaries from the peaks of the Divide and Mount Cook. About six miles from the terminal face of the Tasman Glacier, at the inflow of the Ball Glacier, the Government in 1891 built an iron hut, and formed a few tracks for the use of climbers, and from that date mountaineering may be said to have assumed a civilised form, for previously a start had to be made from the Hermitage Hotel, and camping necessaries had to be carried on our own shoulders over trackless moraines. Since the building of the hut I have only been for two expeditions in this district, and rough as the present arrangements are, as compared with Switzerland, they are luxurious when contrasted with our experience before 1891. Even now in the Tasman, our best known district, any expedition entails, for one not accustomed to it, a large amount of very hard work. We have no guides, and porters are difficult, or almost impossible to get. The few men who have gone in for systematic work have had to learn the art of mountaineering without help, and necessarily at considerable risk. Consequently we can boast of three or four climbers who are almost first-class men, never having climbed with guides, and yet able to top some of our finest peaks.

Alpine workers, especially in a new country like New Zealand, may be divided broadly into two classes—exploring climbers, and climbers who wish only to top peaks. Of course many do a little of both. But one class makes exploration its hobby, while the other cares for climbing only, and is not particular about the topography or geography of the country, often adding very little to our knowledge of the mountains. Of the two classes I think the explorer does the most useful work. True, he gets little credit for the hardships endured, because, after many weeks of hard work, he can often only prove which routes to avoid, and some one learning this important point, appears on the scene with all his predecessor's knowledge, thus saving days of reconnoitring, and completes the climb or exploration. On his return we hear the first man mentioned only as having failed at a certain place, or having made such and such mistakes, there being no acknowledgment of the benefit derived from those mistakes, or of the time saved by making use of his experiences. In another way, too, the first man has to take a second place. He may, in the course of his exploration, bring information as to a likely pass; the other makes the said pass and writes a glowing account of "First pass by So-and-so," with no mention of the fact that Mr. Explorer gave him the whole facts as to the route. The result is that many who are better men with their pens than their axes gain great *kudos*, while the really hard worker, who has borne the brunt of the battle, is unknown except to a few, and has the misfortune of seeing the results of his work not only ignored, but, to a great extent, appropriated by someone else.

In January, 1890, Mr. G. E. Mannering and I made an

expedition to this district, originally with the intention of trying Mount Cook. We formed our main camp on the site of Green's "fifth camp," which was close to the point at which the Ball Glacier joins the Tasman, some six miles above the Terminal face. The above-mentioned hut now stands on this site, and has a horse track to it. But in 1890 no sort of track existed, and we had to carry our heavy loads of from 30 to 50 lbs. to the camp. The route, after reaching the terminal of the Tasman Glacier, had to be taken along the bottom of the V-shaped valley, formed on the left by the hillside, and on the right by the huge lateral moraine of the glacier.

In places this valley is broken or half filled up by large shingle fans from the hill, and between these the bottom is filled with large boulders of 10 ft. or so in diameter, which have fallen from the moraine or the hillside. Consequently our progress was painfully slow, for we were always more or less in bad training at the commencement of our trip. I remember that I used to think at the time that there could not possibly be any worse ground to travel over, but my last two seasons' work, on the West Coast rivers and glaciers, have caused me to modify those ideals considerably. Yet from my knowledge of Switzerland I can say without doubt that this district presents far greater difficulties on low ground than the former would present, even before it had reached its present state of good tracks and huts. But as compared with some of the West Coast valleys, it is easy country to travel over.

From our main camp we established a bivouac on the Hochstetter spur, near the one used by Mr. Green in 1882,* and from there intended to establish another on the lower snows of the Linda Glacier, which flows down from the northern slopes of Cook, between it and Mount Tasman. The weather looked threatening, and I did not at all care to risk so high a sleeping place, but after some discussion we went on and reached the Glacier Dome, a rounded peak, over which the route lay to the great Ice Plateau. While climbing the last rocks and pulling our loads up after us, one of the straps broke, and the "swag" made a rapid descent for some 700 ft. into a *bergschrund*. This put an end to the plan of sleeping out on the Linda Glacier; therefore, after reaching the great Ice Plateau we made a return to the lower bivouac at 6,500 ft. The delay caused by the recovery of our lost load proved beneficial, for a howling north-west gale sprang up that night and made us most uncomfortable, but would have been almost fatal had it caught us at our proposed bivouac on the Linda Glacier some 3,000 ft. higher. At daylight next morning the gale was so bad that we continued the descent and retired to our main camp, having been so far successful that we could boast of being the first New Zealanders to reach the Snow Plateau and Glacier Dome.

I had done a few climbs in Switzerland in 1887 and 1888, and had, therefore, some slight idea of the work of mountaineering, and was convinced that we had not yet had sufficient practice or experience to attempt such a difficult peak as Mount Cook. Consequently Mannering, much against his wish, decided not to try the mountain again that year, unless

* "The High Alps of New Zealand." By the Rev. W. S. Green. Macmillan & Co.

we could make up a stronger party. This attempt was the only one I ever made on Mount Cook, but Mannering, with Mr. H. Dixon, again tried it the next season,* and nearly succeeded in conquering it, by the same route as that taken by Mr. Green in 1882.

Instead of returning to the Hermitage by the usual route, we made the first pass over the Cook Range, *via* a saddle at the head of the Ball Glacier, 7,426 ft. above sea-level. It was an easy day's climb, and led us into the Hooker Glacier, about $5\frac{1}{2}$ miles above the Hermitage, and has since become quite a favourite expedition for tourists, giving, as it does, good snow and ice work combined with glorious views of the four great glaciers and the chief peaks surrounding them.

Having replenished our supplies, and being joined by Mr. H. M. Hamilton, a tourist whom we met at the hotel, we returned on the 9th January to our main camp. It was decided to give up the idea of climbing Cook, and to spend the remainder of our holiday in exploring the Murchison valley, which joins the Tasman valley just opposite our camp across the glacier. Though the terminal face of the Murchison Glacier had been seen four miles distant from the lower portion of the Tasman Glacier, it had been up to that date entirely unexplored, and was supposed to take its rise from the southern slopes of Mount Darwin. We had no reason to suppose that this was not the case, but wished to make a personal exploration of the valley. Our plan was to proceed up the Murchison to the head, and cross the Malte Brun Range, between Mount Malte Brun (10,421 ft.) and Mount Darwin (9,715 ft.), by the saddle which

* "With Axe and Rope in the New Zealand Alps." By G. E. Mannering. Longmans.

was supposed to be the head of the glacier, and return down the Tasman to our camp. We expected to be able to do this in one day, but on second thoughts decided to take a blanket and a day's provisions.

Starting on January 10th at 9 A.M. with light loads of about 30 lbs. and crossing the Tasman (a distance of $2\frac{1}{2}$ miles), in two hours we found ourselves in the river-bed of the Murchison, which, after the bad surface moraine of the Tasman, proved good travelling. Every step opened up new glaciers and peaks, and we wasted some valuable time in deciding whether these peaks were unnamed or only new views of old friends, with the result that it was 3·30 before we reached the glacier. The ice was covered with *débris* even worse than the Tasman Glacier. It is difficult to give an adequate idea of these terrible moraines, they must be seen by anyone wishing to realise their extent and size. Imagine loose boulders of all shapes and sizes up to 10 or 15 ft. square thrown into heaps and hummocks 100 ft. high and in hopeless confusion, extending for miles, and a faint idea of what we had to travel over may be formed. With this sort of travelling it may be supposed that progress was slow, and at 5 P.M. we had only gone a mile up the glacier. Here a tributary came in from the Malte Brun Range, near which was some scrub for firewood, so we took advantage of such a convenient spot and stopped for the night.

So far nothing had happened to make us doubt that we should be able to cross the saddle at the head of the glacier and reach the Ball Glacier camp the next day; therefore, we did not economise our food that evening or next morning at our 5 A.M. breakfast. Two miles above our bivouac the glacier appeared

to come from the left, off the Malte Brun Range, but on reaching the spot and ascending a rise in the ice, we discovered that it was only a tributary stream, and the main glacier lay in front of us, stretching out for miles, and evidently coming from the northern side of Darwin instead of the southern slopes. A short council of war, as to the advisability of continuing an expedition which must involve another night and day away from camp, with only enough food for one meal left, ended in our deciding to "do or die." Consequently we made for the white ice now just ahead of us, and began to move more easily and quickly. At 1·30 P.M. we saw to our joy a saddle of some 7,400 ft. on our left front, which appeared to lead over the Malte Brun Range to the Tasman Glacier, at the head of a large tributary, the main glacier apparently coming from a saddle a mile or two further to the north. After some rather difficult work amongst snow-covered crevasses, and in a thick mist, we arrived on our saddle at 4.30 P.M. In a short time the fog lifted and we were fairly puzzled to know where we had got to. No Tasman was in sight, but far below us an unknown glacier swept away to our *right hand* instead of to our left as we had anticipated.

Suddenly Mannering saw the Hochstetter Dome, which he had ascended the previous season, and then it all became evident. Instead of being on a pass over the Malte Brun Range, we had ascended a spur round which the Murchison Glacier came. And the ice below us was the head of that glacier, sweeping down to the right, previous to turning at right angles round the spur on which we were. Some distance to our left we could see a saddle leading into the Tasman hopelessly out of our reach, and in front, across the head of the Murchison, another saddle over the Main Range, evidently leading into the Whymper Glacier, which lies at the head of a branch of the Wataroa River on the west coast. Our pass, therefore, only led us into the *névé* of the glacier on which we had been for the last two days. Hamilton was somewhat out of training and wanted a rest badly, so we took an hour's spell and made a rough map. Some time after 5·30 P.M. we began to retrace out steps, having left a record of the ascent of "Starvation Saddle" in a cairn. At 8 P.M. we found a fair bivouac and supperless rolled ourselves in our blankets and were soon in the Land of Nod. At daybreak, after a miserably small meal, which exhausted our supplies, we moved off, and in eight hours reached the head camp—I having gone ahead to cook a meal for the others, who arrived an hour later.

The result of this expedition was topographically important. It proved that the Murchison was a large glacier, as far as was then known, the second in size in New Zealand; also, that instead of coming from Mount Darwin's southern slopes, it came from the main range at a point two miles north of that peak, which is, as I have already explained, on the Malte Brun Range, an offshoot of the Divide. Therefore, the Murchison, with the Tasman, encloses the Malte Brun Range, like a great island in a sea of ice. The Government had this glacier surveyed during the next season, and proved our topographical conclusions to be correct, and also showed that our sketch map was practically right in all its features.

In the early part of the next season, December, 1890, I formed a party consisting of Messrs. R. Blakiston, W. Beadel, and myself, but owing to some terribly bad weather and heavy snow, we did nothing till January, except twice reach the Ball

Glacier, and on each occasion being driven back by terrific storms. The season was notable for one or two things only, but all of them important. In that year Mr. Brodrick, Government surveyor, completed the survey of the district, and Mannering nearly succeeded in ascending Mount Cook,[*] in company with Mr. Dixon, a most plucky attempt. And lastly, R. Blakiston and I made the first complete traverse of the Hooker Glacier and ascent of the saddle at its head, since called "Harper Saddle" (8,580 ft.). The upper basin of this glacier had never been visited, though two or three attempts had been made to reach it, rendered unsuccessful by the enormous crevasses about five miles up the glacier. The previous three weeks' bad weather and heavy snow, however, had so covered the ice that I decided to make the ascent.

On December 29th Blakiston and I left the Hermitage with a light camp, which we pitched some two miles above the terminal face on the western side of the glacier. On the morning of the 30th an unfortunately late start was made at 6·30, and after an hour or so on the lateral moraine, we took to the snow-covered ice, which rose in a succession of ice-falls, on which the snow was disagreeably soft. Thanks to the heavy fall, we were able to cross all the broken ice, but not without considerable care, as some of the crevasses were of great width. Eight hours' floundering above our knees in the soft snow brought us to the foot of the saddle, which lay at the top of an ice-wall of 250 ft., rising very steeply to within 60 ft. of the top. A large *bergschrund* skirted the foot of this ice-slope, and delayed us a good deal, as it was not easily negotiated. I took the lead,

[*] "With Axe and Rope in the New Zealand Alps." By G. E. Mannering. Longmans.

for Blakiston was new to ice-work, and after cutting some one hundred and twenty steps we stood on the saddle. I have never experienced in any other climb such difficulty in the way of step-cutting. For the first 180 ft. the slope was so steep that I had to lean my chest against the ice while cutting the next steps, and could see Blakiston below me by looking between my feet.

In New Zealand there is the same trouble with fog as in Switzerland, that is to say, it is very rare that a clear view can be obtained over the west coast after 10 A.M. because a low dense bank of fog drifts in from the sea and fills the valleys, only allowing of 6,000 ft. and upwards to be seen. This is, I imagine, very much like the fog so often seen on the Italian side of the Alps. The saddle led into the La Perouse Glacier at the head of Cook River on the West Coast, but we could see nothing of the valley, owing to the fog, which lay 500 ft. or so below us, and which, though we tried to descend, prevented our completing a trans-alpine pass. The day had been intensely hot, which made it highly probable that several snow bridges would be gone and new crevasses exposed, hence it was necessary to waste as little time as possible, and to reach them before dusk. At 3.30, after leaving a record of the ascent, we began to descend, Blakiston going first, and both descending backwards. The steadiness of my companion on this ice-slope is beyond praise, considering that this was his first expedition on ice or snow. Unfortunately, also, it was his last, for he has never been free to climb since, and we have lost a promising mountaineer.

Opposite Baker's Saddle—which lies south of Mount Stokes, and leads into the Copland River on the West Coast—we found the crevasses very much exposed and bridges gone, no less than ten had appeared which were invisible in the morning. One crevasse we crossed on the snow by crawling was of great breadth—I believe it was fully 25 ft. wide. So large and numerous are these that, except early in the season, I feel convinced a route up the Hooker would be a most difficult thing to find. At 7 P.M. we regained our camp, and next day, in heavy rain, retraced our steps to the hotel, fearfully burnt and sore from the glare on the fresh snow.

This climb was topographically of importance, and had we had a clear view over the West Coast, we could have answered some interesting questions, which, however, I was able to decide two or three years later, as will be seen in a future chapter. The actual result was that the map of the Hooker was proved incorrect as regards the head basin and the position of Mount Cook, which had been placed on the main range. As a matter of fact, it is on the eastern side and sends no drainage on to the West Coast at all. Mount Cook branches off at Mount Dampier (11,323 ft.), which drops on one side into the Linda Glacier, on another into the head basin of the Hooker, while its third side falls precipitously into the La Perouse Glacier on the West Coast. From Dampier the main range goes to Mount Hicks or St. David's Dome (10,410 ft.), and thence past Harper's Saddle (8,580 ft.) to Stokes (10,101 ft.), whence it bends away sharply southwards to Sefton (10,359 ft.) and Mount Burns (8,984 ft.), which lies at the head of the Mueller Glacier. Though our climb finally settled the position of Mount Cook as being off the main range, it is only fair to say that Mr. Roberts, of the Westland Survey Department, had practically decided the point, and only wanted to have it confirmed by more sure evidence. When sitting on the saddle,

I planned a route up Mount Cook, which seemed to be far easier and more direct than that followed by Mr. Green, but unfortunately I never had an opportunity of attempting it. However, Mr. Fyfe, who also considered it the best route, followed it when he made the first ascent of the peak on Christmas-day, 1894.

Later on in the same season, namely, February, 1891, Mr. P. H. Johnson and I made another expedition to this district, intending to climb De la Bêche (9,815 ft.) and the Minarets (10,058 ft.), part of the same mountain. Unfortunately, my companion fell ill, and we did nothing for a week or more, and then only made two small climbs, namely, a pass over the Malte Brun Range—the first climb done on that range—and an attempt at Mount Sealy, from which we were driven by a terrific north-west gale when near the top.

The following summer I made three attempts at Mount De la Bêche, but had the most extraordinary bad luck. The first attempt was in company with H. M. Hamilton, and we reached a point close under the main peak, some 9,000 ft. above sea-level, when my companion became helpless, owing to sickness. I then returned and obtained Jack Adamson from the Hermitage, and with him reached the same point in such a gale of wind that we could not stand. And two days later we again went for the peak, when my mate was seized with the cramp in the stomach, which forced us to return at 8 A.M., within 900 ft. of the summit. The only fact worth recording with regard to these climbs is that I obtained the first photographs ever taken overlooking the main range. I have the somewhat melancholy satisfaction of knowing that my route, which lay up the Rudolph Glacier, and up the rock face of the peak,

was the correct one. Fyfe, who made the first ascent of this mountain later, wrote and told me he had followed my route, and it presented no real difficulty.

Mount De la Bêche is one of our most beautiful peaks, and stands between the Tasman Glacier and the Kron Prinz Rudolf Glacier, a large tributary flowing into the main glacier some twelve miles up. At the point where these two ice streams join, a deep triangular hollow is found, bounded on two sides by the high lateral moraines of the two glaciers, and on the third by De la Bêche. This area is filled with large masses of rock, and under one Adamson and I built a first-rate shelter, which is really as good as a hut, forming a convenient point from which to ascend fifteen or twenty of our highest peaks.

For a really successful expedition in this district, a party should be composed of four men, who are willing to do a considerable amount of rough work, and ready to carry their own loads. They must also have plenty of time at their command, as nearly all our old failures are due to want of time, which prevented our waiting for good opportunities, and compelled us to attempt all sorts of difficult expeditions in the face of doubtful weather. There are only two parties who have done any extended work in this district in one season, and both owe their success to having plenty of time at their disposal. Those of us who used to try and climb with only a short holiday, always prophesied success to the first man who could spend a month or two at the Hermitage, and that prophecy turned out to be true. In 1893-1894 season Fyfe spent a considerable time in the district, and could afford to wait for his weather, consequently he made the first ascents of three or four of our best peaks. Again in 1894-1895 season, Mr. Fitzgerald, with his Swiss guide, Zurbriggen, had a successful season, making several ascents, and owing his success as much to the fact that he could await fine weather and good opportunities, as to the fact that he had Zurbriggen to guide him.

Fyfe's climbs were of course guideless, and considering that he is—like all of us—a self-taught man, they are greatly to his credit; in fact, so far as peaks are concerned, his record exceeds that of anyone who has climbed in New Zealand for *bona-fide* merit.

## CHAPTER III.

#### WESTLAND.

The West Coast of New Zealand—The Forest and its Plants—Birds.

In August, 1893, I applied to and obtained work from the Westland Survey Department, in conjunction with Mr. C. E. Douglas, to continue the exploration and mapping of the rivers and glaciers with their surrounding ranges. Mr. Douglas had been working for some twenty years, following and traversing rivers to their sources, but none of the larger glaciers had been explored, except the moraine-covered Strauchon on the Copland River, and Balfour Glacier on the central branch of Cook River; this was owing to the want of a man experienced in ice work, Douglas having, as a rule, only carried his work to the snow-line, and having neither companion nor Alpine equipment, was unable to go into high altitudes.

Before relating my own experiences amongst the Westland Glaciers and Alps, it will be as well to give a short description of the country. This will allow my readers to form some idea of the conditions under which our work had to be carried on.

Westland, or "West Coast," as it is more commonly called, was rushed by gold-diggers in the early sixties, and a large amount of gold was found and exported. Now, however, it has become, from a digging point of view, a field of far less importance. True, there are still many working the alluvial ground, but those making more than "tucker" are few, and it is many years since "a rise" of importance has been made by anyone. The country itself, except for a few clearings made by settlers, may be said to be covered with dense evergreen "bush" (forest) up to 3,000 ft. above sea-level, which gradually merges into a low, impenetrable scrub, growing perhaps 500 ft. higher until it gives way to luxuriant snow-grass and other Alpine plants.

There is a narrow strip of more or less flat country (that is, rough, low hills, with patches of actually flat land) between the ranges and the sea, varying from 25 to 5 miles in width. It is of little value from an agricultural or pastoral point of view, covered as it is with bush (forest), and costing more than its value to clear. Here and there are large tracts of swampy ground, useless to man or beast at present, but which may prove valuable if properly drained. These large swamps are usually to be found between the rivers on the flat country; and, with few exceptions, confine the settlers to the river flats near the sea, where the best land is to be found.

To a casual visitor, there would seem to be in Westland an inexhaustible amount of marketable timber, both on the flat country and in the ranges. The truth is, however, that beyond a certain amount on the low country there is very little. In the ranges, and up the rivers, there is practically none of value, and those trees which are worth cutting are so scattered that they would be unworkable by any mill fixed in one locality. It is doubtful if the timber up the rivers will be more than sufficient to build and keep in repair culverts and bridges, when such are constructed. On the Arawata and Blue Rivers, in the far south of the country, there is a very fine patch of birch (really a beech) bush, which could be worked with advantage from one centre. Douglas speaks of trees 42 ft. in circumference, with a clean trunk of 90 feet to the lowest limb, growing on the Arawata. At present, however, the means of communication with the rest of the colony are very poor, a fact which adds greatly to the difficulty of making either farming or any other industry remunerative.

The gold industry is the mainstay of the southern part of Westland, and there is little doubt that, should the output of the precious metal cease, there would be small inducement for a population to stay in the district. A few, possibly, who prefer a free and unfettered existence in a part of the colony where they can easily make a small living, may consent to dwell in such an out-of-the-way locality. It is, however, more than probable that the minerals of Westland will continue to give employment to some number, especially when better means of communication are provided, which will allow them to be worked at less cost with more chance of profit. The only connection with the rest of the colony is by steamer and coach, while south of Ross, the communication is precarious to say the least, only a pack-horse mail running at present. In my opinion, Westland has a great future before it, if properly and energetically pushed, as a tourist resort. Nowhere else in New Zealand is there such magnificent scenery, equalling, if not surpassing, that of Switzerland and Norway in grandeur. But it is out of reach of the ordinary tourist, unless he is willing to rough it considerably, while to see the finest views in the Southern Alps on this side, days and weeks of hardship must be faced, which would frighten most people. Before any noticeable benefit can be felt from tourists, some steps must be taken to make means of transit easier. At present, owing to the unbridged state of the rivers and frequent rain, there is great risk of loss of time by being "stuck up" by floods. But until we have a large neighbouring population, a government would hardly be justified in going to great expense in making roads and bridges.

The "bush"* or forest of New Zealand has often been described, but even had nothing been said on the subject, it would require a more gifted pen than mine to depict its beauties. The fascination which it has over all those who see or work in it cannot be understood by one who has not experienced it. I will not attempt to describe the innumerable beautiful ferns and mosses, and the wonderful colouring of the bush, which never cease to exercise their power over even the oldest "hand," if he has any love of fine effects. When toiling through dense undergrowth, cutting a track, or carrying a heavy load, I found time to enjoy the lovely effects and fairylike scenes met with at every turn. Yet, in spite of its many attractions, it is a serious drawback to such work as ours, or, in fact, to any which entails much travelling. Even the oldest bushman may find himself temporarily "bushed," but a good man can, by use of common-sense and coolness, generally find his way out somewhere, not, necessarily, at the place he wants to go to, but at least to some locality from which he can easily reach habitation.

Common-sense, unfortunately, is not a strong point with

* In New Zealand the forest is always spoken of as "bush" as opposed to lower growth of vegetation, which is called "scrub."

some, if we may judge by the frequent absurd actions of persons lost in the bush. For half the year it is easy to build a shelter with bark, and at all times with ferns, while no one need be without a good fire, unless, of course, he has no matches. Those who have in the past suffered from exposure have done so for want of a little thought. But many when "bushed" seem to lose their reasoning powers, for there are cases in which it has not occurred to men in such a plight to kindle a fire, even though they have a plentiful supply of matches, nor to try and snare a bird, or eat some of the edible plants in the bush when suffering from hunger. When, however, we hear that there have been men who, on being lost in hilly country covered with timber, have on reaching a river actually gone *up stream* in order to get into the low country, it is hardly surprising that the misfortune of being "bushed" is often serious in its effects.

Though there are several edible plants, they are not very nourishing, nor can I honestly say very nice. However, a hungry man must eat what he can get, and I have often been glad of even a small feed of Piki-piki fern (*Asplenium bulbiferum*). This is, perhaps, the best of our natural foods, and the curled, crozier-like shoot is quite passable when boiled for an hour. In addition to this is the head of the young "supplejack" (*Parsomsia albiflora*), a vine which grows in immense quantities up to nearly 2,000 ft. above sea-level, and is about as bad an obstacle to force a way through as I know. The kihi-ki (*Freycinetia Banksii*) which grows on the lower hills near the sea, wild parsley (*Angelica geniculata*), spinach (*Tetragonia expansa*), and root of the bracken fern (*Pteris esculenta*) are also eatable. In the low country, that is, below 1,500 or 2,000 ft., the undergrowth in the bush is bad beyond description, especially where " supplejacks " and " lawyers " (*Rubus australis*) abound. For the benefit of those who have never been in New Zealand, it may be explained that a " lawyer " is a bramble which grows in very dense masses, and is covered with small thorns. It is so named because, when once a man is unfortunate enough to get into its clutches, he finds it hard to free himself. These most obstructive plants are fortunately not found often above 1,500 ft. from sea-level, unless the hill has a sea frontage.

Besides the plants already mentioned as eatable, there are others possessing valuable medicinal qualities. The best known of these is, perhaps, the koromiko, a shrub belonging to the veronica tribe, which makes a good tonic, useful in cases of dysentery, and has already been used to make a patent medicine. A certain portion of the flax plant (*Phormium tenax*) has an opposite effect to the koromiko. For external use, we have the gum of the miro pine (*Podocarpus ferruginea*), the finest healing ointment for an open wound that I have ever used, and a sure cure for warts. The Maoris often take the leaf of the pepper-tree (*Drimys axillaris*), and after chewing it, apply it to a wound, which it is said to heal very soon, leaving a blue tattoo mark. The leaf, I think, is more or less poisonous, and should be avoided, like all those shrubs which have leaves with white undersides and dark above.

For camping purposes it would be difficult indeed to surpass the New Zealand forest, and in the mountain ranges of the West Coast, though we grumble at the work it involves, we really have great cause to be thankful for it. The eastern slopes of the Southern Alps are open and grass covered, a great contrast to the densely timbered ranges of the West Coast. In the one district the want of firewood for camping purposes is felt, and in the other too much timber gives a party a great deal of heavy work when travelling. If it were possible to "split the difference," each side would be all that could be desired for explorations—easy travelling, combined with good camping grounds. Between October and March in the mountains, within 3,000 ft. of sea-level, it is really not necessary to carry canvas, unless, of course, one is fastidious as to shelter. It is always possible to build a good "wharé" or "mai-mai" with bark stripped from the rata (*Metrosideros robusta*), totara (*Padocarpus totara*), or cedar (*Libocedrus Bidwillii*) trees, all or some of which are to be found up the rivers. Of firewood there is such an inexhaustible supply and good variety to select from, that it is always possible to keep a fire burning, without any necessity to economise, a great consideration in wet weather. There is the rata tree, the prince of firewoods, very hard, and burning almost like coal, dry or green, miki-miki, ake-ake, kamahi, or so called red-birch, white and black birches (which are really beeches), the mountain broom, ribbon wood, broad leaf, totara, and many others, all burning in a green state, though the first six or seven are the best, and always available in the Ranges.

While enumerating thus shortly the advantages and disadvantages of the bush, I cannot pass over one of the greatest charms of camp life and work in unexplored country—namely, the birds to whom man is a stranger. They are not only useful as food, and enabled two of us to do work which really required four men, but they provide us with endless amusement when together, and are especially welcome when one is working or camping alone.

First and foremost of these is the weka (*Ocydromus Australis*), wood-hen or Maori hen, as he is variously called, as good a camp companion as one could wish for, with his tameness, impudence, and almost human power of expression. I have never studied a weka in or near civilisation, but as found in the hitherto unvisited valleys, in which my last two years have chiefly been spent, he is only approached by the kea (or mountain parrot) as a source of amusement and interest. Often have Douglas and I sighed for the powers of the artist, whose "Zigzags at the Zoo" in the *Strand Magazine* helped many a wet day to pass, wherewith to depict the many knowing expressions of the weka and kea.

Perhaps it is almost unnecessary to say that the weka is a bird with small unformed wings, unable to fly, and varying in size from a partridge to a pheasant. In plumage he is not unlike the former, sometimes dark brown and sometimes a very light colour, according to whether his habitation is in narrow and gloomy valleys or open grass country. He walks with a "very genteel" step, and bobs his short tail up spasmodically; his whole action suggesting the exaggerated motions of a teacher of deportment, if such a person exists outside novels. The male and female only keep together during the breeding season, and if the place they choose for their temporary abode happens to be productive of the necessities of weka life, the cock drives his mate and family away at the end of the season, remaining in solitary possession of a good feeding-ground. Should, however, the locality be indifferently productive, Mr. Weka bids the family a glad farewell on the completion of his domestic duties, and seeks happier hunting-grounds for himself. As to food, he is omnivorous, eating everything, from a pea-rifle cartridge to the remains of one of his own tribe, or even family. I remember an instance of this when our dog unfortunately killed a young bird before we could prevent it, which was too small to eat. The parents made a decent show of grief over their loss, and then, being quite sure that the little one was dead, they proceeded to eat its still warm remains!

In camp the birds are useful as scavengers, but they are incorrigible thieves, trying to take away everything at all white or glittering; and as they are able to move a weight of two or three pounds, it can well be imagined that a careful look out has to be kept. The glance of mingled triumph and contempt which a weka gives over his shoulder, as he walks off with your pipe, is inimitable, and his whole attitude would make a most laughable picture, if well drawn. One of these birds will take full possession of a camp as soon as he discovers it, generally within a few hours of its being pitched, and rarely have we been without one or a pair. No other birds or rats are allowed to come near if he can help it, but are attacked without hesitation. And if another weka dares to intrude, the one in possession will—nine times out of ten—manage to make good his claim, though sometimes the combatants seem very unevenly matched for a fight. Possession is nine points of the law. They even rush wildly at a thrush or crow, though far out of reach above them, and often resort to stratagem to induce the object of their attack to come within reach.

I have seen a weka run under a shrub on which a thrush was

sitting, and try to frighten him. This had no effect, so our friend walked away out of sight, and in a few minutes returned, and when he had come under the thrush, he suddenly tumbled down, and with stiffened limbs and ruffled feathers feigned to be dead. It was a fine piece of acting, but he had one wicked little eye open. The thrush looked at the motionless weka for a second or two, and then began to sing, as much as to say, "I've played this game before!" leaving our friend to get up and try not to look foolish. The thrush never seems to fall into the trap. The weka, though very clever in carrying out his scheme, sometimes tries it on two or three times in succession, which shows some want of intelligence.

For downright impudence, too, the weka is unequalled, and no doubt this fact will help to preserve him against his new foe, the weasel, so kindly turned loose by a paternal—or shall I say "maternal"—government. Though really no match for such an antagonist, he will by mere "bluff" frighten it, for if he sees the weasel first he will charge it, though I fear if *vice versâ*, he will run away. The weka will figure often in these pages, so for the present we will leave him.

The robin (*Miro albifrons*) is a constant companion in some localities, as far as the bush limit; he differs from his English namesake very little, only having a yellow instead of a red breast. They are quite tame, and generally called "dear, gentle little things," but in reality they are the most vicious and quarrelsome little birds it is possible to imagine. A family of four or five seem to spend their whole time in fighting—a great contrast to the weka family. When one is cutting or climbing through the bush, a robin nearly always follows close behind, picking up grubs exposed in the footsteps, and depositing them under moss or in holes in a tree, for future use.

Of song-birds we find a great number in the back country, away from the haunts of men, notably the crow (*Glaucopis cinerea*), which has a note like a rich-toned flageolet, the most beautiful I have heard in our ranges. Besides him are the bell-birds, mentioned by Captain Cook, and getting very scarce; the tui, canary, and many others, all of which swell the chorus heard every morning and evening. The canaries (*Orthonyx ochrocephala*) and the little mountain wrens (*Xenicus filviventris*) are useful as foretellers of weather, for they always collect in flocks, and keep up a lively chirping, some hours before an approaching storm, a warning which we never allow to pass unnoticed.

For the camp-pot there is a varied choice. The weka is perhaps the most nourishing, having a large amount of oil when in good condition—over a quarter of a pint can be obtained from a fat bird, which, though not very palatable, is sustaining, and can be baked with flour to advantage. The kiwi is passable when one is hungry, though personally I do not like him, but being more nutritious than savoury, it is not to be despised, and is almost nice when boiled with piki-piki fern and rice.

The kiwi is a wingless bird, and still fairly plentiful in out-of-the-way places, but on the whole is fast becoming extinct. The West Coast kiwi (*Apterix oweni*) is a small grey bird, differing from the North Island species (*Apterix mantelli*), which is dark brown and more coarsely made. With the help of a good dog they can be generally caught asleep in the daytime, being entirely night birds. Sometimes in the spring, one, or generally two, eggs are to be found with a pair in their retreat, but, chiefly owing to cats and weasels, there are more solitary birds than originally. The only way to account for this is that, owing to the unknown enemy which has appeared, they become frightened, and are unwilling to pair, "and," to quote Douglas, "Mrs. Kiwi probably says: 'What is the good of my laying that awful egg if a weasel sucks it while we are actually sitting on it?'" The size of the egg is well known, and it is hard to believe that so small a bird can lay one so large; however, not one but generally two are produced. Both birds sit to hatch this, which is nearly as large as a black swan's egg,* for one could not possibly cover it alone, and there is little doubt that the warmth of decayed vegetable matter contributes largely to the hatching. Though laying two eggs, they only hatch one, and I have heard it suggested that the second is laid later and used to feed the young one, for though there is only one young bird, there are generally the remains of two eggs, and two are frequently found before hatching. During the daytime they sleep in a standing position, with their heads tucked down between their legs, looking like a fluffy ball on two sticks. When taking a kiwi from its hole, great care must be observed if the skin is required for stuffing; for while the body is warm the feathers or hair fall out in handfuls wherever they are touched, but after it is cold it is the hardest bird to pluck I know.

The kaka (*Nestor meridionalis*), kakapo (*Stringops habroptilus*), and kea (*Nestor notabilis*) of the parrot tribe, the wood pigeon, blue, grey, and paradise ducks, are all excellent for

* See Appendix, Note III.

eating, and if one is hard pushed for food, the smaller birds, such as the crow, tui, paraquet, and saddle-backs, are all acceptable.

The kakapo is found in South Westland, the Sounds country of Otago, and the Nelson Province. He is rarely, if ever, seen away from the birch forests. He is a large, ground parrot, with a bright green plumage, and, except for descending from a rock or bluff thirty feet in height, his wings are useless to him. Like the kiwi, he is a night bird, living in holes and under rocks all day. As food he comes second only to the weka, having a large quantity of fine oil in his body, of a light straw colour. We capture him with the help of our dog, and he shows a great deal of fight before he surrenders. This bird apparently performs an operation on his food akin to chewing the cud; that is, he collects a large amount of grass in his crop, and retires to his refuge to chew it, and when all the juice has been extracted, he throws the grass out in dry balls. After feeding, these birds make a booming noise, not unlike the grunt of a pig, and though it can be heard for a great distance, it is quite impossible to locate it. Probably the fact of the bird being in a hole will account for the deceptive nature of the sound. I have heard the noise apparently within a few yards of me, and have been surprised and angry at the dog not looking for the bird where I pointed, but instead of doing so he has run off up the hillside for some considerable distance, and in a few moments the shrieking of the bird and barking of the dog will show that the noise had deceived me completely. The crop of a kakapo, when freshly killed, makes a capital poultice if applied to a sore, drawing out all poisonous matter quickly and effectually, so the Maoris say. Though one of our largest birds, it has an egg not much bigger than that of a pigeon, a great contrast to the enormous egg produced by such a small bird as the grey kiwi. It would be both reasonable and convenient, I should imagine, if they could change eggs!

Blue, or mountain ducks (*Nestor rotabilis*), are not now found in any numbers except in the upper parts of hitherto unvisited rivers, and make a very welcome addition to our supplies, which are generally at a somewhat low ebb by the time we reach the head of a river. They appear to have the rivers and creeks marked off in regular divisions, never encroaching on the preserves of another, or allowing intrusion by a strange couple. I have seen many instances of this rule of division, and proved it by driving two or three pairs down stream with their broods, and finding them all in their own "claims" next morning. Many a fight can be seen between two pairs, when a strange couple try to "jump a claim." Their chief weapon of attack is a horny growth on the second joint of the wing. Unlike most New Zealand birds, the male and female are partners all the year round, but the female alone sits on the eggs, while the male keeps guard and feeds her.

The Paradise duck (*Casarca variegata*) is too much like a tough goose, in my opinion, but the "flappers," or young ones, are very good indeed when roasted. Here, again, we find a peculiarity; these ducks will sometimes build their nest in a tree 30 ft. from the ground, but by what means they bring their young ones to terra-firma or water, I cannot say. Possibly they carry them on their backs, but, if they followed the usual happy-go-lucky laws of nature in New Zealand, it is as likely as not that the promising brood is allowed to tumble out one by one, and trust to providence.

Scientific descriptions and names of our birds can be found in Sir Walter Buller's "Birds of New Zealand." The above short description is not intended, by any means, to be complete, for that would be unnecessary. But certain interesting habits of the birds can be noted by those who see them in their undisturbed and natural haunts, which scientists may not have been able to obtain, having had few opportunities to go far from civilisation.

It is a sad fact that most of the native birds of the country are gradually disappearing. In the early days, those who went into unknown country found thousands of birds of all kinds; but now, even in localities hitherto unvisited by man, birds are scarce. Sometimes, of course, they are as numerous as formerly, but I have been into valleys where hardly a bird was to be seen of any kind. This is largely due to cats and weasels. The digger is very fond of his cat, and nearly always carries one with him; but in the past, when new "rushes" were frequent, he would go off at a moment's notice from his camp or hut, and if the cat was not at hand it was left behind, and naturally became wild. These have increased and multiplied enormously, and I have seen their tracks miles up unexplored valleys. It has been several years since the coast was overrun by wild cats, and now weasels are added to the list of enemies which the birds have to contend against. It is, therefore, only a question of time before our most interesting birds—those that cannot fly—become extinct.

The Government has wisely set apart two large islands on which to preserve birds and plants, and they seem to be answering their purpose. These are Little Barrier Island in the north, near Auckland, and Resolution Island, near the Sounds in the south-west. No doubt, in the unexplored country behind the Sounds, there are still plenty of birds; but there, again, it is only a matter of time before they are exterminated. Though there are wild dogs, escaped from civilisation, they are in no great numbers, as a wild life does not seem to suit them, and they soon die out.

## CHAPTER IV.

### WAIHO RIVER—FRANZ JOSEF GLACIER.

Journey Southwards—Waiho River—Lake Maporika—Terminal Face—Camp 1—Attempts on Glacier—Hot Springs—Camp 2—Camp 3—Ice-fall—Baffled—Return.

On the 6th October, 1893, Mr. C. E. Douglas and I left Hokitika, with instructions to map Lake Ianthe, some 40 miles south along the road, and thence traverse the Wanganui River to the sea from the ferry on the road, after which we had to make our way further south to the Waiho River and explore the Franz Josef Glacier. A daily coach runs to Ross, a small mining township of 500 inhabitants, 20 miles from Hokitika, and thence there is a weekly pack-horse mail service to Gillespie's Beach, 88 miles south of Ross, and near the mouth of Cook River. We therefore put our small supply of clothing on the coach as far as Ross, and here obtained three weeks' stores and a pack-horse to carry them to Lake Ianthe.

It took us to the 20th to finish our work on the lake, and on the 22nd we started in a small "dug-out," or canoe hollowed out of a tree, down the outlet, which flowed into the Wanganui River, and on the 24th went down the river to the sea, having some very narrow escapes in the foaming rapids. Our craft was only 6 ft. by 2 ft., and very clumsily made, so we had a good deal to be thankful for in getting down safely; it was largely due to luck, helped by Douglas's steering. Next day we returned on foot to our camp, some seven miles up the river, and thence carried our impedimenta five miles on to Hende's Ferry, which is on the main south track, 30 miles south of Ross.

This road, after leaving Ross, skirts along the foot of the hills, and crosses the Waganui at Hende's Ferry, 30 miles, the Wataroa River at Gunn's Ferry, 50 miles, and at 60 miles branches off to Lake Maporika on the left-hand and to Okarito (64 miles from Ross) on the right-hand side. From the latter place, which lies on the sea-beach, the road is non-existent, and it is just possible to take a wheeled vehicle to that point, the journey occupying about three days from Hokitika. From Hende's Ferry, where we slept, we carried our loads and tramped to Gunn's, on the Wataroa, and on the 20th of October went on to the "Miner's Rest," at the Forks, a settlement at the point where the road branches.

The Forks is a "township" which can boast of a publichouse and one digger's hut, though in old days it had a large population, when plenty of gold was being obtained there. Now, however, only two or three parties are working near it, and, on mail night especially, the whole neighbouring population (of perhaps ten) assemble at the "Miner's Rest." I am sorry to say they do not confine themselves to tea! On these occasions politics form the chief topic of conversation, because numbers of diggers, having Hansard's Parliamentary Reports sent to them "gratis," and religiously reading every word, are keen politicians. I cannot conceive anyone wading through these Reports, for when it is remembered that there are some members in the House who speak for no other reason than to see themselves (or for their constituents to see them) in "Hansard," it can be imagined what sort of reading they afford.

One evening, when we were waiting for pack-horses to take our stores as far as possible up the Waiho River, I became involved in a political discussion. One of the diggers charged me with being " a capitalist."

"How can I be a capitalist when I've no money?" I answered.

"Money," he explained, "has nothing to do with it."

I remonstrated.

He said: "Well, I don't know about your money, but you speak like a capitalist."

I again objected that I could hardly be called a capitalist if I had no capital. So he changed his ground, and said, " Well, you're a Conservative, anyway."

Being of opinion that there were no Conservatives in this colony, and objecting to the expression, I thought this a good opportunity to find out what politicians meant by it; so I replied, "Ah yes, I may be a Conservative, but you must tell me what a Conservative is, before I can answer."

" A Conservative," he said hesitatingly, " is—er—is a man you don't agree with "!

I always suspected this to be the truth of the matter, for each party generally dubs itself the " Great Liberal Party," which I suppose implies that the other side are Conservatives!

On the 31st we obtained two horses and went on towards the Franz Josef Glacier. About three miles from the Forks is Maporika township, which consists of a store and a publichouse, with a small population of ten or twenty diggers; here we procured our necessaries. A horse can be taken right up to the terminal face of the glacier, so there was no need to procure all our stores at once, we therefore only ordered enough for a month or six weeks, for we might perhaps finish our work in that time if favoured with fine weather, and if not could easily have more sent up. After leaving the township the road, or horse-track, skirts the beautiful Maporika Lake, and many lovely views are to be seen through openings in the bush. To see this lake to advantage it is necessary to stay a day or two at the township and hire a boat. I camped on a promontory half-way up the lake for a week in January, 1894, when surveying it, at the time of the full moon, and the views day and night were glorious. At the southern end the snowy peaks of the Bismarck Range tower into the sky, with Mounts Cook and Tasman just appearing over them; and, at a distance of nine miles, the Franz Josef Glacier is seen coming out of the valley, between bush-clad hills, and apparently pushing its way into the bush at the head of the lake. In the foreground are numerous promontories, with great trees overhanging and reflected in the perfectly still water, or perhaps the limb of some fallen giant stands naked out of the placid surface of the lake. After my day's work I used to get into my boat, and drift about on the lake, smoking the pipe of contentment, and watch the last rays of the sun throwing a pink glow over the great snow peaks, and the gloom gradually deepening over the glacier and lower valleys. Then the moon would rise and shed its white light over the whole scene, and make me loth to return to my camp in the bush, with its mosquitoes.

About eight miles from Maporika township, after leaving

the lake, the track passes a farm on the river flats of the Totara and Waiho Rivers, on which sheep and cattle are grazed, and which is one of the few farms in the south where more than a living can be made. This is chiefly owing to the fairly large number of diggers in the district. The homestead is only a small house, but it is surrounded by a few acres of cleared land laid down in grass, and forms a pleasing contrast to the sombre-coloured bush and hills behind. Crossing the Totara River, the track continues for two miles to the Waiho River, where some four or five parties are gold-digging, and have their huts; one of them, Mr. Jim Nesbitt, having been there for over twenty years. His hut is on the north side of the river, just below where the " Left-hand " branch, or Callery River, joins the " Glacier branch " or Waiho. From Nesbitt's hut a small foot-track runs along the bank of the former river for half a mile to a wire suspension foot-bridge, which spans the stream some fifty feet above the water, at the mouth of a magnificent gorge.

This is one of the finest gorges I know, within easy reach of tourists. The river is a large glacier-fed stream, and descends very rapidly through a deep and narrow, rocky gorge, above which the mountains rise abruptly to the height of 3,000 or 4,000 ft. The contrast of dark-green bush on the almost precipitous hillsides, with the grey rock walls of the gorge, rising 100 ft. sheer, and overhanging, out of the river, which comes boiling and roaring down over immense boulders, is very grand ; while in the distance, between the bush-clad hills, can be seen the glaciers of Drummond's Peak, some miles up the Callery River.

On the small level piece of ground between the two

branches, and at the foot of a rounded hill (The Dough Boy), there is a digger's hut called the Hospital, and a few chains further on the bank of the glacier or "right hand" branch, are some hot springs, of which more will be said. The County Council bought this hut for the use of tourists and others who visited the hot springs, but as only one or two come in the year, Andrew Gordon and A. Woodham, working a claim close by, had taken possession. By the hot springs another footbridge spanned the glacier branch, but that was swept away in February, 1894, by a flood; however, we used it constantly while there. The Government are now building another across the Waiho, below the junction of the two rivers, from Nesbitt's hut to the south bank, and have formed a fair horse track to the terminal face of the glacier.

After crossing the second footbridge, we only had $1\frac{1}{2}$ miles to go to the spot chosen for our head camp, which we pitched on November 1st, in some tall scrub within 400 yards of the glacier. To this point numerous persons had been in the past, but the glacier and the upper valley had not been touched, presumably because no one having any knowledge of ice-craft had been there.

Our camp has not yet been described, and as it is the simplest and best form of shelter for a party of two, working in rough country and near forest or "scrub," an exact description of it may prove useful. It is an invention of Douglas's, and we call it a "batwing." In the ordinary course of camp life, survey parties can have their loads packed on horseback, and carry tent and fly, with a second smaller fly to pitch at the end of the tent to shelter the fire. We, however, have to carry all our goods and chattels

on our backs, and over very rough, unexplored country, so could not afford to take such a weighty camp. We therefore pitch an ordinary 6 ft. by 8 ft. canvas tent, on a ridge pole, with an 8 ft. by 10 ft. fly six inches above it; and cut the tent in half along the ridge, and taking away one half, leave the other standing. This is just large enough to allow two men to lie "heads and tails." The front, or side, is left open, and one side of the fly, which was over the half taken away, is raised about 4 ft. in the middle, and the two corners slightly less. Under this the fire burns about 3 ft. away from the remaining half of the tent, so that in wet weather we have shelter for ourselves and fire, and save more than half the weight, and though rather cramped for room are fairly comfortable. Should a heavy gale of wind make the shelter too cold, or cause discomfort by blowing the smoke into the batwing, we make a "breakwind" of ferns or branches across in front to protect us. We never have more than this to cover us, and often when necessary to travel in "light order" trust to finding some friendly rock to sleep under, or build a "mai-mai" with bark and ferns.

Our stores arrived by pack-horse next day from Maporika, a ford rather below Nesbitt's hut having been found for the horses. Having made ourselves fairly comfortable, and ready for a long stay, I spent the afternoon in looking about the terminal face and reconnoitring, to determine our best mode of attacking the very rough glacier in front of us. The exact position of the terminal face of the Franz Josef Glacier is lat. S. 43° 25′ 30″, long. E. 170° 10′ 58″—or rather nearer the Equator than Florence in Italy. It comes down to within 14 miles of the sea to an altitude of only 692 ft. above sea-level.

It is about half a mile broad, and showed an upper layer of white ice pushing its way over a lower layer which carried dirt and stones.

There are five isolated *roches moutonnées* standing at intervals across the valley at the terminal face. On the right-hand side is the Sentinel Rock, 236 ft. high, the largest; a few feet to the left comes the "Mueller" Rock, 60 ft. high; the "Strauchon" Rock lies nearly three chains further to the left, and is about 160 ft. high, and lastly the "Barron" Rock, 50 ft. in height, lies near the river, which flowed out on the extreme left or east side of the glacier. Behind the Sentinel Rock, with the ice still pressing against it, is a rock—since named the "Harper" Rock—about 170 ft. in height, with some moraine débris on its summit, which must have been deposited within the last few years, as no moss or vegetation was to be seen there. Some eight chains to the left and still surrounded by ice, the "Park" Rock, 190 ft., lies behind the "Strauchon," and is raked by a running fusilade of falling ice from the towering pinnacles behind. For the purpose of understanding this interesting array of rocks across the valley, reference can be made to the sketch plan of the "Terminal face of the Franz Josef Glacier," given in Chapter XI.

The best point from which to get a general idea of the valley and glacier is the Sentinel Rock, and thither I went as soon as possible to form a plan of attack. The glacier being in such a warm latitude and low altitude, and having such a rapid descent, is naturally very much broken and crevassed. From the Sentinel the great ice-fall can be seen, at a distance of $2\frac{3}{4}$ miles, descending in a little over a mile 1,800 ft. Even from such a distance it presents a grand appearance.

Terminal face Franz Josef Glacier, from Camp I.

Below it the glacier sweeps round a slight bend and comes straight down in gigantic waves to the terminal face. There are evidently rocks, of the same kind as those exposed at the "snout," under the ice for some way up the valley, as the glacier has the appearance of heaving or lurching, from side to side, on its way down between high rocky walls, which rise out of the ice. The idea conveyed to my mind was that of water forced at an angle into a narrow rocky channel, and forming waves which rebound from one side to the other, obliquely across the course of the stream. The extent and height of these "waves" may be seen from some measurements taken just above Cape Defiance; assuming the south bank to be 0, the heights taken at every 100 yards across the glacier were as follows :—0, 21, 80, 40, 95, 55, 177, 229, and 205 ft.

The glacier flows from south to north, and after leaving the *névé* and coming down over the steep slope which forms the ice-fall, it enters a narrow rock-bound valley of a little over half a mile in width. On the eastern or left-hand side (looking up), the rock slopes back for some 200 or 300 ft., and then disappears into luxuriant timber, which clothes the hills up to the usual limit. This rocky bank is cut, here and there, into deep gorges and bluffs by streams from the hills. On the western side the range rises abruptly out of the ice, for the first 300 to 500 ft., a bare ice-worn precipice—fringed with scrub and bush, growing on almost precipitous hillsides, for some thousands of feet above. Here and there fine waterfalls drop over the cliffs into the ice.

The surface of the glacier, contrary to the general rule with New Zealand glaciers, is practically clear of débris, with exception of a narrow strip along the western side coming from a patch of rocks near the head of the ice-fall. This accumulates in the bend above Cape Defiance, a promontory of rock which obstructs the flow of ice on the western side about 2 miles up the glacier, and continues until it joins a larger piece of surface moraine about half a mile from the terminal face, evidently caused by a slip a year or two previous. The débris left by the slip will no doubt have fallen over the terminal face and entirely disappeared by the end of 1898. The very broken nature of the glacier is the real cause of its cleanness and freedom from surface moraine, as the débris falls into crevasses and comes out at the terminal face in the lower layer of dirty ice.

From the general appearance of the valley, it was evident that the best plan would be to cross the river and get on to the eastern bank, for the ice looked too rough for a practical route, and the western side was too precipitous to attempt. Accordingly, on November the 4th, after some heavy rain, I went across to the outlet and endeavoured, without success, to pass over the river on the glacier, while Douglas went down to Nesbitt's hut to bring up the remainder of our stores, which had been left there owing to a flood in the river. I found that the ice was very soft and broken all along the side, and that it was unsafe to attempt a landing on the bank near the terminal face; in fact, it was a decidedly difficult business to get up the sheer ice face on to the glacier. The only course left open to us was to try and force a way straight up the glacier. On the 7th we managed, after some gymnastic feats, to reach a point about one mile up the glacier on the western side, but the last 120 yards having taken an hour, amongst very bad seracs, we gave up the attempt and returned to camp.

The following morning was spent in again trying to get over the river on the ice to the eastern bank, without success, and in the afternoon we went on to the glacier behind the Sentinel Rock, which appeared from subsequent examination to be the only possible route to reach the more level ice in the centre. From this point we made our way up and across the glacier by slow degrees, crawling between crevasses, and cutting steps up and down high and almost perpendicular hummocks, and, after three hours, were able to step ashore on the eastern bank, about a mile from the terminal. For two or three hundred feet above the ice, the hillside is bare, ice-worn rock, sloping back at an angle of 25 degrees, and along this we went for a short distance, until a deep gorge stopped us. As it was late we decided to return to camp and move it up to a suitable place on this bank, at the same time bringing up a spare rope to fix at the gorge.

We always take a dog with us, to catch kiwis, &c., for food, but as our work for some weeks would be on the ice, it was necessary to dispense with the dog's company. When I joined Douglas, I found he had an old friend, "Betsy," a black "pure-bred mongrel," as he called her, and up to this point she had been a faithful, though somewhat useless, companion. Accordingly, while Douglas took her down to the beach for an old digger friend to look after her for a time, I went off to the small farm on the Totara River, obtained half a sheep, and returned to the "Hospital" to sleep. Before returning to camp on the following day I had a bathe in the hot springs.

On nearly every river on the West Coast there are mineral

hot springs. Their heat is not due in any way to volcanic agency, and though I have tried to obtain an analysis of the water, some accident has always happened and I have failed to get particulars. It is generally the case that a mile or so before the river emerges from the hills, a mineral spring is to be found in the bed of the stream, in which case the water will be hot. Sometimes, however, the spring is a few feet above the river level and only warm. The two best I know are those on the Waiho, a mile and a half below the glacier, and on the Fox River, a mile from the Fox Glacier. In each case they are situated in the river-bed, covered at flood-time, and often after the river has resumed its normal level, they are completely buried in gravel. On the flat near the Hospital, hot water can be found almost anywhere; at the depth of six feet it would be warm; at eight feet below the surface or on the edge of the river-bed the temperature is 120°, and at ten feet, or two feet below the river-bed, the temperature is 130°, the hottest I obtained. Their rise and fall correspond with that of the river, showing great activity when the latter is high.

In order to have a good bathe, the plan was to take a long-handled shovel, scoop out a hollow, and letting it fill with water, lie down in it and stew. If, however, the bath proves uncomfortably hot, it is easy to let in a little ice-water from the river a yard or two away, or even catch a piece of floating ice and place it in the pool. It was a new and pleasing sensation to lie in a hot spring, under the shade of tree ferns, and enjoy the glorious view of a glacier within a mile and a half ploughing its way down between steep hills clothed in luxuriant forest, and backed by high snow and ice-clad peaks. When

going up a river, there is no difficulty in locating these springs, for their smell is strong, and rather objectionable. Douglas said that "you smell as if you've been having tea with the Evil One inside an old gasometer," after having a bathe in one of them. I cannot vouch for the correctness of the comparison, as I have never had tea under such conditions, but can quite imagine the combination would produce much the same effect.

On Douglas's return we moved camp and some three weeks' provisions across the glacier, and along the eastern side, to a point about a mile and a half up the valley, and ascending 400 ft. up the ice-worn rocks, found a capital camping place amongst great rata trees, and alongside a clear stream of water, which ran in a deep, water-worn channel down to the glacier, with many small pools in which to bathe.

Situated as we were at Camp 2, in fine rata bush, with a luxuriant undergrowth of tree-ferns and other plants—which in England would be called semi-tropical vegetation,—it was difficult to believe that we were a mile and a half up and 300 ft. above a glacier. Through an opening in the trees in front of our batwing, lofty snow-capped peaks could be seen a mile away across the valley, rising in precipices from steep slopes, clothed with dark green bush; while below, a pure white glacier flowed at our feet, presenting as fine an instance of crevassed and broken ice as could be wished. A near view of Alpine peaks with a foreground of trees is, of course, met with in many places, but it is doubtful whether the beautiful combination of tree-ferns, semi-tropical vegetation, glacier and snow-clad mountains, can be seen anywhere else, except on the Fox Glacier. From the rocky platform at the edge of the bush, a few yards from the camp, we overlooked the glacier flowing past, in great broken waves, down to the terminal face, beyond which were glimpses of the river as it wound in and out of the old moraine hillocks, covered with luxuriant timber, to the large river-flats below. And fourteen miles away, the blue sea was plainly visible, with the "white horses" raised by a squall of wind.

One result of the neighbourhood of the ice is that Alpine plants, such as the nei-nei, broom, daisies, and edelweiss, are found growing amongst the vegetation of the low country. I found one plant of the last named growing within 800 ft. of sea-level on the Sentinel Rock. It does not appear to grow more luxuriantly at so low an altitude, but on the whole is rather stunted.

Finding the ice at the side of the glacier very rotten, we attempted to continue along the side, and succeeded in reaching a rocky "cape" which rose about half a mile further up the valley. On ascending the point, we discovered that the rock side had lost its gentle slope, and rose out of the ice in a perpendicular face of several hundred feet—smooth and ice-worn. There was no route along here, so we returned, looking out for a place where we could cross the rough side ice and reach the more level surface in the centre of the glacier. The whole of the 16th was spent in trying to find a route on to the glacier. At seventy or eighty yards from the side, broad crevasses ran across and along the line of flow, consequently, though the surface was fairly level, it was cut up into huge seracs and hummocks. After five unsuccessful attempts we found a fairly good route, which, however, necessitated some peculiar acrobatic performances.

Twice or thrice I had to let Douglas down bodily into a

crevasse, so that he could cut steps up to me, the side being too perpendicular to allow us to cut downwards in comfort; and then I had to cut steps up again on the other side for perhaps 40 ft., using the axe with only one hand, and holding on to the ice with the other. No doubt, had the glacier been at a higher altitude there would have been no difficulty in finding several routes, but here the ice was terribly rotten. Occasionally we would hear a report like a pistol-shot, or louder, and feel a tremble under our feet, or see a large serac fall down which looked strong enough to stand for days. Under these circumstances, therefore, we had to be most careful to choose a good line, because it had been decided to move camp again to Cape Defiance, a mile or so further up on the opposite side, in order to have a good point from which to attack the great ice-fall and do our work on the *névé*. If bad weather came on and delayed us in the upper camp for a week, it would be possible that our retreat to Camp 2 would be cut off by reason of the frequent changes in the surface ice.

Having spent some days in survey work and wet weather, on the 22nd we each took 40 lb. loads, including camera and instruments, and made for Cape Defiance (2,864 ft.). It occupied just an hour and a quarter to go some 200 yards before we reached the good travelling in the centre. When "fossicking" for this route the week previous, our gymnastic feats were most interesting and amusing, as we had only a camera to carry; but now with our loads we found it not only trying, but most difficult. The "swags" had to be lowered and pulled up again frequently, receiving very rough handling, regardless of their contents.

The centre of the glacier was fairly good going for a short

distance, and then we got amongst some bad crevasses again, with long narrow ridges between. Often after crawling along several of these razor backs, we would find our way blocked by a break in the ridge and be compelled to retrace our steps and try another line. Luckily, anticipating some such work as this, I had brought a bundle of leafy twigs of rata to stick into the ice and mark our route, to save time on the return, because had we taken the wrong razor-back at the start, we might have had an hour's work for nothing. Consequently, when we emerged from the rough ice close under Cape Defiance, there was a trail of rata twigs behind which would insure more speedy travelling in the future.

At Cape Defiance we found the only real piece of lateral moraine on the glacier—about eighteen chains long. This cape, or point, is formed by a spur which projects across the flow of the glacier, and, narrowing the valley by a quarter of a mile, causes the ice to "back up" behind it to a considerable height. On the upper side of the spur the lateral moraine lies at right angles to the general flow of the glacier, the ice having swept down into the bend, and then, turning in an eddy, flowed along and round the cape. In the valley formed by the moraine and hillside, we built a level floor of large stones on which to place out batwing. Heavy rain had set in at noon, so we were fairly wet through and uncomfortable by the time we had pitched the camp. Behind us the hillside had dense Alpine scrub on it, and rose very steeply to the rocky pinnacles of Mount Moltke; to the right a stream ("Harper's Creek" it has since been named) came down from the ice-fields of the same peak. The valley down which this creek flows is very steep, and on the upper side has sheer rocky precipices, which

THE UNSER FRITZ FALL, 1,209 FEET, FROM CAMP III.

*To face page 61.*

are 2,000 ft. high near the glacier, and as the valley rises they gradually become lower, until at the head they are only some 500 ft. Over this rock-wall, a waterfall, the Unser Fritz, descends in one leap 1,200 ft., being the drainage of the Andermatten and Baumann Glaciers on Mount Roon.

In front of us was the grand ice-fall in all its glory, 1,800 ft. or more in height, and a mile wide, presenting a dazzling array of towering seracs and deep blue crevasses. I have seen many fine ice-falls in Switzerland and New Zealand, but very much doubt if any, except perhaps the Haast Glacier on the Tasman, is as grand as that of the Franz Josef. Though I call it 1,800 ft. in height, it may be said that for 3,000 ft. at the least, the glacier is really an ice-fall.

On the 24th we made an attempt to force a way to the *névé*. After three hours we reached the head of the ice-fall by means of a fairly smooth strip of ice, caused by the inflow of the Almer Glacier on the left. It is generally the rule that where two glaciers join, the crevasses and seracs are much smaller than elsewhere. But after passing the junction nothing could be done. The *névé* snow was within a quarter of a mile, smooth and white, but between us was a field of ice broken into seracs and crevasses in a manner which it is impossible to conceive without seeing. Douglas said it looked like a bird's-eye view of an Eastern town, with a deep blue street between each and every house. The seracs were all square and flat topped, but surrounded by apparently bottomless crevasses. I could see that the only way to make a successful traverse up this glacier was in the early spring, when the winter snow would form bridges over this impassable piece of ice. It would only be waste of time to attempt to go any further, because nothing could be done without a ladder of at least 25 ft. It was also raining heavily, so we returned to camp and spent the afternoon in making sundry observations, &c.

On the following morning we went up the spur behind the camp to 5,000 feet or so, in order to get some compass shots into the upper basin of the *névé*. From this point the outlook was splendid. Immediately on the right, across Harper's Creek, within a few chains, was the great Unser Fritz Waterfall, with its two small glaciers and enormous precipices on each side. To the south-east we got a clear view for a short time into the main *névé* coming off Mount De la Bêche and the saddles leading into the Tasman Glacier. Opposite us was the Almer Glacier, a fine open icefield coming off Stirling Rock, behind which Drummond's Peak showed a peculiar array of tooth-like rocks rising out of a field of snow. On the other side of this range lies the Callery River, which joins the Waiho by the Hospital. Over the low country to the north, the view was good, but limited. The glacier to the Terminal face lay 2,000 ft. below, at the foot of great precipices, over which a grand series of waterfalls fell with a roar into the ice. Beyond it lay Lake Maporika, and the sea-coast was easily visible to the Wataroa bluff. The clouds, however, soon hid everything, and more heavy rain compelled our descent to camp.

Next morning, in still bad weather, we retired down the glacier to Camp 2, having decided that no route lay up the ice to the *névé*. The ice on the line of route had altered very much, even during the last three or four days, and had it not been for my rata twigs left on the way up, we should have had hard work to find a way. Sometimes we would see a piece of rata 30 feet away and take a quarter of an hour to work round to it. The ice at the place where we had to leave the glacier was even more altered than elsewhere, and it was difficult to recognise the way which we had followed when getting on from the rocks. However, by lowering Douglas to cut steps once or twice, we were able to come off safely and reach Camp 2 at 4 P.M. pretty wet and hungry.

We now decided to try a high-level route along the top of the range behind the camp on to the Almer *névé*, and across it, over a shoulder of Stirling Rock, to the main *névé*. This would involve a considerable amount of track cutting or "blazing" in the dense bush and scrub, and probably, with the bad weather we were having, would take some time. I therefore went to Camp 1 at the Terminal face, and Douglas went on to the township at Maporika for more stores. Unfortunately, while there, he had a bad attack of influenza, lasting nearly three weeks, and so, beyond perfecting the survey and taking some observations of glacier motion, little could be done for the present. In naming the tributary glaciers and peaks which had not already received names from the low country trigonometrical stations, we used those of Swiss guides, in Almer, Croz, Baumann Glaciers, &c. It is often hard to find names, so we use those of one class for one valley, and another class for another locality, as far as possible.

## CHAPTER V.

### WAIHO RIVER—THE HIGH COUNTRY.

Track Cutting—Dry Camp (No. 5)—Wekas—Another Failure—Maporika—Mount Moltke Spur—Camp 6—Camp 7—Gale and Shipwreck—Return—Callery River—Heavy Flood—Marching Orders.

On Douglas's return we began to "blaze" our track to the grass line behind Camp 2. This very trying business is so constantly necessary, that I must try and convey some idea of the work.

The undergrowth in the bush is as a rule so bad, that progress is very slow, even without a load on one's back. But when carrying anything it is almost impossible to make any way at all. It is therefore a saving of time to take a billhook and "blaze," or cut a narrow track, before attempting to carry any load through the undergrowth. When climbing a hill to reach the grass line this is more necessary than when travelling on flat country, and an ascent of 1,500 ft. is a good day's work. Often in the Ranges the bush is fairly open from 1,500 ft. to 2,500 ft. above sea-level, consisting of large trees and little undergrowth, but at the latter altitude mountain vegetation begins to appear amongst the trees, and at 3,000 ft. the true impenetrable mountain scrub has to be faced. This varies from ten to three feet in height, and its denseness can hardly be appreciated by those who have not experienced it. I have seen it thick enough to walk and crawl on the top of, and in nearly every locality a 500 ft. ascent is a good day's work. Sometimes it is literally too tangled to force a way through without a bill-hook to clear a track, even when carrying no load; and any attempt would leave very few garments on the back of the man who tried. The only stuff I know which is impervious to the stiff pointed ends of the stunted vegetation, is "Gabardine," made by T. Burberry and Son, Basingstoke, England.

The track which had to be cut from Camp 2 to the grass line was my first experience of this sort of work, and I can safely recommend it to any one wishing to test his vocabulary. Five hours' hard work only took me 600 ft. up the hill, and now, after considerable experience in "blazing," I have decided that a distance which takes an hour to cut, will only take four or five minutes to go with a load on one's shoulders after it is cleared. We only clear a width of about two feet, sufficient to get our loads along in comfort.

Owing to wet weather and various other delays, it was the 23rd of December before we had our camp pitched in the last piece of mountain scrub, some 4,000 ft. above sea-level, on the opposite side of the glacier to Cape Defiance and the Unser Fritz Fall. This we named Dry Camp (or No. 5), because there was only one small drip of water from an overhanging rock, which took some hours to fill the "billy." A thousand feet above the camp there was a small peak, from which the finest panorama in the district—without going above the snow line—can be obtained.

Looking south from here was the great *névé* basin of the Franz Josef Glacier with its tributary ice falls, the Agassiz, Melchior, &c., and beyond them were the fine rock peaks of the

Dividing Range, including Mounts Spencer (9,157 ft.), Jervois (8,675 ft.), and another (9,511 ft.), which I named Conway's Peak, lying on the Divide at the point from which the Bismarck Range branches to the north. Across the valley this Range, with its peaks, glaciers, and waterfalls, was seen for its whole length, and to the north the coast line could be followed, bluff after bluff, to the Wanganui River, and still further we could see the Paparoa Ranges north of Greymouth between ninety and a hundred miles away.

When Douglas had rejoined me on the 16th December, we brought up some ten days' stores only, thinking that would be ample for our projected expedition to the *névé*; however, the rain and Douglas's illness had kept us back, so we were compelled to economise our food. On Christmas Day we were in fog and could do nothing, so we reluctantly decided to kill one of the pair of wekas which had honoured us with their presence. As they had two young ones we were unwilling to kill either of the birds, but a Christmas dinner looking very doubtful we shot the male. Previously I had shot a crow, and on opening the weka's crop we had evidence of their extraordinary ideas of food, for in it was the copper cartridge-case which had been used for the crow, already partly polished by the stones. Mrs. Weka seemed to take a great interest in our method of preparing her late husband for the stew, and, on my throwing the remains aside, her reason was obvious. She at once seized the discarded parts and carried them in triumph to her young ones, no doubt saying, "Here, my dears, is part of your poor old father for a Christmas dinner." She then returned, carefully picked up and gave her promising young family all the remains of the stew.

In the West Coast Ranges it is the exception if hill tops are clear of fog after noon in the summer, and generally the clouds form on them as early as 9 or 10 A.M.; consequently, though the weather is fine in the valleys, we are often unable to do any work on the tops except in the very early morning. For three days fog prevented our taking observations at or near Dry Camp, and till we had done this it was useless to go on to the *névé*. The delay necessitated further supplies, and was the more inconvenient because our drip of water had ceased.

On the 27th, Douglas went to Camp 2 for some flour, and I took the two billies down to a creek, 600 ft. below, for water, and shot a bird or two. The 29th saw us, with light loads of 30 lbs., pushing along the rotten rocky spur towards the *névé* of the Almer Glacier, but again we were doomed to disappointment. At noon we came to a deep gorge walled by rotten cliffs, down which stones were constantly falling. After an hour's work we managed to find a fair route into the gorge, but the other side was too rotten to ascend. There is no doubt a party of three could traverse this side without much trouble, but we did not consider it safe for two men to put so much dangerous ground behind them if any other route existed, because should any accident occur to one I doubt if the other could have got out alone; also Douglas had been shaken by his recent attack of influenza, and was not fit to do such a difficult and long day as we should have before us. Wherever the schist formation ends and the slate begins, we find terribly shattered rocks, and when this occurs in a precipitous locality, it is often quite impossible to traverse the steep faces with real safety. The gorge that turned us back was near the point of junction of the two formations, and had enormous masses of rotten rock ready to fall; in fact, we could hardly touch any projecting stone, however large, without dislodging it.

Having christened the gorge "No Go" Creek, we returned to Dry Camp, and, gathering all our goods, left them at 5 P.M. for Camp 2, which we reached at 8 P.M.

On the last day of the year we moved Camp 2 down to our old terminal face quarters, and found that the ice behind the Sentinel had so changed, that it gave us great trouble to find a route off the glacier at all.

During the next three weeks we had some very bad weather and floods, which considerably delayed my work on Lake Maporika, which I had been sent to survey before we did any further work at the glacier. This, and other lakes on the low country, lie between high moraine hills left by ancient glaciers. They are all supposed by the inhabitants to be bottomless. I do not know why, except that people seem to look upon a bottomless lake as a luxury, and are very angry with the man who destroys the illusion. The general rule is, that they are not quite so deep as their height above sea-level. Maporika lies about 275 or 300 ft. above the sea, so I offered to bet that the lake was under 300 ft. in depth, but no one would accept, for they said they knew the lake was bottomless. When I sounded in fourteen places, and found bottom always within 280 ft., many of the inhabitants of the district took it as a personal insult, and have never quite forgiven me. While camping on the shore of this lake, I heard the cry of the rua, or large brown kiwi, now nearly extinct and very valuable; I believe there are one or two pairs in this locality.

Thanks to a flood putting one of my camps four feet under

water, and otherwise delaying my work, it was the 25th of January, 1894, when I rejoined Douglas at the glacier. He had been laying off a line for a horse track from Nesbitt's to the terminal face.

We now decided to go along the spur on the western side of the glacier, and if necessary ascend Mount Roon, so as to complete our map of the *névé*.

As Douglas was yet feeling far from well, we asked A. Woodham, one of the diggers, to come and give us a helping hand for the ten days we expected to be away. It was two days before we had our track blazed and camp pitched 2,700 ft. above the flat. The view from Camp 6 of the glacier was quite the prettiest picture we saw, for the glacier could be seen from the *névé* to near the snout through a framework of nei-nei and other trees. The nei-nei is a mountain scrub, and grows up to 30 ft. in height; its foliage is like a large pineapple head. Some plants have only straight stems and one head, while others have gnarled and twisted limbs with a hundred heads. The shape of the tuft on the end of the branches gives a tropical appearance to the scene, and as it only grows in any quantity near the grass line on the West Coast, it is rarely difficult to obtain a foreground of apparently tropical vegetation with a distance of snow and ice—a combination at once curious and beautiful. The grass line was 1,000 ft. above Camp 6, and it took Woodham and me two and a half days to cut through the scrub for that height. I never experienced before or since such an impenetrable tangle of vegetation, of stunted, hard, stubborn akeake, broom, &c. This mountain scrub, to a great extent, grows downhill, that is, when ascending you have the branches pointing towards you, consequently it is difficult to get into a shrub to cut a limb off near the ground. In places it is not unlike meeting a number of fixed bayonets pointing at you, and trying to cut the rifle off at the stock with a bill-hook without room to swing it properly.

On the 1st of February we shouldered our loads, and made along the high ridge towards Mount Moltke, but at noon a fog came up, and at 3 p.m. the dry fog changed to a wet mist, a sure sign of a storm. We could not see thirty yards ahead, so decided to go down on our right and camp, because it was the lee side of the ridge, and also because the slopes towards the glacier were practically precipices. After descending 500 ft. in the fog we came to a precipice, and on going to the right and left, found more sheer rocks. The mist was too thick to see how deep, or of what kind these faces were, so having found a small patch of scrub growing on the hillside, we decided to stay where we were. It took an hour to cut a flat shelf 6 ft. by 8 ft., out of the hillside with our ice axes. On this shelf we pitched our fly, stretched on a rope between two ice axes, and tied down in every possible direction to the long snow-grass. We were thoroughly wet by this time, and the wind was whistling over the ridge above us from the northwest.

Douglas had a dry shirt, I had a pair of light canvas trousers to put on, and Woodham had a complete change, so we hung our wet garments outside, there being no chance of a good enough fire to dry them, and put our blankets round us. We were, however, able to make a small fire of scrub for boiling the billy, and having had a good drink of hot cocoa, turned in. All that night and next day it blew a hurricane, but this did not affect us much as we were on the lee side of the ridge. Over our heads we could see the grass and lily leaves whirling about, having been literally torn up by the roots, and between the blinding squalls of rain we watched the sea, whipped into one sheet of foam by the squalls. The high wind and heavy rain dispersed the fog of the previous day, and enabled us to look at our surroundings and see where we had got to, a point which we had been unable to decide the previous evening.

From Conway's Peak, at the extreme south corner of the Franz Josef Glacier, the Bismarck Range branches off in a north-westerly direction towards the coast, dividing for a mile and a half its névé from that of the Fox Glacier. At this point, a short ridge, "The Chancellor," branches off for five miles nearly due west, and a mile and a half further on the Bismarck Range is Mount Anderegg (8,360 ft.), which sends an offshoot to the west for about seven miles. Between these two diverging ranges the Victoria Glacier lies, and beyond them the Fox Glacier flows, first along the Chancellor ridge, and then passing the snout of the Victoria Glacier, continues along the foot of the second range. Anderegg's Peak and Mount Roon (7,344 ft.), which lies a mile north of it, give rise to the Fritz Glacier, which is bounded on the south by the second range, and on the north by a spur which comes off Mount Moltke (6,509 ft.), a peak a little north of Roon. The Fritz Glacier is the source of the Waikukupa River. On Mount Moltke is a small icefield, which sends its drainage to the east down Harper's Creek, by Cape Defiance, and to the north gives rise to the Oemerua River. After leaving Moltke, the Bismarck Range continues north for four miles, sending off several short abrupt spurs to the west, between which are valleys of some 1,500 ft. in depth, walled by high precipitous sides. These are drained by "Dry" Creek, which flows into the Waiho River, six miles below the glacier. Some idea of the great steepness of these valleys and ridges may be gained by the fact that, near the head of Dry Creek, a straight line could be taken for a mile and a quarter in length, which would cross three ridges of 5,090 ft., and two valleys 1,500 to 2,000 ft. deep. This is often the case on the West Coast ranges. The main chain of the Southern Alps sends off more spurs and branch ranges of considerable altitude on the western slopes than on the eastern. All these have deep valleys between them, and descend from 10,000 ft. and upwards to within 500 ft. of sea-level in a distance of less than ten miles. Those valleys in which there are glaciers present high precipitous sides of rock, and in the lower portions, the rivers descend through dark bush-clad or bare rocky gorges—beautiful scenery, but ugly from the unfortunate explorer's point of view.

On the 2nd of February, when the fog cleared, we found ourselves camping on a very steep hillside, near the head of one of the branches of Dry Creek. The other side of the valley, for 1,000 ft. or more, was almost a precipice, with grass and stunted scrub clinging to it in places.

The storm still raged furiously, and as our aneroids had fallen 1·10 inches during the night, Douglas and I put on our wet clothes, made the fly ropes taut, gathered some bits of scrub for the fire and retired again to our blankets. So long as the wind came from the north-west it was fairly warm, and we were more or less sheltered by the spur above us; but, about two hours after dark, it veered round as usual to the south-west, and blew with all its force on to our shelter, bringing with it hail and sleet, instead of rain.

There is a fixed rule, which rarely has an exception, as to weather on the West Coast, namely, that north-west wind always brings heavy rain, followed by south-west hail and rain storms for a day, and then fine weather again till the next nor'-wester. As soon as the wind, therefore, veered round to the south-west we knew that twenty-four hours would see fine weather, and, as the temperature fell, our spirits rose. Douglas had turned in, in his dry shirt, I was in my thin canvas trousers only; but Woodham, luckily for himself, had on plenty of clothes. Towards midnight the gale increased, and the wind howled round us in furious gusts, trying to dislodge the fly which was flapping about in an alarming manner. Douglas had just said, "It is deuced lucky that we tied her down so well," when a squall struck us again, and after a brief struggle with the canvas it broke a rope, and in half a second the whole arrangement had gone away in the darkness. Up we all scrambled, Douglas and I in our airy costume, as there was no time to find and put on our wet clothes, and began to struggle with the canvas. The wind seemed literally to leap on us, driving the hail with almost irresistible force, and making it very difficult to rig up any kind of shelter. After nearly a quarter of an hour battling with the fly, tumbling over one another in the dark, and slipping down on the wet and steep grass with our bare feet, we managed to put up a rough shelter. Cold as I was, with my almost naked body, I almost smiled at Douglas's wild appearance, seen at intervals in the uncertain light, when we came near one another, his solitary garment fluttering in the wind, and every moment a hasty remark would be heard as he slipped with his bare legs on the wet grass. Neither Douglas in his long years of exploration, nor I, have had our shelters blown away before. And if the hail stung his bare legs as it stung my bare back and chest, I feel sure neither of us will ever neglect a precaution which would prevent another such experience.

As soon as we had any shelter at all we got under it, and allowed Woodham to finish fixing the ropes. We then donned our wet garments, having wrung them out, and, rolled in our wetter blankets, lay waiting for dawn. Poor old Douglas was chilled to the bone, and I really feared he would be unable to face the storm and journey down at daybreak. As soon as the first streak of light allowed us to see, Woodham began to kindle a fire. Everything was wet as possible, but by burning a candle and dropping the grease on to a piece of rag, and lighting that, he gradually charred and dried enough twigs to make a blaze. In two hours we had a billy full of boiling cocoa, and with the help of that soon made Douglas warm. My young bones and blood did not get the cold into them like his, for there is a great difference in the staying powers of a man under thirty and one over fifty years of age. At noon the wind was still blowing a gale, so we decided to go down to the Hospital and leave everything where it was. When we reached the top of the ridge the fog came again, and we found the force of the wind very great; several times we had to lie down for some seconds, or we should have been blown away like flies. Whenever possible we descended and traversed the steep face on the lee side of the ridge. At one time we must have been in a thundercloud, as our axes hummed. In three

or four hours we reached the shelter of the bush, and at 7 p.m. arrived at the Hospital, where dry clothes, a good fire, and hot tea made us happy.

This was Woodham's first experience on the higher country, and he said it would be his last. He thought it a "Very poor game." But his disgust was only temporary, he was far too enterprising a man to be so easily daunted. In two days the weather cleared and we returned to the scene of our late discomfort, to complete our work and bring down the things. On the way we called in at Camp 1, at the terminal face, and found it blown down, and all my photographic plates which had been exposed up the glacier, had been exposed a second time to two days' rain. Eventually it proved that not many were spoilt, but this is an instance of the difficulties which I had to contend against for my photographs.

Having gone along the ridge beyond our camp to a point from which we could get observation into the *névé* and complete the map, we picked up our camp and returned to the diggers' huts. The only incident worth mentioning which occurred on our second trip along the ridge was one which might have been a serious accident. The outer ranges often have deep and narrow fissures in the rock after reaching the grass line. Sometimes these are 300 ft. deep, or more, and only a few feet broad, easily hidden by the long snow-grass. On this spur there were several small ones, a foot or two broad, and perhaps 20 to 50 ft. deep. Coming down the grass ahead of Douglas, I heard a "coo-ee" from above, and being unable to see him on looking up, I returned and heard another below me, so I went down again, thinking I had been mistaken, when a third cry came from behind. Putting down my load, I was again ascending, when I heard a voice on my right, "You might pull a chap out of a hole!" It appears that poor Douglas had walked into one of those fissures, which was luckily narrow, and his load had jammed, preventing him from falling below his shoulders. We soon had him out, none the worse for the mishap. On reaching the diggers' huts with our various belongings, a day or two later, we were greeted with news of the gale, which had done an immense amount of damage all over the district. Roads were blocked, houses blown down, and no prospect of the mail getting through for some time.

Douglas now had another attack of his influenza, brought on by the recent chill, and he retired down to more comfortable quarters at the Lake. I stayed on the Hospital with the diggers, and spent my time in preparing the map and going up and along the "Burster" Ridge on the north side of the Callery River, to get bearings and photographs, into the head of that river and the Totara. There is gold in the reaches of the river above the gorge, and several diggers have been into the upper valley. No possible route exists through the gorge itself, owing to the very precipitous sides, so a track has been blazed up Mount Mueller (3,700 ft.), and along the ridge to the grass line. This ridge is easy but tiring, yet the inhabitants of the district look upon it as a breakneck and difficult journey. Several young fellows have been so frightened by the travellers' tales told by the older diggers, that they would sooner do anything than try to "go over the Burster."

The Callery River drains Mount Elie de Beaumont (10,200 ft.), which sends down two fine ice fields, the Burton and

Spencer, both primary glaciers. The saddle at the actual source of the river, a mile or two above the Burton Glacier, leads probably into the Wataroa River, nearly under the Lendenfeldt saddle, which lies at the extreme head of the great Tasman Glacier. At present the topography of the upper waters and tributaries of the Wataroa River is very uncertain, but I think it safe to assume that the Lendenfeldt and Callery saddles lead into the same valley. I have never been on the former, but knowing the Western Ranges so well could easily decide the point, and hope before long to be able to do so. From the Burster, Mount Elie de Beaumont is a beautiful cone, rising out of the two glaciers, to its right Mount Green (9,325 ft.), and the Minarets are seen rising out of the *névé* of the same glacier, the Spencer. A pass could be made between Green and Elie de Beaumont on to the head of the Tasman Glacier, opposite Mount Darwin.

About the middle of February we had five days of heavy rain, and several slips occurred on the Glacier Branch, causing the bed of the river to rise eight or ten feet, with gravel and other débris. The result was that the water overflowed its usual flood-channels, and, cutting in behind the wire bridge above the Hospital, washed away its supports. The bridge consequently gradually became less taut, and at last touched the water; strong as the wire ropes were, they hardly resisted the rushing torrent for a second, but snapped like twine, and the whole structure collapsed.

A flood of such magnitude is worth seeing; on the Glacier Branch great icebergs which had broken off from the glacier careered madly along, crashing and colliding against one another, and huge boulders could be heard bumping down under the water. In the Callery Gorge, the water was thirty feet above its normal level, and on emerging from its narrow rock-bound channel on to the more open ground, it spread out right and left in huge waves. Trees and stones were swept along with tremendous speed and force. After the river subsided we found a mass of ice blocks stranded amongst the trees in the bush by the hut. All the claims were filled with débris, and unworkable for days, and in some cases the men had to wait for weeks, until the river had scoured out some of the gravel in its bed, and lowered its level, thus enabling them to get sufficient fall to carry away their " tailings."

As soon as I could find a horse on which to ford the river, I went up to the glacier to see what damage the flood had done. In places the terminal face had retreated five or six yards owing to the masses of ice which had broken away, and at the outlet on the east side there appeared the finest ice cave I have ever had the pleasure of seeing. It was 100 ft. high, and about the same breadth, while quite fifty yards inside a ray of sunlight could be seen coming through some crevasse which had opened through the ice above. At that point the cave seemed to still maintain its dimensions, but beyond was inky darkness. This glacier had since 1867 been well known at its terminal face, as it only necessitates a ride of fourteen miles up an open river bed from the sea; beyond, the snout only had been unexplored. Twenty years or more before our visit, Douglas says he remembers hearing of some Maoris, who were prospecting for gold with the early diggers on the river flats, going up to look at the ice. At that time it came down to the Sentinel Rock, and the large cave, out of which the river flowed, was between the Mueller and the Strauchon

Rocks. The Maoris, on seeing this, imagined that it was a tunnel through the Ranges to some unknown country on the other side from which all the gold came. So they brought up a large "dug out" canoe, and having obtained some short poles with steel hooks on the end, they started into the cave on a voyage of discovery, using the hooks against the icy walls. After they had gone in some little distance it is presumed a block of ice fell near them, or they heard one of the cracks or groans which we so often heard on this glacier, because the canoe suddenly shot out into daylight again, and her crew jumped ashore, saying the "Taipo" (devil) was in the cave.

I ought, perhaps, to have mentioned before, that "Waiho" means "smoky waters"; it is difficult to decide whether the Maoris named it because of the very milky appearance of the water, or because of the peculiarly thick white fog which hangs over the stream, not encroaching at all on the banks, but only covering the actual water. The river has more silt coming down it than any other on the coast, and its water is very milky at the mouth.

## CHAPTER VI.

COOK RIVER—BALFOUR GLACIER.

Old Moraines—Beach Travelling and Digging—Gillespies—Ryan's Range—Balfour Glacier—A Race with the Clouds—"Topsy."

At the end of February instructions came for us to go without delay to Cook River, and explore all its branches. Some years ago the track or road which skirts the outer hills southwards from Ross, was continued from Maporika, across the Waiho River, some three miles below the glacier, and thence over the Oemerua and Waikukupa Rivers to Cook River. The distance by this road does not exceed twelve miles, but it had been allowed to grow over, and is now worse to tackle than bush in its natural state. Why the authorities should have allowed a track, which cost a good sum of money, to grow over, is hard to say; possibly because the powers that be in Okarito and Gillespies had sufficient influence to prevent its being kept open, for it diverted all the southern horse traffic from these two "townships." However, the fact remained that, instead of being able to ride in an hour or two from the Franz Josef Glacier to Cook's River, we had to go down the Waiho to the sea beach, and along it to Gillespies township, and strike inland some eight miles to a small farm on Cook River flats—thirty-five miles of bad going, taking a day and a half. Having procured a horse on which to carry our property, we left

Mouth of Cook River and South Bluff.

the Hospital and our digger friends on the 7th March, and following the Waiho river-bed to the beach, went to Mr. Gibb's store and farm at the Waikukupa, where we slept.

Beach travelling is a distinct feature at present on the West Coast. At low tide the sand is generally good, but at high tide the traveller is forced up into soft sand or gravel, and the going becomes tedious and painful. The whole of the lower country is formed of low morainic hills and terraces, reaching 400 ft. in height, left there by the ancient glaciers. These have been cut through here and there by the rivers, and, in many places, they form high bluffs along the sea-shore, at the bottom of which large erratic boulders, loosened by the sea, are lying in confusion. At high tide the surf, which is nearly always heavy, dashes over this mass of rocks, and beats against the hard mass of moraine above them. Some of the bluffs are practically impassable except at low tide, and these have had narrow tracks cut over or round them; others are in their natural state and are impassable at high water. Consequently, travelling along the beach has its excitement, for seas have to be dodged amongst the loose masses of rock strewn along the shore at the foot of a bluff.

Frequently, after a storm, the sea throws up sand and gravel to such an extent that no rocks are visible, and the bluff can be passed on a good beach, but the next tide may destroy the good ground and leave the rocks naked again, or possibly the bluff may be "filled up" for weeks. Two bluffs have to be passed before reaching Gibb's house, both easy ones, and the Oemerua and Waikukupa Rivers have to be forded at their mouths.

The rivers often have large lagoons behind the sea wall, and these have an outlet into the sea, the lagoon filling up at high tide, and nearly running out before the next tide. To cross the water, rushing down over shifting sand, is never pleasant, and can only be done at low or half tide, for the surf causes a strong undercurrent when it runs up the narrow channel against the stream. Fording, when the river is in dangerous condition, or without due experience, has been the cause of many deaths; hardly a river or creek on the coast exists which has not been answerable for one or more lives. From the Waikukupa we reached Gillespies by noon, a township consisting of two publichouses, a store, and a few huts.

It is, indeed, difficult to imagine a more dismal or depressing place than Gilliespies Beach, or "town" as they call it in the district. Some six or seven huts and houses are scattered along the old sea wall of sand hills in a row, facing the sea. These include two publichouses, a Government school, and one store, the other store being part of one publichouse. On approaching it no one is seen about the sandy track which connects the scattered houses, but suddenly one of the many canine mongrels which are plentiful here, becomes aware of a stranger's presence. He gives tongue to his indignation, and, followed by other "curs of low degree," notifies to all whom it may concern the fact that someone is coming. Up to this moment nothing worthy of notice has occurred, but no sooner has the signal been given, than children of all ages and sexes spring up on every side, and, after a short stare to see if they know you or not, bolt like rabbits to their houses, leaving the place again deserted. The stranger then, feeling that he cannot so insult the publican as not to look in for a "drink," turns up from the beach to the sandhills, and proceeds down the "street" towards the "hotel." As he passes each house out come the inhabitants, and, by the time he has reached the shelter of the bar-room, the whole available population of some ten adults and thirty children are gazing at him.

A few diggers live here, working for gold on the beach, or just behind the old sea wall, and the rest of the population practically owe their means of livelihood to supplying these men and others working in the district. This "beach combing" is sometimes profitable, as a great deal of "surfacing," or black gold-bearing sand, is now and then deposited after a storm, and can be taken above high-water mark before the next tide washes it away again. The gold obtained from this sand is very fine, sometimes not much coarser than flour. Above high-water mark, on the sandhills forming the old sea wall, gold-bearing sand is worked in many localities, but is not on the whole profitable, only 15s. to 30s. a week being made. The average, however, is increased when a rich patch of "surfacing" is thrown up by a storm, and good gold obtained from it by those who are on the *qui vive*.

When journeying along the beach, huts belonging to men working the black sand are passed at long intervals, in lonely seclusion on some flat amongst the tall flax or scrub above high-water mark. Behind these is generally a piece of swampy ground to the foot of the morainic hills, which are covered with tall bush; beyond again, within twenty miles, the great snowy ranges can be seen towering up to 10,000 or 12,000 ft., with dark, gloomy valleys, and rocky spurs descending very rapidly to the lower country.

It is a wonderfully fine effect to see this magnificent panorama of mountains so close, clothed with bush at their base, and rising range upon range to their ice-clad summits, while standing on the sea-beach, with the heavy rollers just at one's back, crashing on to the shingle, and roaring as they retire and draw the stones after them. From the beach near the Waikukupa to the summit of Mount Cook, is about 20 miles as the crow flies, and is 8 or 9 miles to the foot of the outer flanks of the ranges, 500 ft. above sea-level. Therefore the Southern Alps and their many buttresses rise at this point 12,000 feet in eight miles, and can be seen for their whole height.

A track has been formed from Gillespies township up to Cook River flats, where Mr. Ryan has a small farm, about eight miles distant, at the foot of the hills; to this we made our way in the afternoon, after two hours' delay at the store, ordering provisions and necessaries.

All the way down the coast our ice-axes had created great curiosity, and Douglas, who is of course known to every man, woman, and child, south of the Wanganui River, overheard some remarks concerning these dangerous-looking implements. Four or five men were standing round the "swags," speculating as to the use of the ice-axes. The first suggested that they were "grubbers which had been sent down for Ryan," another believed "they were picks for fossicking gold in the ranges," and so on *ad lib*. At last a brilliant idea struck some one, and he said, "Why, they are fixings Charlie has invented for spearing eels." This appeared to solve the difficulty, as they adjourned for a drink.

Cook River has, as I have already explained, three branches —the Fox, the Balfour, and the main branch. The first named comes from the Fox Glacier, which drains the Dividing

From Ryan's Spur overlooking Cook River.

Range from Conway's Peak to Mount Tasman, and is bounded on the east by the Bismarck Range and its branches, on the west by Craig's Range, a high offshoot from Mount Tasman, running north-west. The Balfour River flows from the glacier of that name, lying between the latter range and the Balfour Range, which branches off the Divide from near the Silberhorn of Tasman, and runs due west for nine or ten miles. The main branch takes its rise from La Perouse, a fine glacier, which drains the Divide from the Silberhorn of Tasman to Mount Stokes, and flows west between the Balfour and Copland Ranges. The latter range is an offshoot of Mt. Stokes, and runs a little north of west, past Mount Copland (7,895 ft.), and Lyttle's Peak (7,386 ft.), to Ryan's Peak; at this point it branches in two directions, the northerly spur coming down close to the lower extremity of Craig's Range, having curled round past the lower end of the Balfour Range. The main branch of the river is joined by the Balfour stream, about three miles before it leaves the hills, and after flowing for three or four miles on the flat country is joined by the Fox River.

The hut to which we went on Ryan's farm, after leaving Gillespies, is situated a mile or so above the inflow of the latter river. At the point where it leaves the hills the main stream is spanned by a wire rope and cage, placed there for the benefit of three or four men, who are digging a mile further up on the south bank. Gold has been obtained in the main branch and Balfour River, but is now nearly all worked out, only two claims existing at the present.

Our plan of campaign was, firstly, to make an ascent on the lower end of the Copland Range towards Ryan's Peak, in order to get some general observations and photographs, into the upper portions of the two branches and the surrounding peaks, and then make our way to the Balfour Glacier, taking the Fox Glacier and the main branch afterwards.

On March 12th we took our camp to near the diggers' huts, and began to cut the track up a spur behind them. It took two days before we had cleared a track and pitched our camp at 3,000 ft., and, owing to wet and foggy weather, it was the 17th before we were able to do our work on the top of the range. Even then we should have been unsuccessful had we not made a point of reaching our station by 7 A.M., so as to finish the bearing before the fog came. However, luck was on our side, and we were able to fix the station and return with the camp to the diggers' huts by the evening of the 17th. From the shoulder of Ryan's Peak we got a good idea of the topographical features of the watershed of Cook River, and could see the Dividing Range from Mount Elie de Beaumont to the Footstool. This is a good example of West Coast work, as compared with that of the eastern slopes of the Southern Alps. It will be seen that to fix a station at 5,000 ft. took us six days, necessitating a camp at 3,000 feet, whereas on the eastern side of the main range, with its open grassy slopes and more certain climate, the whole thing could have been done in one day from our lower camp.

On March 18th we moved off again, crossing by the cage to the opposite side of the river, and pitching camp, in a perfect deluge of rain, about half a mile above the diggers' huts. Everything we had was wet, so the following morning was spent drying a few things before a large fire, and at noon we continued up the river to the inflow of the Balfour stream, at

which point another, Craig's Creek, also joins the river, flowing from a small ice-field on Craig's Peak. Douglas had explored this branch some years previously, and found the gorge impassable; the route, therefore, lay up the creek for a mile or more, and thence over the spur which comes from Craig's Peak to the gorge, a climb of about 4,000 ft. Accordingly we turned up the creek, which comes down very rapidly over large stones and between rocky sides—a stiff piece of going for us with our usual handicap of 50 lbs. Towards evening we reached a large erratic boulder, about 40 feet high and 250 feet in circumference, under which we could find very fair shelter for the night, so we kindled a fire and turned in.

Even this little valley had signs of ancient ice; the sides were 2,000 ft. high, and showed terraces of smooth ice-worn rocks. It is possible that a glacier originally came from Craig's Peak down here, and joined the main ice stream; but the valley is so short that it is difficult to account for a body of ice large enough to leave such distinct marks and so many erratics.

Half a mile above the bivouac a tributary stream comes off the spur, over which we were going; we therefore, next morning, followed it up for an hour, and then pitched the batwing in the last patch of mountain scrub. Douglas, on his previous visit, had found some good crystals on this spar, so we spent the day crystal hunting, and found some nice specimens. I took my camera to the ridge, some 1,700 ft. above camp, but failed to secure views owing to the inevitable fog. On the 21st I made an early start with my load, in order to obtain some photographs before the fog obscured the higher ranges, leaving Douglas to follow at his leisure.

The view from the ridge will ever live in my memory as one of the most striking I know from a long range, because, not only was it of surpassing grandeur, but of more than ordinary interest. In the first place, no one would suppose —from a distance—that there was room for more than a small valley here; but on closer inspection there proved to be, not only a broad valley and glacier, but a comparatively large tributary valley. The reason of this is, that the ranges are of exceptional steepness, and very narrow, allowing room for broad valleys between. The point on which we were standing was upwards of 5,000 ft. above sea-level, and overlooking a quadrangular basin, seven miles in length, and increasing in breadth from one mile at the upper to two miles at the lower end, the floor of which lay 2,500 ft. below.

A spur from the Balfour Range, and that on which we were standing, forms the western wall of this basin, a deep gorge having been cut through it by the river; Craig's Range and the Balfour Ranges form the northern and southern sides respectively, while the eastern end is blocked by the stupendous buttresses of Mount Tasman. On the north and south of the valley the sides rise in rocky precipices to the height of more than 2,000 ft., and at the eastern end Mount Tasman rises fully 7,000 ft., its black and frowning cliffs only relieved by one small ice-field which lies half-way up its sides. This small glacier is apparently of second-rate importance, but so far as was then known, it formed the *névé* of the Balfour. That a large glacier six miles long should draw its supplies from so small a *névé* was more than doubtful, and I was of opinion that the snow field which we could see between the Balfour Range and Mount Dampier would prove to be the real *névé*

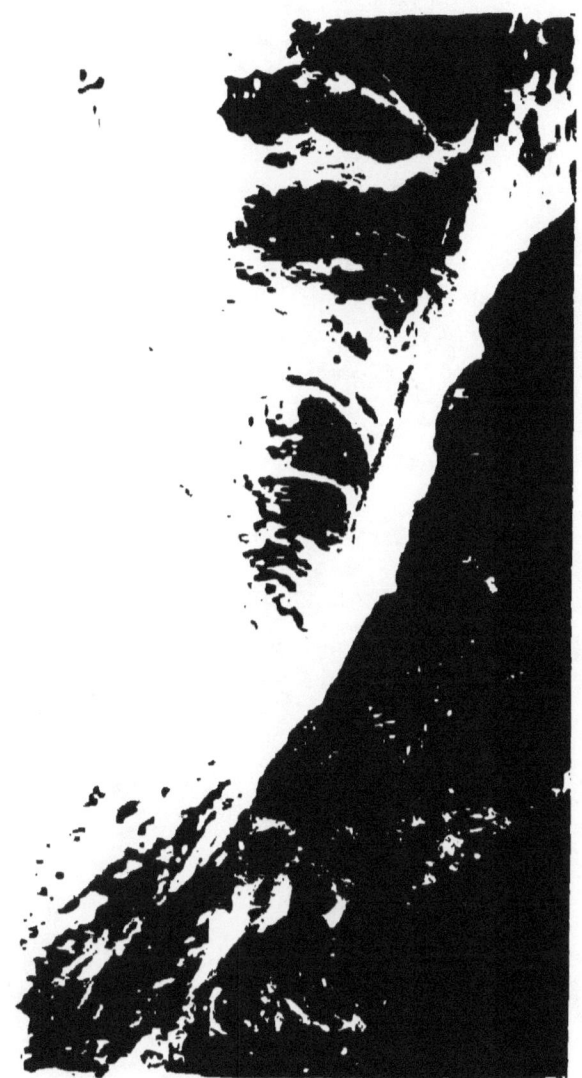

OVERLOOKING THE BALFOUR GLACIER FROM CRAIG'S SPUR.

*To face page 56.*

coming through some unsuspected gap in that range. This point we could not determine from here and hoped to finally settle it by going up the glacier.

There is only one small flow of ice joining the *névé* and trunk of this glacier, most of the ice drops over a cliff over 1,000 ft. in height, bringing with it a great deal of débris, which covers the glacier with heavy moraine for its whole length.

Over the Balfour Range, Mounts Dampier, Hicks, and Stokes could be seen, with Harper's Saddle at the head of the Hooker glacier, and behind again, dominating all, was the upper part of Mount Cook. These great peaks rose in apparently a wall, within seven miles of us, 7,000 or 8,000 ft. of their height being visible.

The original name given to Mount Stokes was "La Perouse," and it seems a pity to have changed it. How appropriate the latter name is cannot be realised better than from Craig's Spur, because from this point there is a group of peaks standing alone, and from their position dwarfing all others. This group could hardly be surpassed, and being all closely connected, should have similar names. At present the name Stokes spoils the uniformity, and, if "La Perouse" were again adopted, we should be able to call the group the "Five Navigators," namely, Tasman (11,475 ft.), Dampier (11,323 ft.), Cook (12,349 ft.), Hicks (10,410 ft.), and La Perouse (10,101 ft.).

Fortunately I had an hour or two on the top to obtain photographs before 9.30, when the fog closed in upon us. Douglas having arrived in due course, we began our descent over steep, treacherous grass slopes and bare rocks, and in two hours arrived at the terminal moraine of the glacier, and pitched our "fly," having left the batwing behind to lighten our loads.

When travelling with a "fly" only, we arrange it as follows:—Placing a pole horizontally, about five feet from the ground between two uprights, we hang the canvas over, and peg it to the ground behind, giving it a slope of 45°. The front is then stretched out, and the corners made fast at three feet, and the centre at four feet from the ground. The two ends of this "lean-to" are blocked with screens of scrub and fern, making walls of about three feet in width. Under the back part we place our bedding, which consists of twigs, branches, and grass, and kindle our fire in the shelter of the front portion. The bed is about the same size as in our batwing, namely, six feet by four feet, and on turning in we lie "heads and tails" in our blanket bags. This shelter is practically the same as our batwings, only, with walls of fern at the ends instead of canvas; but it has the disadvantage of only a single, instead of double, canvas roof. To remedy this, in heavy rain, we make a large screen of ferns or grass, and fix it about six inches above the back portion, letting it act as the "fly" does in the batwing camp. However good the quality of canvas, a certain amount of moisture always comes through in heavy rain, either in drops where the roof has been touched, or in fine spray, hence the necessity of an extra roof over the portion in which we sit or sleep. A single piece of oiled canvas would be water-proof in any weather, but has not sufficient lasting qualities, for it dries and cracks in a few weeks, and being nearly twice as heavy as ordinary canvas, it is just as convenient to take two pieces of the latter, if one takes any.

Our camp was situated on the bank of McKenna's Creek, which drains some ice fields on Craig's Peak, and the range to the east. The valley, in which the creek flows, is broad and flat for two and a half miles, and is separated from the Balfour Glacier by an ice-worn narrow ridge which we named " Hen and Chickens," descending from 1,500 ft. at the upper end of the valley to 500 ft. at the lower end. This ridge has been abraded by ice on both sides, and on the top for a greater part of its length. A few chains below our camp the creek joins the Balfour River, at a point about a quarter of a mile below the glacier. After leaving the ice the river flows on a fairly level course, through a series of terminal moraines, some of no great antiquity. There are five terraces of old lateral moraines along the lower part of the glacier, and three of these have their corresponding, semicircular, terminal moraines, from which the position of the glacier at different periods of its existence can be determined. The highest terrace of these five was formed by the ice when the glacier reached the present gorge, or possibly when it pushed its way still further through the narrow outlet.

Almost immediately below the inflow of McKenna's Creek the valley begins a rapid descent, and the river becomes a rushing torrent over, under, and through large erratic boulders, until half a mile below it leaps into a gloomy gorge walled by sheer rocky precipices of fully 1,000 ft. Though I could see generally that the gorge narrowed and descended very rapidly, and also the enormous precipices overhead, it was impossible, owing to scrub and boulders, to obtain a photograph of more than a general idea of the gorge. It is a most helpless feeling to get mixed up with the large boulders met with in such places. One feels like Gulliver in his journeys amongst the giants, and can often neither get under or over one of these smooth-sided obstacles. The Balfour joins Cook River about three miles from the glacier, and must have a descent of 1,500 ft. in a little under two miles while passing through the gorge.

On March 22nd we traversed the glacier from the terminal face to the foot of the precipices off Tasman, Douglas taking the southern and I the northern side. Rain, however, set in at noon, and by 3 P.M., when we reached the foot of Tasman, the clouds were so low that we could see nothing. It was, therefore, impossible to clear up the doubt about the *névé* of the glacier, but we still inclined to the opinion, that the snow field from Mount Hicks found an outlet into the Balfour, otherwise it was difficult to account for so large a trunk. The ice was completely covered with surface moraine, nearly every stone of which sparkled with minute crystals, and some of the larger stones bristled with crystals an inch long.

My diary entry for March 23rd begins as follows:—" $2\frac{1}{4}$ miles of creek bed; 700 ft. climb at end; 55 minutes' exciting race with fog; thought I'd done it; sold!"

Such races with the fog to obtain bearings or photographs from a high point, were constantly taking place, and I think the fog has won as often as I have. On this particular occasion I wanted to get a clear view, from a point at the head of McKenna's Creek, which should finally settle the doubt with regard to the Balfour *névé*. My route lay through some rather bad scrub for 200 yards, and then along an open creek bed for $2\frac{1}{4}$ miles to the foot of a saddle which lay nearly 700 feet above the creek. I took "Betsy" the dog, who, by the way, rejoined us after leaving the Waiho, and travelled at a jog-trot to the foot of the grassy slope to the saddle, because I had seen a small insignificant piece of fog form and disappear again on Ryan's Peak below the gorge. By the time the foot of the saddle had been reached, a dense bank of fog was crawling through the Balfour gorge, and had apparently met an opposing current of air from McKenna's Creek, as it remained stationary to all appearances at the lower end of the valley.

The saddle I was making for lay on the above-mentioned ice-worn rocky ridge, between the creek and the glacier, and as it would be only three or four miles from Tasman's great cliffs, it ought to command a grand view of the western face of that peak. I had just begun the ascent, when a wisp of fog came over the top of the ridge through another saddle, and I realised that though it had stopped at the end of McKenna valley, it was passing up the Balfour Glacier on the far side of the "Hen and Chickens." Never did I travel up hill so fast before; Betsy now barking and biting my heels, now running ahead, was madly excited, while I scrambled frantically up to get at least one photograph.

The fog now crept along the McKenna valley, and was close up to me when I reached the bridge thoroughly done, having travelled just over two miles along the creek, and climbed 700 ft. in 55 minutes, with 20 lbs. of camera, instruments, &c., on my back. It was all to no purpose, however, for though I had raced the fog behind in the McKenna valley, it had crawled up along the Balfour Range, and only allowed me a momentary glimpse of Tasman's giant buttresses, obscuring everything above the 6,000 ft. level before I could get my camera out of its case. "Did you swear?" I am generally asked, when relating this experience. No, I did not say anything at all. I merely upset a large rock lying near me over the 800 ft. precipice on to the Balfour Glacier to relieve my mind, and then lay down to recover my wind. It happens so often—this mad rush uphill to forestall the fog—that one gets used to disappointments.

The only way to secure good photographs is to reach the point by 6 or 7 o'clock in the morning, and sit down quietly until the light improves. Directly the first bit of fog forms anywhere in sight, a set of plates ought to be exposed, whether the light is good or bad. Never wait till the last minute, but secure one set at least, and if the fog does give a further chance of exposing in better light, then take another set. I have seen the whole landscape blotted out within three minutes of the first sign of fog, and as I was waiting till the last minute to let the light improve, I was on that occasion badly sold, and never again did I omit to make one complete set of exposures on arrival.

The rocks above me on Craig's Range were broken into very fantastic shapes, and numerous detached blocks lay on the "Hen and Chickens," which I believe to have been left by the ancient glacier. "Betsy" and I spent two hours on the ridge, trying to catch some keas, and also dropping stones over the great precipice on to the glacier below. A most fascinating occupation is this, of rolling stones from a great height. Douglas and I have spent hours, when waiting for a fog to lift, in various places, rolling down large rocks, and working as hard as if our lives depended on it, to dislodge one of exceptional dimensions. We often used to try and suggest some reason which would account for the fascination, for I suppose it may be said to be universal. I have never met a man, even amongst those who spend their whole lives on these hills, who did not only thoroughly enjoy seeing a stone career madly down a slope, but who would not go to considerable trouble to start one rolling.

On returning along McKenna's creek we got two ducks, but the dog took them both to the far side of the creek and left them there, compelling me to wade across for them—a cold task, as the stream was ice-fed, and took me up to the waist.

Douglas, some years before I joined him, used to work alone, and had a wonderfully clever and useful dog named "Topsy," which used to keep him well supplied with birds. She would go away to hunt as soon as he began to pitch camp, and return with three birds, two for her master and one for herself; it would be a very poor locality for birds if she couldn't find any, a better forager never existed. In another way, too, she proved useful. Douglas says, that when going up a river, he might find a rocky bluff rising out of the water, which seemed likely to necessitate a high climb. In order to avoid the risk of going forward some distance, and being compelled to return, owing to an impassable corner, he would send "Topsy" ahead, and sit down for a smoke till she came back. On her return, he could always tell from her manner whether a route was practicable round the bluff. So well did she know what he could do, that on one occasion she gave him to understand that there was no possibility of going round, but as he was anxious to avoid the high climb, through the bush, over the bluff, he picked up his load and started off to find his way round. "Topsy," who was lying down, merely looked up, and seeing him going where she had been, stayed where she was, and made no attempt to follow, knowing her master would have to return to that spot to begin his climb over. When Douglas came back, having failed, he said Topsy got up, stretched herself, and followed him up the hillside, "with a superior smile on her face."

The weather became very threatening on the 24th, so we decided to get out of this valley, before a storm came on and stopped us, as provisions were coming to an end, and we had done all that was necessary. The very steep grass slopes, and smooth rock faces, up which we had to go to reach the spur again, were treacherous, and would have been very dangerous but for our ice-axes. It was annoying to have to take such a high and roundabout route to and from this glacier, when, had the gorge been passable, it would have only taken an hour or two to reach the junction with Cook River instead of a long day. On Easter Sunday the storm came on, so we pushed along from our bivouac, where we slept on the previous evening, and reached Ryan's hut before dark. A week's bad weather followed, putting all the streams into high flood, therefore we had good reason to congratulate ourselves on having got out of the Balfour valley in time, for another day's delay and we should have been cornered like rats in a trap, without the cheese.

One evening some of the diggers working up Cook River, above the cage, who had been down to "town" (Gillespies), called in at the hut on their way back, and stayed for the night. Conversation turned to ice work, and after explaining the use of our axes, I began to give them a rough idea of the effects of glaciers. In course of the conversation I spoke of the Tasman Glacier, and one of those present said, "Is the Tasman as large as the Fox Glacier?"

"Oh yes, much larger," I said.

"Is it on a big river, too?" said another.

To which I replied, "Yes, the Waitaki."

"What a rum thing," said the last speaker, "it is that nearly all the glaciers are on rivers."

"It *is* curious," I said humbly, feeling ashamed that my discourse had not conveyed a better idea of the causes and effects of glaciers.

## CHAPTER VII.

COOK RIVER—FOX GLACIER.

Slight Mishap—Douglas—The Chancellor Ridge—Victoria Glacier—
Keas—Fogged again.

EVEN when out of the ranges our communication with the civilised world was casual. A weekly pack-horse mail came as far as Gillespies Beach, and was generally punctual, except when rain put some of the rivers in flood, which occurred about twice out of five trips, and then we had to be thankful if there was only a week's delay. In addition to this, many of the inhabitants at Gillespies are not on speaking terms, and as we relied on the thoughtfulness of some one coming up to the hut to bring our letters, it often happened that the person who came had not been to the post-office, because he was not on good terms with the people there. On returning from the Balfour valley we found letters awaiting us in the hut, urging that our reports be completed and sent up to the office in Hokitika before we again went into the ranges. This took some days, and when I had completed my portion of the writing I decided to go to the Fox Glacier and work there until Douglas had finished his report and could join me.

Regardless of possible bad luck, I left Ryan's hut on All Fools' Day, 1894, with Johnny Ryan, taking food for a fortnight, batwing, &c., in two 40-lb. loads on a pack-horse.

The snout of the Fox Glacier, which lies 670 ft. above sea-level, is easily reached, but at present a horse cannot be taken within a mile of the ice; if, however, a track was cleared through the bush, there would be little need of formation, and a horse could go to the terminal face with little trouble. At a mile and a half below the glacier, I sent Ryan back with the horses, as they were of no further use, and leaving one load to bring up later, I started up the river with the other. The travelling was rather rougher than I expected, and it was two P.M. before I found a good camping place amongst some rata bushes near a tributary creek. Returning for and bringing up the second load occupied another two hours, leaving just enough daylight to clear a space and pitch the batwing. When there is a probability of staying more than one night in a camp, we put some flat stones under the fire to keep it dry, and also a few between the bedding and the fire, as it is more comfortable and cleaner than the bare, damp ground. Intending to be here for a week at least, I made the camp as snug as possible before dark, and having had a meal, proceeded to read the papers which had come by the mail before I left Ryan's.

The Fox Glacier had been visited during the previous twenty-five years by many who were either in search of fine scenery or gold, but no one had been beyond the terminal face. The map then existing, as in the case of most of the western watershed, was made from distant trigonometrical stations on the sea bluffs and lower hills, and I anticipated some interesting work on such a large field of virgin ice. It was a decided drawback being alone, but still one man can do a great deal by himself with due care, even on a glacier.

The valley is broader than that of the Franz Josef; the

northern side rises nearly sheer from the ice in high precipitous hills, a considerable amount of bare ice-worn rock showing here and there through the dark vegetation. The southern side for the first three miles slopes gently back from the glacier for some distance, showing several old lateral moraines and terraces, to the foot of Craig's Range, which rises abruptly for some 3,000 or 4,000 ft. The terraces and hillsides are clothed with dense bush and scrub to the usual altitude. On the right-hand side of the terminal face, when approaching the glacier, a large isolated rock stands in the centre of the valley, which appears to be a perfect cone from below, but is in reality a narrow glacier-worn ridge of nearly a mile in length. The ice, which at a comparatively recent date divided and flowed down on each side of the rock, now only flows along its northern face. The "Cone" Rock (as we named it) is 825 ft. from base to summit, and shows marks of abrasion by ice all over it, with a number of huge erratic boulders strewn along its narrow ridge. These, however, are not seen until one is on the top, because the trees grow to a considerable size wherever they can obtain a hold.

On the south side a large creek coming off Craig's Range, down a steep course, flows against the Cone, and is turned at right angles to its original direction, and, continuing along the foot of the rock for a mile, joins the main river a few yards below the glacier. About half a mile from the river, up this creek, I made my camp, at the foot of the Cone Rock, in a nice patch of rata-trees.

The first thing to do next morning was to ascend the rock and obtain a good general view of the glacier, to form some idea of the route to take up the ice. On reaching the top I found

Fox Glacier, from the Cone Rock

it heaped with large erratic blocks, lying in hopeless confusion on one another along the narrow ridge, and sometimes from their size and position rather troublesome. Fine rata-trees were growing amongst and on the top of these, and prevented my getting a clear view, or opening, for a photograph.

I generally use my ice-axe, by an arrangement of my own, for a camera stand, never carrying a tripod, as we must economise weight in every way. Here, however, a stand would have been useless, for the trees were too large, so climbing a rata until I could overlook its neighbours, I arranged cross-sticks between two branches, and made three exposures, one of which ultimately proved very good, the others having been spoilt by movement.

From such a central position as the Cone a capital idea of the glacier can be obtained. Of the Dividing Range, Glacier Peak and Haidinger could be seen rising out of the *névé*, while more to the right the top of Tasman was visible over Craig's Peak. From the *névé* the ice descends over a good ice-fall, part of which is in view from the Cone, and thence for three or four miles the glacier flows white and smooth to the terminal face. Two small portions of broken ice form the only apparent obstacles to easy travelling as far as the great ice-fall. In the map then existing the Fox Glacier was shown as flowing down in two large streams, divided by the Chancellor Ridge, a branch of the Bismarck Range. The southern ice-flow drained the Dividing Range, and the northern came from the snowfields of Bismarck's Peak. I had fully anticipated a magnificent view of two great ice-falls descending on each side of the Chancellor Ridge, and joining at its base, but there was nothing of the kind visible from the Cone, presumably because the northern stream, or Victoria Glacier, flowed at a lower level and joined the Fox without an ice-fall. Below the Chancellor Ridge the descent of the glacier is gradual, not nearly so steep as the Franz Josef, and its course is over a smoother bed, no obstacles apparently to cause such broken waves and undulations as were seen on its neighbour.

Having decided on the best route to follow in order to reach the Chancellor Ridge, I climbed from my high perch in the rata-tree to the ground. Though not very superstitious, I have one or two harmless ideas about luck, and one is that the 1st of April is an unlucky day to start on an expedition. However, up to this point all had gone well; I had a good camp, plenty of provisions, the promise of a day or two of really fine weather, and a fine glacier to explore. But such good fortune was not to last, for on descending from the top of the Cone I had to go along a ledge, overhanging a drop of about 25 ft., in the middle of which a single tree had to be passed. Catching a branch in one hand, I was in the act of swinging round on the outside, when the limb broke, and sent me backwards over the drop, at the bottom of which I landed with one leg somewhere under my back. Before rising I naturally looked at my camera, which was under me, with some apprehension, and found it unhurt, but on getting up to go on, the pain in my ankle showed that it had been twisted badly.

There is only one thing to do in a case like this, namely, *keep moving*, to prevent the joint from stiffening. An hour's hobbling brought me to camp, where I filled the billy with water, cut two days' supply of firewood, and generally fixed up the camp before resting. Within a quarter of an hour of sitting down I could not put my foot to the ground, and had the pleasure of lying in camp during the 3rd and 4th, before I could move about at all freely.

An accident like this, though slight, would be quite enough to lead to fatal results if it occurred far away from camp, because no anxiety would be felt by those on the low country for a week or two at least. Generally, indeed, two or three months might pass before a search party would be organized, as we often do not know how long we are going to be away. Even allowing that a search party was sent out within a week or two, they would not know where to begin operations, as the country would only be known to the object of their search. Douglas, who has in the past done most of his explorations alone, has been fortunate, except in one or two cases, one of which would have proved fatal but for his extraordinary pluck and determination.

It was, if I recollect rightly from his account, in the seventies that he was crossing the swamp between the Karangarua and Cook River, jumping from "niggerhead" to "niggerhead," when he slipped and sprained his ankle badly. He only had a little oatmeal with him, and was nearly two weeks before he could get to Hunt's Beach—the nearest habitation. On coming some days after to the river Karangarua, he found it was rising—for rain had been falling—but in spite of his ankle, and the fact that he couldn't swim, he crossed that evening, and reached the hut thoroughly exhausted. He says it was a case of "neck or nothing," because had he not crossed that night the river would have been too high, and a day or two more of exposure would have been too much for him. Had he had any matches to kindle a fire, he would have got on much better; but even though it had been raining most of the time, he was without fire and only a little shelter. Making a crossbow, he killed two pigeons, but the bow soon "lost its spring," and except these two birds, he had to rely on three pounds of oatmeal and "a chew or two of tobacco." Had the accident occurred in the bush, probably more birds could have been obtained and a good shelter built, but this was in an almost open swamp.

The fact that my little mishap, and Douglas's accident, turned out to be harmless, is no excuse for working alone, nor does it alter the rule that a man should never go into rough country, away from habitation, by himself. But we cannot always act according to rules, however sound they are; it is often a choice of doing the work alone or not at all, and if no one took any risk, the country would be unexplored for years. I must plead guilty to having done a fair amount of solitary work, and to liking it quite as well as—if not better than—with a companion, but I admit that it is a mistake.

On the 5th I went up the glacier some three miles, to a point where the ice-fall could be seen to advantage. The route lay up the creek, from camp, for half a mile or so, to the upper end of the Cone Rock, though at the time I did not anticipate more than 300 yards before reaching the ice. A few chains below the end of the rock the creek-bed turns at right angles up Craig's Range, from which it flows, and at the bend there is an old water-course from the glacier into the creek, down which there has been an outflow of water from the ice at no distant date. By taking this route a rough piece of going is avoided, caused by the Cone Rock having compressed the glacier into a narrow channel. As far as the ice is concerned one can get on or off almost anywhere along the sides,

Looking down Fox Glacier from one Mile up.

except where high rocky precipices render it impossible to land. Travelling on the glacier is easy to anyone accustomed to ice-work, and it only has to be left once, in order to skirt a small ice-fall, nearly three miles up; here there was, so late in the year, a short piece of complicated work amongst crevasses. About a mile and a half from the terminal face, there is a quarter of an hour of roughish ice, which had to be manœuvred rather carefully, but which would give no trouble whatever earlier in the year.

Soon after mid-day, I had reached the small ice-fall, and having thus far seen no sign of the ice of the Victoria Glacier, I began to suspect some great error in the map. Landing on the south side, immediately below the rough ice, thirty minutes' climbing and crawling over large boulders, forming a lateral moraine, brought me to the rocky point of a spur off Craig's Peak, round the foot of which the glacier bends. From this point of vantage looking across to the Chancellor Ridge, it was evident that no tributary ice stream joined the main glacier, nor indeed did it appear that any glacier existed behind the ridge, because no water was visible coming over the rocks. The glacier is narrower here than its neighbour, but its total average width is slightly more; the surface ice is good, and though hummocky, is fairly free from crevasses. The only surface moraine is at the terminal face, which is covered from side to side for perhaps 150 yards up the glacier.

It would be necessary to cross over the Chancellor Ridge in order to settle the doubt concerning the Victoria Glacier, but my ankle was still too weak for a long day's work, so I returned to camp. On the following day I got up at dawn, intending to take blanket and provisions for a bivouac on the Chancellor Ridge, but the foot was still stiff, and required another day's spell; therefore, after going half-way up to the small ice-fall, I "gave it best" and went back to camp.

It was evident that the sore ankle would not allow much work if I carried even a light load, so I decided to only take the quarter-plate camera and one day's food, and trust to luck in the shape of a good stone, if necessary to sleep out on the Chancellor Ridge. Leaving camp at dawn, or 6 A.M., on the 7th, I reached the rock bluff below the ice-fall in two hours, and went on to the foot of the fall to see if any practicable route could be found up to the *névé*. Though not stupendously broken as the upper part of the Franz Josef, the ice-fall of the Fox Glacier would be better left alone, as the seracs are large and constantly falling. Turning back again towards the lower end of the Chancellor Ridge, I intended to cross it, and if possible go up some peak or saddle on the Bismarck Range, to command a view of the Fritz Glacier and head of the Waikukupa River. At the lower end of the ridge it was easy to reach the side, which is of smooth rock sloping gently under the ice; about, above and below, the glacier is lined by sheer and, in places, overhanging precipices of 400 or 500 ft. in height. At the foot of this rocky wall the ice flows level and unbroken; it was not rotten or crevassed as is usually the case at the side of a glacier. In one place it was possible to walk up to the foot of the cliff and, standing on the ice, lean my back against the rock, only a foot or less space intervening. The ice is evidently of great depth at the side here, which accounts for its unbroken surface, and the rock must be perpendicular for a considerable distance below the level of the glacier.

It was now evident that there was a fair-sized glacier in the valley between the Chancellor Ridge and the Bismarck Range, as a large stream of dirty water fell over the precipices, making a fine waterfall. It had worn a curiously shaped funnel down the face, which completely hid the stream until quite close to it, and which accounted for my not seeing it from the opposite side of the glacier.

The old saying, "More haste, less speed," is generally true, but never more so than in new country, as I have often found to my cost. After leaving the ice, and being in too great a hurry to reach a good point of view into the valley beyond the Chancellor Ridge, I began to climb up and across the lower end of the spur. This is very steep and rotten, and the whole face being shattered rock, it was not without considerable trouble that I reached the *arête*, having got into one or two decidedly ticklish places. In half an hour I topped the ridge and could see into the valley beyond, where lay—300 ft. below me—the Victoria Glacier, slightly over four miles in length, and about thirty chains in breadth, covered with a very heavy surface moraine for a third of its length. This glacier comes off the Bismarck Range, from Bismarck's Peak and Mount Anderegg, with two tributary glaciers, from the Chancellor Ridge on the south and from a long offsho t of Anderegg on the north. It flows past the end of the Chancellor on to a plateau (3,685 ft.) lying at the top of the perpendicular rocky wall already described, which rises out of the Fox Glacier. Large erratic boulders lie scattered on the plateau, amongst dense mountain scrub and grass, showing that in the past the

Victoria found its way over the cliffs to the main iceflow of the Fox. As it exists at present, the Victoria is as perfect an example of a small primary glacier as could be found, with its little *névé*, tributary ice-streams, and complete system of surface, lateral and terminal moraines.

I had been looking for a likely Alpine pass to the Tasman Valley since the beginning of the season, and had come to the conclusion that, for all practical purposes, the Franz Josef Glacier had better be left alone, so far as its lower extremity was concerned. There now appeared to be a good route up the Victoria Glacier, over a low "col" to the head of the Fritz Glacier, and thence behind Roon to the head of the Melchior, a branch of the Franz Josef Glacier, and then across the broad *névé* basin of the latter over Graham's Saddle near De la Bêche, down the Rudolph Glacier to the Tasman. I had been close up to Graham's Saddle, from the Tasman, and knew the Franz Josef Glacier and the Victoria, so excepting the "col" over the Bismarck Range, there was little new ground to cover. Therefore, while I was in Christchurch during the winter following this trip, I tried to persuade someone to come and make this pass, and though Mr. Fyfe arranged to join me, he was at the last moment unable to do so. However, I am glad to say I ultimately had the satisfaction of being one of the party to make the first complete pass, as will be seen later, when I told Mr. Fitz-Gerald of the route, and with him and Zurbriggen crossed it a year later.

Ever since sunrise, I had been the object of considerable attention from some keas, or mountain parrots, at first only two or three, but afterwards their number had increased to fifteen or more. They joined me on the south side of the Fox Glacier, and annoyed me considerably by their inquisitiveness while I was taking some bearings and photographs, one of them alighting on my back just as I was looking through the compass. These birds are not found except in high country, and their eggs are very rare, as they probably choose some crevice in the face of a precipice for their nesting place. They have cruel beaks and great power in them, being able to tear any cloth with a single stroke, but are tame and harmless, except in certain localities, where they kill sheep. This weakness of theirs has given them a bad name, and it is generally supposed that all keas are naturally inclined to attack sheep. Such, however, is not the case. The fault lay in the first instance with the shepherds or persons who had to skin the sheep on a station. Keas naturally feed on berries, but they are possessed of an intense desire to investigate everything they see, and if possible tear it with their beaks; consequently, near homesteads, in Otago and Canterbury, when they see sheepskins hanging up to dry they go down to examine them. If the skins are carefully cleaned little harm results; but if not, the keas have a chance to taste the fat, and when once a kea tastes fat he is a ruined bird, and would sell his soul—if he had one—to get more. To satisfy this craving he attacks the sheep with fatal effect, causing, in some localities, very heavy loss to the stations.* The birds are not migratory, and as far as I have been able to ascertain, rarely leave the valleys they live in. This is evidenced by

* These birds, when attacking live sheep, settle on the back of the animal and deliberately drive their beaks into the skin until they have reached the kidney fat. They never wound a sheep in any other part of the body.

the fact that while some stations lose many sheep, owing to the keas, an adjoining owner may suffer no loss whatever, owing to the fact that the birds have not learnt the taste for fat.

When crossing the Chancellor Ridge, the keas which I referred to followed me on the wing, but owing to the ice being very slippery my progress was too slow for them; therefore, alighting on the ice, they began to follow on foot. Whenever a kea makes its appearance we are prepared for some good fun, as their actions are most ludicrous, and their conversation, which is incessant, is almost expressive enough to enable one to understand what they mean. I have had considerable experience with these birds, but have never seen such an intensely funny proceeding as on this particular morning. The keas having settled on the ice began to follow in a long straggling line, about fifteen of them. They have a preternaturally solemn walk, but when in a hurry they hop along on both feet looking very eager and very much in earnest. To see these fifteen birds hopping along behind in a string, as if their very lives depended on keeping me in sight, was ridiculously comic. The ice was undulating, with little valleys and hummocks, and the birds would now, for a second or two, disappear into a hollow and now show up on a hummock, pause a moment, and then hop down again out of sight into the next hollow. To judge by their expressions and manner, they were in a great state of anxiety on emerging from a hollow on to a hummock, as to whether I was still there. Now and then the one in front would appear, craning his neck, and on seeing me still ahead, would turn round and shriek " K-e-e-a," as much as to say, " It's all right, boys, come along." And the others, putting their heads down, would set their teeth and travel "all they knew," a fat one in the rear evidently making very heavy weather of it!

On the Chancellor Ridge they became offensively inquisitive, and I really could hardly take any photographs, owing to their anxiety to ascertain the maker's name on my camera. However, such is the perversity of affairs in general, that it was only when it occurred to me that a picture of ten or fifteen keas examining my ice-axe would be interesting, that they suddenly seemed to remember an appointment elsewhere, and disappeared. Had the idea occurred a few minutes earlier, a good picture could have been obtained.

After having descended to the Victoria Glacier, I saw a small cloud appearing on Craig's Range, which warned me that the usual fog was coming, so I hastened back to the ridge, and along it to a point from which I could get a view over the *névé* of the Fox Glacier. The climb gradually developed into a race with the mists creeping up the valley behind me; on reaching the top I was rewarded by a momentary but magnificent view of Haidinger and the great northern face of Tasman, before the fog descended like a curtain and shut everything from view, leaving no time to take a photograph. I have been fortunate enough to have been all over the central part of our Alps and to have seen the great peaks both far and near from every side; and I think the northern face of Mount Tasman is as fine as anything I know, except perhaps Mount Sefton. It rises out of the *névé* of the Fox Glacier in great brown precipices, capped with hanging glaciers, and the graceful curves of the summit are unsurpassed for beauty.

When the fog has once closed in and shut out surrounding

objects, it is really little use waiting for it to clear, but for some reason I always hope against hope, and spend a miserable hour or two under a rock, before finally giving it up as useless. On this occasion I stayed for nearly two hours on the side of the ridge, now and then catching a fleeting glimpse of the main glacier far below me, winding in ghostly whiteness down the valley, and beyond it the sea with its two or three lines of breakers crawling in towards the beach. Of the upper portion of the valley nothing was again visible, beyond one tantalizing peep of Tasman's mighty shoulders appearing over the fog. At 1.30 I could not see an object fifteen yards away, and the dry fog changed to a wet mist—a sure sign of an approaching storm—so I began to cast about for a shelter in which to spend the night, and from which to make an ascent on the Bismarck Range if the morrow proved fine. However, in half an hour the drifting mist having wetted my clothes completely, I gave up all idea of staying out for the night, and decided to get back to camp without delay.

## CHAPTER VIII.

### FOX GLACIER—(*continued*).

Return to Camp—Unpleasant Surprise—Result—Wekas—Back to Ryan's—
Remarks on the Glacier.

To return in such a dense fog was by no means easy, especially as I could not think of descending the rotten rocks, up which I had come in the morning; for even had it been possible to find a route, the falling stones would have been too risky. Fortunately my bump of locality is strong, and by dint of dropping, sliding, and scrambling over steep faces of unpleasantly smooth rocks and slippery grass, I managed to hit off the point to a nicety, at which to cross the ice. On reaching the south bank and skirting the small ice-fall, the few minutes' work amongst the crevasses gave some trouble in the fog. It is no easy matter to travel down a glacier—even when one knows it well—in such a dense white mist, but to find a good route, after only once traversing it, was rather a difficult business. After travelling till 5 P.M., it seemed that I had gone far enough to have reached the point where I first took the ice in the morning. There are no large stones on the glacier by which to guide one's course, so it was not surprising to find, on turning towards the bank, that I had gone about 100 yards too far, and was abreast of the precipice under the Cone Rock. Another half-hour, however, saw me on my way to the camp, and though wet to the skin, decidedly pleased at being well out of an awkward position, and looking forward to dry clothes, good fire, and snug camp. Hurrying along in the deluge of rain which had set in, splashing down the creek and clambering over the boulders, I arrived at the camp about ten minutes before dark.

Instead of my comfortable little shelter and dry clothes, I found only a wreck. The batwing and a corner of the fly had been burnt, the little canvas bags of food and the pea-rifle, which usually hung on the ridge pole under the fly, were lying scorched on the ground. In one corner a heap of ashes, a button or two, and a large hole in the scrub bedding, were all that remained of my dry clothes. This was the crowning disaster of an unlucky expedition. A man familiar with his Virgil would probably have consoled himself by saying :—

"Forsan et hæc olim meminisse juvabit."

I fear, however, that I made some other remark—not in Latin—and did not think of Virgil till afterwards!

With only a few minutes of twilight to work in, I commenced to fix up some sort of shelter out of the remains in which to pass the night; a more weather-proof shelter would have to be left till the morning, in spite of the heavy rain. The fly I pitched as we had had it on the Balfour Glacier, and one end was blocked to a height of two feet with a few branches. This was all that could be done that night, and having kindled a fire and put the billy on to boil, I sat down to see what remained out of the wreck.

The first things to be missed were the candles, which had of course been burnt, and their loss at once put an end to further investigation till daylight. Fortunately, I had a few matches in my pocket, and could manage with care to hold out for a few days as far as they were concerned. Having had something to eat, and some half-burnt tea without sugar to drink, I put on "kilts" (*i.e.*, wrapped the blanket round me) and proceeded to dry my clothes. By 10 o'clock some of the garments were fairly dry, so—thoroughly tired after the long day—I rolled myself in the blanket, and in spite of the storm soon forgot this miserable world in a sound sleep.

However long or hard a day's work has been, we cannot sit down and have a spell on returning to camp at night, because possibly there is firewood to gather, bread to bake, and a meal to cook; indeed, sometimes a meal has to be found with the pea-rifle. It would be to either of us a luxury beyond belief to have a third man whom we could occasionally leave in camp, and to find things ready on our return in the evening. The extra work in the evening is far harder than one would imagine. Even supposing a permanent third member to the party was impossible, it would have made our work considerably quicker and less trying had we been given a man who could carry a good load of provisions, for two or three days, from habitation, and then be sent back. This would give us a good stock to fall back on, and possibly save a long tramp back for food or else a period of starvation. It is a trial to one's powers to have to do mental work and heavy packing at the same time in such terribly broken country, and for a prolonged season of seven or eight months. The authorities, however, did not consider it necessary, not having any idea of what rough work it really was; in fact, on one occasion when mention was made of the necessity of carrying heavy loads, someone asked, "Why do not you employ a spring dray or pack-horse?" Imagine a spring dray over 50 foot boulders or along a narrow arête! It was often difficult to get the dog over the country.

The driving rain and high wind whistling under the fly woke me early, and at daylight I set to work to build a more satisfactory shelter. The creeks and river were in flood and uncrossable, so there was every prospect of two days' delay before I could get away. It did not take long to put up two good breakwinds with branches and ferns at each end of the fly, and to generally "fix up" a shelter in which I was "as happy as a sand-boy" in spite of the storm.

There was now time to examine the effects of the fire, which had been very erratic. In the first place it is hard to explain why the fly had not been totally destroyed, for it was only pitched six inches above the batwing; it would seem impossible for the latter to burn from the bottom so completely as it had without setting fire to the fly, which is the most inflammable portion of the camp, owing to the fire always keeping it dry. At each end of the batwing we have two pockets, a large one for field books, &c., and a small one for watch, matches, and so forth. In the two large ones I had left some photographic plates, note books, and a pound of candles; the books and plate boxes were charred a little, and the candles had disappeared. In one of the smaller pockets were a box of fifty pea-rifle cartridges, and two boxes of matches. The cartridges were unhurt, while one box of matches had exploded and the other only melted in a solid mass. On the bedding my dry clothes and tobacco were in one corner, and within a foot of them the blanket, with the half-plate camera and some newspapers on it. Of these, the clothes and tobacco had gone absolutely, leaving a hole burnt to the ground in the scrub which we slept on; the other heap was untouched, except the papers on the camera, which were burnt to an ash.

Douglas has only once been burnt out, and his experience is the same as that of others, namely, that nothing escapes. My misfortune was, therefore, not as bad as it might have been, and there was good cause to be thankful that some provisions were still left since my retreat was cut off; shelter was not of so much importance, because had all the canvas been destroyed I could have knocked up a "mai-mai" of bark and ferns in an hour. It is impossible to say how the fire originated, unless I had left the candle burning when leaving camp at dawn—in which case, no doubt, one of the wekas had pulled it over while looking for buttons or some such digestible food; the white candle would be an irresistible temptation.

After all, it is of little consequence how the thing happened, the fact remained that I had to "sit and sigh in idleness" for three days. Whilst turning out the contents of one of my pockets I came across a scrap of an old *World*, on which was a most appropriate poem entitled, "Every hour has its end"; this fact is often too true to dispute but was open to argument under the present circumstances. With nothing to read and very little to smoke the hours appeared to have at least one hundred minutes!

The family of wekas which had taken possession of the camp were very welcome, and I was able to watch their mode of procedure when dissolving partnership for the time being. As already stated, when the male bird thinks he has done his share in the education and bringing up of the family he dissolves partnership. If in a good locality for food he drives his mate and young ones away, but if in a poor locality he departs to happier hunting grounds himself. The parent birds while rearing their young hardly eat anything themselves and grow as poor as a church mouse, everything they find is carried to the youngsters. When a pair has only one chick it is very ludicrous to see them rushing up to it and jostling one another in their eagerness to give it a piece of bacon or bread, and sometimes asking it to try a piece of a jam tin, or tempting it with a choice copper cartridge-case. The parent finds some such rubbish and rushes off to the over-fed fledgling which is sitting and squeaking under a fern, and holds the tempting morsel out in its beak. The old one looks sideways at it as much as to say, " So good," while the youngster having got it successfully down sits with ruffled feathers and looks at the world in general as if it would say, " That old fool will be the death of me one of these days! "

The first intimation I had that the pair at camp were going to dissolve partnership was when I threw out a piece of bread one morning. Paterfamilias instead of passing it to one of the chickens swallowed it himself, while the rest of the family looked on reproachfully and seemed to know they must " look out for squalls." After the old boy had got all he could he suddenly turned round and attacked his wife and then the male youngster—the female chick having wisely disappeared, *pro tem*. When I saw he was going to drive the family away and stay at the camp to enjoy all the good things himself, I decided to put a stop to his little game, and gave him a rifle bullet to digest. He made a capital stew, and his sorrowing family thoroughly enjoyed his remains!

The next day Mrs. Weka found the two half-grown chickens rather "a large order"; in the first place they both tried to shelter themselves under her from the rain, which upset her mentally and physically, and secondly, the task of feeding them was too much for her; she therefore proceeded to drive away Master Weka. That young gentleman, however, was not going to leave his family home without a struggle, and seeing his sister still petted and fed, he used to give her a good peck when the old hen was not looking, and then run for his life before she caught him. I again interfered in the proceedings, and by dint of some coaxing persuaded Master Weka to come on to the bedding in the shelter, where he would eat from my hand. By degrees he gained confidence and came in without fear, having a good feed while the old hen remained outside waiting for him; on his finishing the meal he used to dodge about inside trying to make his escape, and the old bird dodged about outside to cut him off. I would then throw a piece of bread away into the bush, and while she went after it the youngster would slip out and run for dear life, rolling his more favoured sister in the mud on the way.

On the 10th the weather cleared and gave me an opportunity to go down to Ryan's hut. Therefore, leaving my friends to settle their own family affairs, I rolled up my goods and started down the river, meeting Douglas and "Betsy," who were coming up to join me. However, my ankle was still weak and wanted a rest, so we went back to the hut to make a new batwing and generally repair damages. It required another ten days' work to map the glacier, so we returned on the 16th and took the camp three-quarters of a mile further up the creek than my first camp, intending to make some observations as to motion, &c., and complete the map of the valley. Fate seemed to be against us on this glacier, for out of the thirteen days away from Ryan's hut we only had two fine ones, and those were the day we came up to camp and the day we returned to Ryan's. We were, however, able to make a more thorough exploration of the Fox and Victoria glaciers below the *névé* and take a few more bearings. On the 29th our stores had come to an end, so the weather cleared and the sun shone out beautifully; but one or two snow-falls had taken place during the previous week, warning us that winter was approaching, and that if we intended to reach the head of Cook's River and La Perouse Glacier we must do so at once and waste no more time over the Fox Glacier. In any case there was little left to be done there, while Cook River might prove troublesome, and there was a danger of further snow preventing our expedition. Consequently we packed up and carried our loads back to Ryan's hut.

The Fox Glacier is more attractive than many places much advertised and visited. It certainly has not nearly such a grand terminal face as the Franz Josef, but it is in every other way superior for tourists. It is quite as easy of access, it has fine surroundings, and there are hot springs within a mile of it; but the chief attraction to my mind is, that anyone with ordinary care can go a mile or so along the ice, or three miles along the south bank on the old lateral moraines. This would enable many who have never seen a glacier to gain some idea of an ice-fall at close quarters, for though not so fine as that of its neighbour, the ice-fall of the Fox is by no means a poor one. An easy and safe expedition could be made to the Chancellor Ridge, from which a grand view of the great peaks and the *névé* can be gained; if the Government desired to open up the district, a track could be taken up to the glacier and even along its south bank at a small cost, and a hut placed on the Chancellor. To go even a short distance on to the Franz Josef Glacier with safety would require an expert at ice work.

There are many interesting features on the Fox Glacier which are more marked than on other ice-streams in New Zealand. On no other glacier in the Southern Alps is the veined structure of the ice so apparent; in fact, I have never seen such a fine example of this anywhere. The ice is laminated to such an extent just above the Cone Rock, that it resembles a ploughed field, and the furrows being from six inches to a foot in depth and the same distance apart in places, are very troublesome to walk over. The lamination does not run in one direction, and though most of the lines are longitudinal they sometimes curve gracefully towards the margin of the ice. Wherever a crevasse occurs the effect is beautiful, and the lines can be seen, descending perpendicularly, as far as there is light to see.

Another peculiarity on the Fox is the number of *moulins* or funnels in the ice. Abreast of and above the Cone Rock they are most noticeable, and though not as fine as many I have seen elsewhere, they are very good specimens—from six to ten feet across at the top and two or three feet a little lower down.

For *roches moutonnées* this valley does not equal the Franz Josef, but has a splendid example of a great isolated rock in the Cone. The northern bank too, from the terminal face to the ice-fall, presents a good instance of steep faces of rock abraded by glacier action. Lateral moraines of various ages can be examined on the south side of the valley, and large erratic blocks found on the top of the Cone Rock.

The individual points of interest may be surpassed, with the exception of the first mentioned, in other localities, but nowhere else in New Zealand can they be seen to such perfection, collected in one valley, easy to reach, and easy to inspect and examine owing to the smooth surface of the glacier. In addition to this there is the fact of still more peculiar interest, namely, a glacier in (approximate) lat. 43° 29′ 30″ S., descending for over nine miles to 670 ft. above sea-level, within ten miles of the beach. This can be also said of the Franz Josef, but it does not at the same time possess all the other interesting features mentioned above, nor is it so easy to travel on.

The very easy travelling and unbroken surface of the Fox Glacier shows, I imagine, that the ice is of greater depth than that of the Franz Josef; it may be that this smoothness is due to the bed of the valley having fewer obstructions. That there are several rocky obstacles under the ice of the latter cannot, I think, be doubted, and accounts for the heaving appearance which the ice of that glacier has. I am not aware that the old saying, "Still waters run deep," can be applied to a glacier, but it appears to me that the Fox Glacier must be of considerable depth or it would not flow down as steeply as it does without having a rougher and more broken surface.

At the terminal face the ice pushes its way under the level of the river-bed; in several places holes in the gravel, caused by subsidence due to the melting ice, can be seen towards the end of the summer. The water, too, does not come out in an ordinary manner, but bubbles up like a great spring to a height of three feet in ordinary weather, and five or six feet during rain. This shows that the streams which flow under the ice are considerably below the river-bed level when they reach the terminal face, and on being released from the ice rush up to the surface with great force.

In July, 1894, Douglas and Mr. Wilson paid a brief visit to the glacier, and the former noticed a very marked change in the ice. As will be seen in a later chapter, we anticipated a decided winter advance in the Franz Josef Glacier and were disappointed to find that a retreat only was evident. The fact of these two glaciers descending to such a low altitude would lead one to expect a greater proportional winter motion than is to be found on higher glaciers. For the melting would be less by a great deal than in the summer, and yet the rapid descent and frequent rain would cause a movement greater in comparison to the melting than we should find in the hotter months. This was fully borne out in the case of the Fox Glacier, for Douglas found some of my flags—which had been, as usual, visible from each other—invisible from points where originally they could be seen owing to the ice having banked up considerably. Also on two rocky points or capes on the north side, the ice had completely covered a large portion of rock visible in the summer. I do not know why this advance or increase was visible on the Fox Glacier, while on its neighbour a general decrease was found. It may be, and probably is, due to the different aspect of the two valleys. This one faces slightly north of west, and therefore loses the winter sun for many hours in the day on its lower portion, while the Franz Josef faces due north and receives the whole heat of the day. Again, this glacier has the steep hillsides on the sunny side, while the other has them on the opposite side.

When reliable observations as to the motion of the ice are taken we shall probably find a much higher rate of flow on the Franz Josef than on the Fox Glacier.

An unnamed peak, generally confused with Haidinger from the West Coast, and not visible except from high points on the eastern ranges, stands at the head of the Fox and is the most prominent summit from the terminal face. This I have seen from several different points, and always held that it is distinct from Haidinger. When Fitz-Gerald made his ascent of the latter he left a large cairn on the summit, and he and I distinctly saw this from the Fritz Glacier when we were there during the next season. I had explained my contention to him before we started, and we therefore made a point of deciding the question. Since Haidinger was first named from the Tasman, and the name has been put on the wrong peak by the West Coast department, it should be retained on the summit seen from the eastern side. I have generally called this unnamed peak "The Horn," for it is a distinct horn from the West Coast, De la Bêche, and Darwin. Haidinger (proper) does not show as a peak at all from the Fox Glacier, though one of the finest as seen from the Tasman.

The first impression I received on looking at the surroundings of the Fox névé was, that peaks rising from it would be most troublesome to climb from this side; but the fog cut off my view so soon that the mistake was excusable. Since then, however, a second visit has shown that so far from being more difficult, they would seem to be easier on this side than from the Tasman. From the Chancellor Ridge, the Horn, Glacier Peak, and Haidinger are all accessible, as also are the chief peaks of the Bismarck Range. Good passes may be found between Mount Tasman and Mount Haast, also between the latter and Haidinger; in fact, so many expeditions of interest are to be made from here that I hope it will not be many years before we see a good hut placed on the Chancellor.

# CHAPTER IX.

#### COOK RIVER—MAIN BRANCH.

Rough Work—Large Boulders—Castle Rock—Rata-trees—Shelf Camp—
Bad Weather—Short Commons—Cave Camp.

THE main branch of Cook River had been prospected for gold some years previous to our exploration, but as the diggers never bring out any information concerning the topography or appearance of the country, their visits are not taken into account. In fact it is often quite impossible to find out how far they have been up a valley; sometimes the distance they say they went would land them, in reality, some miles out on to the Mackenzie Plains. I remember one fellow saying he had been eight miles along a certain ridge—a fact which I doubted; but on being pressed he admitted that, when he turned back, he had not reached the open grass, but he had gone quite eight miles by that time. Knowing the ridge well, I was able to say that he had not gone a mile and a quarter, as that would have brought him well up to the grass.

While waiting at Ryan's, on our return from the Fox Glacier, for some provisions which were to come up from Gillespies, the weather was perfect; but the Fates were against us, and on the day the stores arrived, rain set in, and prevented a start until the 29th of April. Sending our camp, stores, and instruments in three loads of 50 lbs. each, by pack-horse

VIEW FROM COOK RIVER FLATS.

to the diggers' huts, we followed on foot, and crossed by the wire rope and cage. With the usual colonial freedom, we boiled the billy, and had a meal in one of the huts before shouldering our loads. Such is the hospitality of the West Coast digger, that the owner of the hut would have been much hurt if we had not made ourselves at home, or had troubled to unroll the "swags" to get out our own provisions.

Leaving about 60 lbs. to bring up later, we took 45 lbs. each, and, starting at 1.30 P.M., travelled till nearly 5 o'clock without stopping, covering a distance of about four miles. This was my first experience of following up to its source a river which came down for any distance through the ranges. Hitherto this year on the Waiho and Fox Rivers, the glacier and ice work predominated, and on the Balfour the gorge prevented our following the actual river. In Cook River, however, we had to follow the valley, and very rough, slow work it proved. The distance covered on our first day was the longest we made during the trip; but on going over the same ground again the time was reduced considerably, as we not only knew the route, but had bush tracks "blazed" where necessary.

The first mile or two were simple enough, merely alternate beaches of small stones (*i.e.* stones under 3 ft. in diameter) and short stretches of large boulders, or rocky bluffs against which the river ran very deep, compelling us to "take to the bush." I have already described what "taking to the bush" involves in the way of track cutting, so need only add that when compelled to leave the open river-bed, the loads had to be put down, a track "blazed" round or over the obstacle, to the next piece of open going, and a return made for the loads. After the junction of Cook and Balfour Rivers, the hard work began. The valley narrows considerably and has very steep sides, covered with dense bush and undergrowth; while below the bush, for perhaps thirty feet to the water, the valley is filled with gigantic boulders, varying in size from 3 ft. to 100 ft., and even 150 ft. in diameter.

These giant masses are not only lying in hopeless confusion in the bottom of the valley, but for some distance up the hill-sides; where it is not too steep, boulders are found, amongst and on the top of which the great trees of the bush are growing. I should thoroughly enjoy a day or two travelling over such ground with nothing to carry, but it is far from amusing with forty or fifty pounds on one's back, even with one man helping the other. I really doubt whether in some places further up the river, a man by himself could have managed to make any progress at all in the river-bed. Often, when an impassable bluff rendered it necessary to go into the bush, one of us would slip down between two boulders into a wedge-shaped hole, concealed by the ferns, and after scrambling out again, probably "bark" a shin in another hole. On finding the bush very bad going we would decide to choose the least of two evils and go back to the open river-bed. This probably necessitated a crawl under two boulders, through a small tunnel, perhaps 10 or 20 ft. long, with a muddy bottom, or trickling water. The aperture would appear large enough to allow one to crawl through with a load; but after going a little way on hands and knees, one would have to lie down, because the load had proved too high for the tunnel. Then, wriggling along, snake-fashion, a little further, and the tunnel becoming smaller, the load would stick again, leaving one lying, face downwards, in mud or trickling water, fairly unable to move. The only way out of the difficulty is to allow the other man to lay hold of one by the heels and to submit—in silence, if possible—to the ignominious and uncomfortable operation of being pulled out against the grain.

I do not know anything more trying to the temper than this operation, and I think it speaks volumes for Douglas and myself that the dog came back alive! After emerging from a hole backwards—with trousers above the knees, shirt ruffled up round the neck, and generally muddy—many men would want to kill something, on the same principle that some men swear at the caddy when they take their eyes off the ball at golf and come to grief!

Having smoothed down the ruffled feelings and feathers, we would take off our loads and go through, passing them in front or pulling them behind. It really makes little difference whether the "swag" is passed in front or behind, because both methods involve sundry bumps on the head and skinned knuckles. In addition to these performances, boulders are met with, to pass which one man has to stand on the other's shoulders and swarm up a smooth round stone; then let down a rope and hoist the loads and the other man. Or the reverse is necessary in other places, followed by more crawling under boulders and so on, *ad lib*. Considering these obstacles, and the necessity of carrying our loads, it is not surprising that in one part of the river we were four days traversing four and a-half miles in the narrowest part of the valley, climbing, crawling, sliding, scrambling, and track cutting most of the time.

So late in the season as it now was, the days were gettting

short, darkness setting in at the bottom of the valley soon after five o'clock, and it was nearly that hour on the first day before we came to a place fit or possible to pass the night, as the sides had been not only too steep, but too rough. The spot chosen to pitch our small canvas shelter was against a large erratic, with a small space of flat ground in front, allowing a passable though poor camp. Some care has to be taken in choosing a camping ground, as sudden rain may cause the river to rise and flood us out.

This great block of stone we measured with a tape; it was 113 ft. high by 384 ft. in circumference, and like all the other masses of rock in the river, was evidently an erratic left by the ancient glacier of which La Perouse is the remains. It certainly did not come off the hill above its present site, because the rock is different, and must have come from four or five miles further up the valley. The river-side of the "Castle Rock," as Douglas named it, was perpendicular and showed a face of about 120 ft. in length by 113 ft. in height, as square as if it had been hewn by man, with the exception of its rounded edges. The top has rata-trees growing on it, which present an instance of what Douglas calls the "reasoning power of trees."

In Westland, there are many examples of this peculiarity, where a clump of trees are growing on a high rock, on which they will necessarily feel the want of water when they have grown to a respectable size. One of the trees in such a position sends down a long arm, which is not a root or branch, but merely a sucker, to the nearest water; all the other trees on the rock then send out similar arms and fasten them on to the one which has first found water, and in this way the whole clump benefits and flourishes. Further evidence of this peculiar law of nature is found in cases where seedlings have been deposited on a narrow ledge on the face of a precipice. Their position is a very precarious one when they grow to any size, for a high wind will probably prove too much for them; they therefore send an arm up the face of the rock, or sometimes along it on the same level, until it finds a crevice, and here it fastens with a wonderfully tight grip. These offshoots are found quite newly grown on trees that must be of considerable age.

Immediately above our camp the river came boiling and foaming out of a gorge, walled by sheer rock cliffs, which would compel us to blaze a track up some height and along the top of the bluff. From here, about two miles further up the river, and some height on the slopes of Ryan's Peak, we saw a rock with scrub growing on the top, which looked extraordinarily like Her Majesty's head on a jubilee coin. Instead of a crown the scrub formed a cap, and with snow sprinkled on the scrub it had the appearance of a black cap with white bands trailing out behind. This rock must be 200 ft. in height from neck to crown, and the overhanging piece forming the nose cannot project much less than 30 ft. It is as perfect a natural bust as I have come across, as seen from this camp and one or two points on the route past the gorge.

The next day, the 30th, Douglas began to blaze a track over the bluff, while I returned to the diggers' hut for the 60 lb. load we had left behind, and making a long day of it, reached camp again at dark. If the journey up to the camp had been hard work with two of us together, it was doubly hard by myself, and the manipulation of the pack at some of the large boulders much more difficult. The down journey without the handicap of 60 lbs. was made in three hours, but the return took a good five hours, chiefly owing to the number of times the load had to be roped up a boulder behind me, and let down on the other side. The worst place of all, to manage alone, was passed far more easily than I had any right to expect, for while making up my mind how to get down without damaging my burden, I overbalanced and fell, thus solving the weighty problem without sustaining any damage. When a man has a heavy load on his back, a fall for a reasonable distance is of little consequence, for the weight always causes him to fall on the "swag," thus having a more or less soft buffer to resist the shock.

On the 1st of May, we had time to look over some papers which we had received at Ryan's a week previously; the latest news in them was three weeks old, but prior to seeing them, we were nearly three months behind time. We here first read the telegram announcing Mr. Gladstone's resignation.

Douglas had not been able to reach the open river beyond the gorge on the previous day, so we spent the 2nd in taking the track on through the gorge. When two work together we generally arrange that while one blazes the track, the other follows and carries a load which we leave at the end of the day and return to camp. The next day, bringing up the remainder of the stores, we camp at the point where the load was left, and while one prepares a shelter, the other, if necessary, continues blazing the track. The route through the gorge had to rise some 700 or 800 feet before we could begin to edge down again to the river. At one point the track followed the brink of the rocky cliff for fifty yards or more, and from here the precipice fell away sheer into the river for 500 ft., while the opposite (or eastern) side was almost as precipitous.

Away below was the river, looking like a small stream, now diving under and now foaming over immense boulders, while above and around us there were towering hills covered with snow to within a thousand feet of where we stood. Opposite us was the deep-gorged valley of McBain's Creek, at the head of which Mount Tasman's ice-clad summit was just visible. Behind, the deep valley, the lower portion clothed with luxuriant bush, could be seen to the inflow of the Balfour River, while Craig's Range and Peak rose abruptly in the background, looking very fine in its coating of autumn snow.

Two hundred feet or so above this we were able to begin edging down, and after crossing two large creeks which fell in fine cascades over large boulders, we descended rapidly to the river, wending our way down a very steep hillside with great erratic blocks scattered on all sides. It is wonderful that some of these stones do not roll over into the river below, so precarious do their positions appear.

On reaching the river we were dismayed at the task before us; it is hardly too much to say that here we found no small boulders at all, they were all of immense size and completely filled the bottom of the valley, the river in places disappearing under them.

In the middle of the stream was one we named the "Egg Cup" Rock. A large boulder, some 40 ft. high, and 150 ft. round (estimated), had a hollow on one side of it, like an arm-chair, in which rested an egg-shaped stone about 15 ft. long, and perfectly loose, evidently left there by a flood. It must not be supposed that a stone of this size is too large for a flood to move. During the great storm in February, there was—as already described—a high flood on the Callery River. After the flood went down, there could be seen a large flat-shaped boulder of some 15 ft. square by 6 or 7 ft. thick, which had been moved from its old position in the middle of the river, and was lying on its side on some other stones— quite ten feet above, and some thirty yards from its original place. The probability is, that during a flood a large amount of débris fills the bed of the rivers, owing to a slip in the valley above, and the boulder is rolled along on the top of the false bed, and then the débris is scoured out again, leaving it high and dry. Whatever the means by which these large stones are moved, I feel confident that any one who has seen a Westland river in an "old man" flood would credit the actual upheaval of any sized boulder. The power, force, and rapidity of the stream is simply appalling, and even the oldest West Coaster will watch the mad career of the river, bringing down large trees, and listen to the boulders pounding and thumping along the bottom.

As it was after mid-day, and beginning to rain again, we left the load we had brought up under a stone, and made our way back over the bluff to our camp.

Some idea of this kind of work may be gained from our experience for the next three days. As the weather looked settled, and in order to lighten our loads, we had taken most of our stores ahead, leaving one day's food with the instruments, &c., in camp, expecting to be able to rejoin the stores again next day. Heavy rain, however, set in and flooded everything, so we were cut off from supplies ahead, and had no chance of returning down the river. Expecting fine weather next day, we finished the remainder of the meat that evening, and consequently had two days in camp with only a very limited amount of flour and rice; the remainder of the stores—namely, flour, rice, oatmeal, suet, and cocoa—was above the gorge.

On the evening of the second wet day we had finished the "tucker" in camp, having made the one day's food last two days, therefore we were very thankful to find the sun shining next morning. Having to some extent dried our things to avoid the extra weight of carrying wet canvas, we went on through the gorge to our other load, intending to have a good meal before going any further. But as soon as we arrived, more rain set in, so, in spite of the fact that we had had nothing to eat since the previous evening, we at once began to make a shelter.

After some "fossicking" and a good deal of talk, we found a suitable place under a large stone, which, overhanging a little, sheltered a ledge of some 6 ft. broad by 20 ft. long. Below this shelf there was a perpendicular drop of 30 ft., and then a slope to the river. Here we decided to rig our canvas in case the wind changed and drifted the rain under the rock.

In camp I always slept on the side away from the fire, which in this case we made against the rock; thus I should have no protection against falling over the thirty feet in my sleep—a very uncomfortable proceeding in a sleeping bag. I therefore stipulated for a substantial barrier. We felled a tree above us, intending to roll the trunk down and place it on the outer edge of the shelf; but of course, with the usual cussedness of things, it slid down nearly to the river. Having got it back to a level with the ledge, we proceeded to put it in position, and had just got it fairly straight, when one end took charge and fell over the side; a fork at the other end hooked Douglas's leg, nearly carrying him over too; but luckily he grasped a root in the ground and hung there, with the whole weight on his leg. To fasten a rope round and secure the log to relieve him of the strain was the work of a minute, and then we had to struggle with the other end, to heave it back into position. In due time, after much unparliamentary language, we had both ends secured with a rope, and the canvas pitched. All this had to be done in a deluge of rain, which, combined with our long fast, did not improve our tempers.

On the way up in the morning we had luckily shot a kaka, which we had prepared and put into the billy to stew as soon as we arrived, having kindled a fire before building our shelter. At 4 P.M., taking off our wet things, we hung them in front of the fire, and having put our blankets round us until our clothes were dry, we sat down at last to discuss the stew, which was by this time ready. It may be imagined that the billy looked very foolish when we had finished; hard work and a twenty-four hours' fast tend to give a man a good appetite.

This camp was no place to stay in, if we could find a better, because it was on a very steep hillside, and there were many loose boulders lying about, which showed that falling stones or slips had to be feared in wet weather. It is never quite safe to camp on a steep "sidcling" in heavy rain, for, in Westland, large landslips are common in the ranges during or after a storm. Consequently we left early next morning, and in three hours had succeeded in advancing about three-quarters of a mile further up the river; here we found a large boulder forming, with two others, a fair cave, which we soon turned into an excellent shelter, and spent several wet days in perfect comfort.

This three hours was, I think, about the hardest bit of travelling we had, and as we toiled along, now crawling, now climbing, under and over the great boulders, I could not help comparing our progress to that of two ants crossing a newly metalled road. The difficulties in our path proved too much on several occasions for poor "Betsy," who had to be hoisted about in the most rough-and-ready manner. Fortunately our loads got lighter by a pound or so every day, so we knew that, on having to face this part of the river again, our burdens would be considerably lighter. Considering the contents of the "swags" we carried, and the usage they received up this river, it is wonderful that so little damage was done. There were 15 lbs. weight of instruments, photographic material, and field-books in each load, before any things in the shape of camp or stores were added. And as these have to be rolled in a blanket and piece of canvas, with a lot of mixed articles, it would not be surprising if damage ensued from the hauling and dumping they received over the large stones which were too slippery to negotiate under a handicap of 60 lbs. But I do not remember having an instrument, camera, or plates damaged once during the season, in spite of rough usage, damp, fire, or floods, with the exception, by the way, of half-a-dozen glass plates broken before exposure, and four half-plates after. The latter, however, were probably damaged in the pack-horse mail up the coast.

The cave camp, though airy, was very comfortable; it had —like our usual shelters—a roof and two walls, but there was only room to sit and lie down, it was a foot too low to allow one to stand up. The weather was now becoming very wintry and cold, snow fell two or three times, but did not lie permanently within three hundred feet of the cave. Our food, too, was getting monotonous—flour and rice were all we had, and a very limited amount even of that, because, having got no birds, on which we always relied, the stores brought up had to bear a double strain, or we had to be satisfied with very small rations.

We used often to wish that we could see the picture which would present itself to a man coming up the river; if anyone had by chance followed us he would have seen a low-roofed cavity under a huge boulder, in which sat two ragged men on a log in front of a large fire, and a hungry-looking dog lying close by. The men would be of doubtful nationality, having long, unkempt hair and beards, and with skins as brown as a penny. In all probability their clothes would be hanging at the side of the fire drying, and they would be sitting, with their blankets wrapped round them, smoking their pipes, and possibly playing a game of cribbage with a pocket-book marked out as a board; or perhaps both would be reading—one lying down on the dry scrub, which served as bedding, and the other sitting up. Periodically the dog would get up, and, stretching herself, would put on a piteous blind-man's-dog look in hopes of coaxing a little something to eat, but without success.

A picture of this kind appears dismal, and I suppose the reality was about as depressing as one could imagine. The hours would drag slowly along because we could only afford two small "dough-boys"—or suet dumplings—for each meal, and only two meals a day. The weather was too bad to allow us to work, and it seemed little use looking at the aneroid barometer, which, however, we did constantly in hopes that it would rise; but even the barometer seemed to have very little effect on the weather. Wet days with plenty of food are not unpleasant, as we could spend considerable time in cooking an elaborate (?) meal, but when hungry and with nothing to cook it is painfully dreary. After consulting our watches periodically during the day, one of us would exclaim, " By Jove, it's six o'clock at last; let's sling the billy."

" Right you are; what are we going to eat ? "

" I vote for grilled chops, some bread and cheese, and a long beer."

" Oh, I'm tired of chops; let's have some steak-and-kidney pie, with a Welsh rare-bit to follow."

" The steak is too tough; what do you say to devilled kidneys ? "

" They give me indigestion."

" Well, then—goose and apple sauce ? "

" I'm sick of geese."

" You're so confoundedly particular; shall we have some dough-boys ? "

" Good idea! Let us have a dough-boy for a change."

Now, we had been eating dough-boys for breakfast and dough-boys for tea for some days, and, even then, only one dough-boy the size of a man's fist; but such is the depressing effect of wet weather and short rations that we were really amused at our little joke, and probably repeated it again next morning! I recollect one evening, when very hungry, telling Douglas of the winter dinner of the Alpine Club in London, at which I was in 1892, and we both felt quite cheerful after thinking of so many good things.

In the evening we generally had a game or two of cribbage, discussed various items of news three or four months old, which we had just gleaned from the papers, and at soon after 8 o'clock boiled the billy again, and made a small drink of cocoa. At 9 P.M., having made up a large fire, we rolled into our respective blankets, and dreamed of city banquets and good living until daylight.

## CHAPTER X.

### COOK RIVER (*concluded*) AND ANCIENT GLACIERS.

Snow-storm—Tony's Rock—Head of the River—Check-shirt Birds—Return Journey—Back to Civilisation—Topography—Ancient Glaciers.

As soon as possible we went on, partly by track cutting and partly in the river-bed, amongst the worst boulders we had yet seen. It was not a case of climbing *over* those stones, because that was impossible, we simply had to crawl and squeeze in and out amongst them, until we could find a place to leave the river, and get on to the hillside, where we blazed a track. This was rendered necessary, because the boulders were practically impassable for half a mile. In three and a-half hours, when we had gone perhaps a mile—certainly not much more—we came to the largest boulder in the river. This is named Tony's Rock, and must have come down on the ancient glacier, from a mile and a half to two miles up the valley. It is not the same formation as that of Ryan's Peak, under which it lies. Behind it, on the slope, and leaning against it, are several other giant stones, but not nearly so large; above it the river-bed is easier and more open, only a few large boulders appearing.

The dimensions of Tony's Rock are: height 156 ft. (aneroid), circumference 843 ft. We were unable to measure more than three sides of the stone, as the fourth had other stones heaped against it; however, we agreed at the time that the figure quoted was not over the mark, as the three sides alone exceeded 700 ft. I do not know the dimensions of known erratic blocks in other parts of the world, so cannot say how this compares with them; Douglas states that he measured one in the Waipara, a branch of the Arawata River behind Jackson's Bay, and it showed slightly over 200 ft. in height, with a girth a trifle under 1,000 ft. In that locality there are several nearly as large, and one, which he could not measure, perhaps a little larger. Of these, however, I cannot speak from personal observation. The boulders in Cook River, between "Castle Rock" and "Tony's Rock," are only approached by some in the Copland River, below Welcome Flat, for number and size.

As the lower side of Tony's apparently gave capital shelter, we decided to move our quarters at once; but before reaching Cave Camp again more rain set in, so we stayed there for the night. Next morning was cold and wet—snow falling at the cave—but at noon we packed our loads, and during a lull in the storm, made for Tony's Rock. Before reaching it, however, another snow-storm came on, and, making the bush cold and wet, drenched us and our loads very quickly.

A short distance below Tony's Rock the whole river goes over a fine fall of some 50 ft. in height, caused by two large boulders obstructing its course; in the middle of the narrow channel a knob of rock, not unlike a camel's head, makes the water rise in a wave six or eight feet high, and spread out in a fan-shaped mass of foam. Behind this fall, I believe one could walk and cross the river dry-shod, for it shoots out a considerable distance. The effect is very striking, as the river is by no means a small one, and in summer it would be even finer, for there would be a larger volume of water.

The difficulty of obtaining a photograph of this fall afforded a good example of the size of the boulders. Hearing the roar of the water, when cutting the track, we climbed a tree to look ahead, and saw the fall some 200 yards or more further up the river. We therefore went to the edge of the bush, and found that, in order to get a good view, the camera should be out in the open. It was by no means easy to get down again into the river from the bank, which was formed of a series of large stones, against which the débris from the hillside has been heaped up. Determined, however, to get my photograph, I slid down the smooth surface of one of the rocks, and landed safely on to the top of another, some 25 ft. below, and was even then 30 ft. above the water, on a flat boulder, off which I could not get—for it was standing in the river separated from the others except on the side I had come down. Having taken the photograph, it was impossible to climb back, without help, up the smooth face down which I had come; and as we had left the rope at the cave, Douglas had to go back into the scrub to look for a pole, which was not easy to find, owing to the vegetation being gnarled and twisted at this altitude. However, he found one which was just long enough for me to catch hold of, and having passed up my boots and camera, I was able, with bare feet and help from Douglas, to scramble to the top again. There is nothing exciting about this incident, but it helps, to some extent, to show how large the stones were.

Just before reaching Tony's Rock, "Betsy" caught us the second bird we had found since leaving Castle Rock a week before; it was a decided curiosity in the shape of a white kiwi, and no doubt its skin would be valuable, but, as usual, hunger for meat overcame scientific ardour, so we made it into stew! The skin is the most nutritious part of a kiwi, therefore we could not afford to keep it for stuffing.

Heavy snow fell again in the night, covering the ground round our shelter, which was some 3,000 ft. above sea-level; and to our disgust we found that this palatial residence was a fraud, for the water trickled down on the inside and wetted us wherever we tried to sleep. I have always noticed that whenever there is a leak in canvas or rock, it always happens to occur exactly above one's face! The night was bitterly cold, as we had left our canvas at a lower camp, and the shelter under Tony's Rock was so large that it was practically the same as sleeping in the open; we had not even our roof and two walls.

The morning broke clear and frosty, but snow was lying a foot or more deep all round, and, instead of melting, would in all probability lie for the rest of the winter, gradually increasing in depth, until the valley would be entirely blocked. It is hard to credit the amount of snow which collects in these narrow valleys in winter, some must have 200 or 300 ft. piled up in them during a bad winter by the heavy storms and frequent avalanches. More snow falls in the winter, in New Zealand Alps, than most persons would imagine, considering the temperate latitude, and in the spring it melts with great rapidity, causing heavy floods in the rivers.

As our stock of provisions was now nearly finished, we

decided to push up the river for one day, lay off the head of the valley hastily, and retreat before more bad weather delayed us indefinitely. Following the valley for some little distance, we turned up a creek off Ryan's Range, on the right, and after a great deal of wading and pounding through soft snow and snow-covered scrub, reached a point from which we could complete the map of the valley. The snout of the La Perouse Glacier lay below us, a mile to two miles further up the valley, and the river flowed over a bed of smaller stones, which were easy to travel on, until Tony's Rock was reached, after which it begins a rapid descent through the boulder-filled valley up which we came.

Such a large basin at the head is unexpected, and like the Balfour valley, is a great deal wider than we had anticipated. This is owing to the very precipitous nature of the Balfour and Copland Ranges, between which the river flows. Above Tony's Rock, the valley turns with a wide sweep to the left, and opens out on the south bank, while on the northern side the Balfour Range continues steeper than before. From the glacier to near the bend in the river, the southern bank slopes back more or less gently for perhaps half a mile, showing three or four old moraine terraces, covered with low, dense mountain scrub. Behind these slopes, Mount Copland and Lyttle's Peak rise abruptly in immense precipices of two or three thousand feet. Mounts Stokes (La Perouse) and Hicks apparently block the head of the valley, while Mount Cook shows over Harper's Saddle. The La Perouse Glacier, however, comes off the main range between Mount Tasman and Dampier, the upper portion lying away to the left round another bend, only the snout, and lower portion of the glacier being visible until a higher point on Ryan's Range is reached.

As seen in May, 1894, the picture defies description. The valley was blocked with snow to the water's edge, the river looking like a black ribbon in the white snow, as it flowed down the valley in graceful curves. The giant cliffs of Copland and Lyttle's Peak were white from base to summit, the snow having been blown against the steep faces, and frozen by the cold wind and frost of the night, formed glistening icicles. At first there was little black rock to relieve the dazzling whiteness of the landscape, but after the sun had been up some hours, the precipices began to shed their white mantle, and the steep buttresses and couloirs began to show their shapes and forms. Now and then the stillness, which was almost oppressive, was broken by a slight hissing noise which gradually increased into a roar as a great avalanche poured down over cliffs of Lyttle's or Ryan's Peak. One descended within 300 yards of us, bounding over a sheer drop of 700 ft. or more, like a great waterfall about 50 yards broad, and lasting for two or three minutes.

Our clothes had become very tattered and worn, owing to the rough usage coming up the river, and afforded us very little warmth; consequently, the morning's work, wading through snow and bruising under and over snow-covered scrub, had chilled us to the bone; yet when we had finished our observations, we were loth to leave such a glorious view, in spite of the cold and hunger. I have often wondered what we should have thought of that scene, if we had been warmly clad and well fed, because my experience is, that discomfort spoils the enjoyments of a view to some extent; and if we admired the head of Cook River, as we saw it in our somewhat wretched condition, how much more beautiful would it have appeared under pleasanter circumstances!

Down the valley to the north, we could see a bank of angry-looking clouds, rolling in from the sea, and already settling down over Craig's Range, so we dared not stay any longer, in case another storm prevented our getting down the river. Therefore, hurrying back to Tony's Rock, we packed our loads without delay, and made for the cave, which we reached about sunset; here a good fire and an extra dough-boy each (including "Betsy") soon made us forget the discomfort of a day's work in soft snow and ragged garments.

On the way down we saw a cuckoo, and his usual companion the "check-shirt" bird. It is not customary to find these birds in the mountains during the early winter, as they generally migrate to warmer latitudes at the end of the summer and return in the spring. The former is the Maori koe-koea (*Eudynamys taitensis*), and like his English namesake, he makes use of other birds' nests. The "check-shirt" follows him in his migrations, and is often seen with him in the lower hills.

I heard a curious story connected with this little wanderer, told by a friend of mine in a digger's hut. He said that sailors believe these birds to represent the spirits of drowned men, and that it is therefore unlucky to kill them. On one occasion he was "down South," below Gillespies, and, with five others, was trying to shoot a check-shirt bird close to the hut of another digger, whom I shall call "Mac." Old Mac came out to where they were shooting, and begged them to desist, for it was bad luck, he said, and meant a violent end to those concerned in the death of the bird. Of course, his hearers laughed at the idea, but he was very earnest, and said he would give them evidence of the truth of his statement.

Taking them into his hut he related his own life's history. He was one of a party of Newfoundland fishermen, who left their homes, in a ship built by themselves, for Australia, in the early days of the gold diggings. When a few days away from land, they discovered that, though all were sailors, they knew nothing about navigation; consequently the ship drifted about aimlessly for weeks. In course of time they fell in with a man-of-war, and discovered that, instead of being near the Cape of Good Hope, they were off the Horn. The commander of the warship put a man on board, with a knowledge of navigation, and he piloted the unfortunate ship to Adelaide, from whence they all went to the goldfields. Mac had no luck, so he shipped on board a trading schooner to the Islands, and all went well till some man "was fool enough" to kill a check-shirt bird. From that day their luck changed, and ultimately they lost the schooner in a gale. Five or six men succeeded in getting away in an open boat, and were afloat for many days. The boat was picked up by a steamer, near Auckland, and in it were four dead bodies, and a living skeleton, almost a maniac from his fearful sufferings—this was old Mac. It was a long time before he recovered, and was able to go down to Westland to try his luck again on a goldfield.

My informant assured me that the manner in which the old fellow related his tale, and the power with which he described his awful time in the boat with the dead bodies—too weak to throw them overboard—exceeded anything he had ever read.

Mac ended his yarn by saying, "Anyway, you can't kill them with shot, you must use silver."

Out of consideration for the old sailor's feelings, my friend took no further part in the proceedings, but he remembers, as he went away, seeing a man cutting up a half-a-crown. Whether they killed the bird or not he never heard, all he can say is that three out of the five died violent deaths, and as the others have gone away he cannot say what became of them. As he said, "It is one of those curious coincidences which tend to strengthen peoples' belief in superstitions."

One long day from the Cave Camp took us to the diggers' huts, where one of our friends insisted on our staying, and we enjoyed a good meal for the first time for ten days; but as he was short of meat we pushed on next morning to Ryan's hut, to find it empty and nothing to eat, only one or two rotten potatoes. These were naturally "hardly good enough," therefore on the following day we started, breakfastless, to Mr. Wilson's Survey Camp at Cook River Settlement, seven miles away over the flats. Here Bill Boyd, the cook, with the help of mutton, vegetables, and plum duff, soon persuaded us that life after all was worth living.

It may, perhaps, be thought that we only had ourselves to blame for short rations and starvation on this trip, but I think it was our misfortune, not our fault. In the first place, the valley was unexplored, and we had every right to look forward to as many birds as we had need of for food; and, as we always rely greatly on these, we only took enough food to last us for the trip, *with help of birds*. Again, we did not anticipate more than ten days' work at the most, so we took flour, rice, oatmeal, tea, cocoa, sugar, a little meat, treacle, suet (for cooking dough-boys), and a tin or two of sardines in sufficient quantity, *plus* birds, to last us for that period. Had we found birds, as we reasonably anticipated, the provisions we took would, with care, have lasted more than two weeks, and even if they were exhausted, we could have lived well with the help of the pea-rifle. Luck was against us in every respect; for the first three or four days we had meat, and went on eating as if there was no need to economise. By that time we had gone some way up the river, and the bad weather not only prevented a retreat, but delayed our advance. Consequently, having only caught the kiwi and kaka, we had to live for ten days, relying *entirely* on the stores which were left, and which, owing to delays, would only keep us reasonably if we had found plenty of game.

To give some idea of the help that we derive from birds, I may safely say that stores which would usually last for ten days comfortably would only give perhaps three days of good meals in the event of finding no birds. It is no joke to be compelled to divide six good meals consisting of flour and rice into rations to extend over ten days, and at the same time do a considerable amount of heavy work.

The less said about our clothes the better; after a long season of eight months in the ranges, the constant wet, rough usage in bush and scrub, &c., soon made havoc of the best materials. The only original garment of mine now in existence is a coat of Burberry's "Gabardine" which lasted me without tearing for the whole of this season and the next—it is now gracing the back of a digger " down South," and he still swears by it! Some valleys are so narrow that, if they run east and west, there are places in them which never get the sun, winter or summer; here the bush, which grows just as luxuriantly, is always wet, and if we are above the bush line, snow or creeks wet us daily; ordinary tweeds therefore become rotten and are easily torn. I find the best costume to be flannel shirt, woollen jersey, and thick knitted woollen drawers—without trousers—and some spare canvas to patch with. It is absolutely necessary to wear flannel or wool next to the skin, owing to the constant wet, and woollen garments underneath trousers are too hot for my comfort, so I generally dispense with the latter. After a few months one may be said to be wearing a number of patches connected together by woollen material!

After leaving Cook River I decided to go north to Hokitika as winter would prevent further work, and there were two hundred or more photographs to develop and print, also sundry work to be done in the office to complete the field work. Accordingly, having spent a few days in photographing the wondrous panoramas and other views from the flats and sea bluffs, I tramped with my goods and chattels some thirty miles along the beach to Okarito. Here I obtained a horse from the mail man, and in three days arrived in Hokitika after a spell of nearly eight months in a batwing, six of which were spent in the ranges chiefly on new ground.

Our work up Cook River finally settled a doubtful point in the topography of the district, namely, the course of the Balfour Range. When in 1890 Blakiston and I made the first ascent of Harper's Saddle, at the head of the Hooker Glacier, we were unable owing to the fog to see clearly down to the West Coast. On our return I was asked by the Westland Survey Department—firstly, what was the true course of the Divide? Secondly, was the Balfour Range an offshoot of Hicks (St.

David's Dome) or Tasman? The first question I answered without hesitation, but the second had to be left for future solution.

On looking at the map, made from distant trigonometrical stations, I was inclined to believe that there was an error in the Balfour Glacier and Range, because, if the latter was an offshoot of the Divide near Tasman, it left such a ridiculously small névé for the glacier, which was shown to be four or five miles long. The La Perouse Glacier had been put in by guess-work, and it was more than probable that it was shown far too large and that its upper basin really belonged to the Balfour Glacier. This would mean that the Balfour Range was an offshoot of Mount Hicks and not of Tasman, or possibly might be a detached range. In the event of the latter being the case the large névé alluded to would supply both glaciers.

However, up Cook River and from Ryan's Peak later on, the truth was evident, and it is now finally settled that the Balfour Range comes off the Divide just south of Mount Tasman. Also the La Perouse is a large glacier, as shown on the map, and nearly clear of surface moraine. The glacier is nearly five miles long and descends by a fine ice-fall from its névé, flowing in graceful curves between high precipices with one or two tributaries from the east. It has but little surface moraine as compared with other New Zealand glaciers, having only a fringe of débris on each side and being completely covered near its terminal face. About a quarter of its length from the snout a peculiar bar of moraine running across it from side to side looks as if a large slip had come down and shot right across the ice.

The course of the Balfour Range having been settled, it only remains to find some reason for so large a glacier as the Balfour, which is six miles long, flowing from such an insignificant névé.

I have already described this glacier with its névé detached from its trunk. The only available theory, so far as I can see, is that the great western face of Tasman, which rises abruptly in precipices for over 7,000 ft. from the glacier, is too steep to hold much snow. It faces the south-west—the cold quarter—and must catch an immense quantity of snow in the winter, which comes down frequently in large avalanches, filling the upper end of the valley and forming the trunk of the glacier. There are also, no doubt, avalanches from Craig's Range on the northern side of the glacier, and these bring down masses of débris and broken rock which completely cover the ice, and to a large extent protect it from the sun's heat. The steep ranges surrounding the valley must also prevent the sun from reaching the glacier in the winter and also part of the day in the summer.

When Douglas explored the left-hand branch of the Copland River (a tributary of the Karangarua) in 1892, he noticed that, though Mount Stokes apparently dropped without interruption to the Strauchon Glacier, the avalanches from the peak never reached the bottom, but appeared to be swallowed up half-way down the slope. This led him to expect one of those peculiar instances of the broken nature of the ranges in the form of a large fissure in the mountain side, or narrow deep gorge with an outlet into Cook River.

We were, therefore, looking out for such a cleft when at the head of the river, and found that his suspicions were correct, for a narrow and dark gorge comes into the valley, evidently

154   PIONEER WORK IN THE ALPS OF NEW ZEALAND.

containing a small glacier formed by avalanches. There was too much snow to see whether a glacier really existed, but we decided that there was a small one. The stream from it flows into Cook River, a short distance below the La Perouse Glacier.

The Cook River glaciers were evidently, in the past, of considerable size, to judge by the numerous moraines and terraces

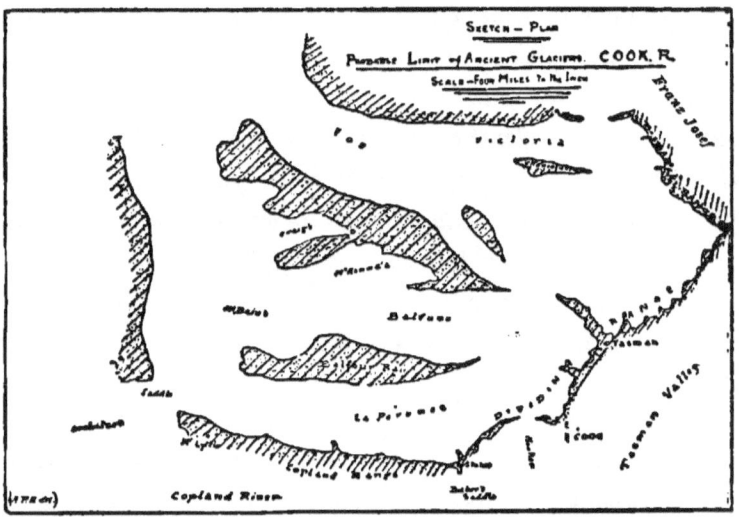

in the upper and lower parts of the valleys. The stream of ice which came down the main valley was probably the largest, and its marks are to be seen on the lower end of the Balfour Range a considerable height above the river. On the slopes under Ryan's Peak, the erratic blocks scattered on the hillside show that the ice must have been 700 ft. thick at the least below Tony's Rock. After forcing its way down the valley of Cook River it would be joined by a stream of ice which came down the Balfour Valley from the Mount Tasman of that day. Between McBain's Creek and the Balfour River is a rounded hill which has evidently been shaped by glacier action, and must at one period have been completely covered with ice. Behind this hill to the east is a low flat depression, showing that the ice after shrinking somewhat had still found its way into the main glacier, down McBain's Creek, as well as the Balfour Gorge; and on shrinking still further it had ceased to flow down the creek, and only found one outlet through the gorge of the present river.

After being augmented by this ice stream, and a smaller one from Craig's Range, the glacier would flow down to the flat country, probably joining the ice from the Fox Valley and from the south.

There is little doubt, from Douglas's observations in the many rivers he has explored, that the general direction of the ancient ice-flow was north. My own observations—small though they are in comparison with his—tend to support his theory. In the south there is, perhaps, as fine an ancient moraine as anywhere in Westland—namely, the Cascade moraine—which begins at 200 ft., and goes back, gradually rising to 1,900 ft. in height. Formerly it projected four miles out to sea to Open Bay Island, which has some moraine débris on it. In this moraine, Douglas, who explored that country some years ago, found several red stones which had come north from the Red Hill country. In no case has he discovered any red rocks lying south of that country—but always north.

An interesting feature about the Cascade moraine, from a geologist's point of view, is, that it is stratified, and in some of the layers sea-shells are to be found well inland.

Other evidences of the northern flow of the ice is to be found in the old Wanganui and Hokitika Glaciers. In the two rivers of these names there are belts of serpentine rock, pieces and blocks of which Douglas has found north of the rivers but never south. In the Waitaha River, for instance, he found several proofs that an ancient glacier came over from the Wanganui country to that valley, carrying with it blocks of serpentine rock. The morainic drift of the ancient Franz Josef and Callery Glaciers is to the north, round Lake Maporika, and could be traced even further than that; and the greatest mass of drift near Cook River lies to the north, and if this theory of the ice-flow is correct, it would belong to the old glacier.

The whole of the low country is covered with morainic hills and terraces of various heights up to 300 or 400 ft.; at intervals along the sea beaches these terraces form the bluffs already mentioned. It has been assumed, from past observations made in the low country only, that the old glaciers flowed direct to the sea between these high terraces. This, however, I venture to think, is the wrong view to take.

My belief is, that the ancient glaciers being some 600 ft. thick at the point they left the valleys, would spread out over an immense area, when the lateral pressure of the hillsides was removed. Probably at one time they joined and formed a vast sea of ice at the foot of the hills, covered with a heavy mass of moraine, caused by constant denudation in the mountains. When the period of retreat began they separated again, and gradually retired up the valleys, leaving a confusion of moraine hillocks all over the lower country. This vast accumulation of morainic drift would be gradually cut through by the rivers, thus forming the high terraces now seen along the river sides, and which have hitherto been taken for lateral moraines.

If the theory here advanced be correct, then the terraces would not necessarily be either terminal or lateral moraines but merely accidental embankments, carved into their present shape by the rivers.

Should, however, the theory that they are lateral moraines be the right one, then I am at a loss to understand what caused the vast collection of morainic deposits between the rivers and in places along the foot of the hills where no valleys exist. It seems that those accumulations of drift hills, lying north of the Waiho River and also north of Cook River, must have been left by the great ice-flow extending all over the low country; and had it not been for the rivers of a later date, cutting broad valleys to the sea, they would have extended over the whole coast in hopeless confusion, and no long terraces would have existed at all.

From the Teremakau River to Bruce Bay—twenty miles south of Gillespies—the rivers have cut through old morainic accumulations, which extend from the hills in many cases to the present sea beach, and from Bruce Bay to Jackson's Bay the sea bluffs are rocky, and the old moraines do not appear again till after the latter place is passed.

There has been in the past a considerable amount of gold brought out of Cook River, but at the present time two or three diggers only make a small living, just above the point where the river leaves the hills. Traces, or "colours," of gold have been found a considerable distance up the main branch, but not payable; and in the Balfour gold was obtained in the sixties which paid well, I believe, at the junction of the two rivers, and was traced right up to the glacier. "Harry the Whale" and Dick Nicoll, two old "fossickers," are said to have discovered the Balfour Glacier in 1866, but it is quite useless to consider the journeys made by diggers, for they never bring out any reliable information. How far up Cook River they went it is hard to say, though a tradition exists of "Harry the Whale," "German Harry," and "Tony the Greek" having gone up some miles and crossed the Copland Range into Architect Creek, which flows into the Copland River.

The enterprising old school of diggers and prospectors is fast dying out, but "Paddy" McKenna, an old man, now and then makes solitary trips up the Balfour, where he is commonly supposed to have located a gold-bearing reef. It is sad to see these old-time prospectors disappearing, and no one to take their places. The younger generation on the West Coast have a strong dislike—I may say fear—not only of the hard work and life entailed by journeys into the ranges, but also have a rooted objection to going off the beaten track. They are good enough men on horses after cattle near their huts, but neither love nor money will tempt them to go far afield.

## CHAPTER XI.

### THE FRANZ JOSEF GLACIER.

Second Visit—Winter Snow—Successful Ascent to Névé—Ice Formation—Moraine Formation—Old Moraines and Glaciers—Advance and Retreat.

JUNE, July, and August being our winter months, it was useless to attempt any hill work, therefore, after six weeks' office work in Hokitika, I returned to Christchurch for a few weeks' holiday. Unlimited golf, and sundry exhibitions of my lantern slides before the New Zealand Alpine Club and other institutions, made the time pass quickly, and before I had well shaken down to civilised life it was time to return. From our work on the Franz Josef Glacier during the previous summer, it was evident that early spring was the best season for attacking the ice fall and upper ice. I therefore obtained permission to try and reach the *névé* in September, and at the same time to make observations as to winter retreat or advance, and generally supplement the former report.

On *September 13th*, 1894, I arrived at the Forks, and after some difficulty obtained a man to accompany me to the glacier, the mere mention of going on to the glacier frightening most of the young fellows in the district; however, one of them joined me in spite of warnings from his mates, prepared to face all sorts of unknown evils.

*Friday, September 14th.*—We pitched the batwing in the

same place as last year at Camp 1, and had everything ready by 3 p.m. While looking about in the scrub round camp in the evening for a straight pole to use in camp, I found a small case for carrying soap, which I had lost last year. A weka must have taken it away from camp before we left in February.

*Saturday, September* 15*th.*—Grand weather, very cold, even here, in the mornings. Made a traverse of the terminal face, which showed general retreat, a new rock appearing by No. 1 (Harper's) Rock. In the afternoon we "fossicked" a route over to the north side landing, a little further up than last year, near the first small ice-fall—ice very broken and troublesome. Went along the side to Rope Creek, and found the ice so far retreated that we could get down without a rope. Left a small load here, which we brought along to lighten the weight to-morrow. Hail-storm in the evening.

*Sunday, September* 16*th.*—Moved up to Camp 2 in the afternoon with fly only. Raining all the morning and showers during the afternoon. Cold quarters up here with only one blanket at this time of the year. Rigged up fly in the usual way with two end breakwinds. Our little female weka of last year still here and seems very glad to see us; very tame.

*Monday,* 17*th.*—Tried all the morning to find a route on to the glacier. My mate did not appreciate the pleasures of being let down into a crevasse to cut steps, nor of going along steep sides of the hummocks in small footholds. After three attempts we found a route 200 yards further up than last season. Not by any means a good one, but safe enough at this time of the year. Went up to Camp 3 to see if we could camp there, also marked our line with rata twigs through the extraordinarily crevassed and broken ice below Cape Defiance. Found deep snow on the bank at Camp 3; should only save an hour and a half by camping there, and should have to break a day if we moved up to-morrow, so returned to Camp 2. Found that the rata twigs saved about one-half of the time taken in going up. The ice here is simply a maze of long ridges, very narrow, between deep crevasses, and in such uneven fashion that I could not see a route for certain more than 100 yards ahead, consequently we were often forced to retrace our steps, having been blocked. Fixed three measurement cairns between camp and point E. (the rocky cape on eastern bank) in the afternoon. Bathed, baked bread, made a stew, changed my plates and lost my temper in the evening! (N.B. I presume the fire smoked when I was baking, but cannot remember!)

*Tuesday, September* 18*th*.—Glorious moonlight last night. Up at 2.45 A.M., but did not leave camp till 4 A.M. My mate did not see much "catch" in getting up so early in the winter, and wanted to know "What's the odds of an hour or two?" Glacier and ranges looked simply magnificent by moonlight; could see everything quite clearly—even on the low country we were able to distinguish some features, and beyond it the sea. Travelled quickly to just below Cape Defiance, when the moon dipped down behind Mount Moltke, leaving us in deep shadow right in the middle of the rough ice. Blundered along slowly, the deep crevasses looking very ghostly as we crawled along the narrow ridges in the dark. Now and then would see a rata twig faintly. As dawn came we got out of the crevassed ice and were opposite the Unser Fritz Waterfall. Had it not been for the rata twigs we should have been quite an hour longer in the rough going. Unser Fritz was silent, frozen from top to bottom in one icicle, 1,209 ft. in length—the absolute silence of so large a fall was very imposing. We put on the rope half-way up the ice-fall and were opposite Almer Glacier at 8 A.M., and had breakfast. Snow covered everything, but all the seracs were standing just the same, the snow bridges being some 10 or 15 ft. below the general level of the glacier. For a few chains above the inflow of the Almer, I thought every moment that we should be stopped, the hummocks and seracs formed a perfect labyrinth, and the crevasses between them were not bridged very strongly. I have never in all my experience seen such a hopeless confusion of broken, crevassed, and generally rough ice.

The snow became painfully soft after 10 A.M., but we pounded along—taking turns in the lead—and as we were now high up in the *névé*, there was little or no chance of going through into crevasses, the snow was so deep. At noon we were well up into the south-eastern corner of the head basin, and there I was able to do all that had to be done for the map. The plan which we made the previous summer is practically correct, and only one or two minor corrections to be made. We went on a little further to within about a mile and a-half—perhaps less—of Graham's Saddle, to the Tasman. I wanted to go on, and, at least, ascend Graham's Saddle, but my companion was a firm believer in the eight hours' day, and would not consent to more, so I had to suit myself to him more or less. I told him that now we had done all that was necessary, and anything else we did would be voluntary work for our own amusement, and asked him if he was willing to go over to the Tasman. He was decided in his objections, as he had "had enough of this blooming work, and didn't give a d―― for the scenery; he

Rough Ice, Head of Franz Josef Ice-Fall (Winter).

was paid for a day's work only, and had done that." I therefore gave up the idea, wondering at such lack of enthusiasm.

We started back at 1 P.M.—travelled as fast as the very soft snow would allow to the top of the ice-fall, and having our tracks to follow, took little time in passing the serac ice. I feared that the snow bridges would be weaker, so lengthened the rope 30 ft., and always kept a hummock of ice between us. This was necessary, for the leader on two occasions crossed a crevasse safely and mounted a hummock, but on going down into the next hollow to be ready in case the second man broke the bridge, he would go bodily through the snow, and the bridge, which he had safely crossed, would let the second man through; thus we were both in crevasses with the rope taut over the intervening hummock. To scramble out was no trouble, and, beyond confirming my mate in his opinion that he had got into most dangerous company, no harm was done! We reached camp about 5 P.M., very burnt with the new snow, the day having been cloudless throughout. I very much doubt if the snow would last for another two weeks of sufficient strength to allow a route to be found in rough seracs at the top of the ice-fall.

The *névé* of the glacier is, roughly, a circular basin of three miles in diameter, and is surrounded by some fine peaks between 9,000 and 10,000 ft. Out of the southern side the peaks of the Dividing Range rise in pinnacles, and knobs of rock out of a sea of ice, affording interesting rock climbs. The first ascents of the peaks from De la Bêche (9,835 ft.) to Conway (9,611 ft.), will probably be done from this glacier, as their slopes towards the Tasman are clothed with hanging glaciers, which send down avalanches night and day during the summer. On the south-eastern side, the range dividing the Franz Josef from the watershed of the Callery, branches from the Minaret (10,022 ft.), and has three nice peaks in St. Mildred's, Drummond's, and Stirling Rock. The two latter are very easy climbs of snow—the former a rock climb entirely. The peaks of the Bismarck Range are, on the whole, disappointing from this side, as they are merely small peaks of rock, standing 500 to 1,000 ft. out of a snow-field, which slopes up to them in a series of broken ice-falls. In the summer the *névé* is almost all broken and crevassed, the lower portion—as it approaches the ice-fall—is, I feel sure, impassable after Christmas. It is quite bad enough in the early spring. To make ascents of the peaks surrounding the *névé*, a party must cross from the Tasman *viâ* Graham's Saddle, or from the Fox Glacier; they can try to reach the *névé* from the terminal face if they wish to, and I hope they will enjoy the experience!

*Wednesday, September 19th.*\*—I fixed some measurement cairns along the side below Camp 2, and we returned to Camp 1 in the afternoon.

*Thursday, September 20th.*—My horse had gone away down the river, so I tracked and caught him below Nesbitt's hut. Returned to camp in the afternoon, and packed the whole of it to the "Hospital," where I found Arthur Woodham alone. Stayed at the hut.

*Friday, September 21st.*—I rode down to Forks, and found instructions from Hokitika, to go at once to Gillespies, and, with Douglas, explore the Karangarua River.

\* See Appendix, Note VII.

This visit, together with our work in the previous summer, was productive of some interesting facts concerning the movement and general condition of the Franz Josef Glacier. In the first place, the ice of the lower portion of the glacier appeared to be very soft and rotten, in comparison to that of other glaciers—a natural consequence of its low altitude; the ice crystals were very large, and easily detached and separated from one another. It was very difficult in some places to form a step, as a blow of the axe would scatter the loose crystals in every direction, and sometimes when a step had been cut, which to all appearance was as strong as necessary, the floor would give way by crumbling under one's weight. In the winter, however, during the last visit, I found it much easier to get about, because the ice was firmer and there was far less likelihood of rapid changes. The constant alteration in the forms and shapes of the crevasses and seracs was in the summer most puzzling, and sometimes an absence of a week would be sufficient for the ice to alter to such an extent as to render a new route necessary. This activity is, no doubt, due as much to low altitude as to the speed with which the glacier descends over its rough bed. It is not noticeable all over the lower portions of the "trunk." After an absence of a day or two, we have found new crevasses open even on the dry "ice," and, as already stated, we constantly heard reports, and felt a slight shock pass like a tremble over the surface. While sitting in Camp 2, we could hear the glacier cracking and groaning on a still night; in fact, one of the first things I noticed on my second visit was the absolute stillness of the nights, compared with our summer experience.

I have already given some idea of the very broken surface

of the glacier, and need only add that I have never seen one with so little good travelling on it. Having had a considerable experience on glaciers, I can generally find a route through rough ice without much loss of time, and certainly never expected to be reduced to leaving a line of marks behind—for use on the return journey—as we did here. It was not really *necessary*, but it saved a lot of time, and was very little trouble. The broken surface will account for the absence of large deposits of surface moraine, which might be expected here, owing to the broken nature of the hillsides and spurs in the upper part of the valley. Below point E and Cape Defiance there is no broken rock at all, save the slip which has recently come down, and is the cause of the single patch of surface débris, now fast approaching the terminal face.

The glacier seems to descend in two, and sometimes three distinct layers; the upper one is pure white ice, and the lower ones generally dirty. The stones which fall into the crevasses are ground up like grain between two millstones; and wherever it finds an opening between two layers, the silt, resulting from the grinding, oozes out in the form of mud. I have found a hollow under such an outlet full of mud, to a depth of two feet or more. Owing to the nearness of the surrounding trees there is a large amount of timber in the ice and lying at the terminal face in the small moraines. Once or twice while cutting steps near the junction of two layers, my axe struck a piece of wood, and stuck fast in it. The timber on the glacier and at the terminal face has a smooth, worn look about it, as if it had been well sand-papered; it is chiefly rata, a very hard wood, and must have undergone a great deal of rubbing and grinding. In some places the upper section of the ice could be seen stand-

ing away from the lower; half a mile from the terminal face I saw a space of three inches, or more, between the two layers, extending back into the ice for some distance; and everywhere on the glacier, if one happened to be cutting a step near the junction, a large piece of ice would break away, leaving a smooth mud-covered surface at the top of the lower layer.

The comparative motion of the ice in a glacier at different depths is little known, and could, I think, be measured at places on the Franz Josef with little difficulty; I fully intended to do it on my second visit, but had no time. It is here perfectly evident that the surface ice moves far quicker than the lower portion, for the upper layer of white ice can be seen at the terminal face pushing its way over the lower layer, and periodically breaking off in large pieces. This possibly is due to the rocky obstacles at the terminal face and underneath the glacier obstructing the flow of the lower portion while it does not interfere with the upper. The layers are horizontal in some places, and in others incline slightly against the flow of the ice.

One very noticeable result of the large quantity of morainic débris falling into the crevasses, and being ground up between the separate layers of ice, is, that the old terminal moraines are composed of a layer of rolled stones, with angular blocks on the top of them in some places, and in others are almost entirely made up of the former. This is, of course, because other slips have occurred in the past, and covering the glacier have travelled down with the ice; a large proportion of the stones having dropped into crevasses come out at the terminal face in a rounded form, while the balance has come down on the surface of the glacier and been dropped over in an angular form on to the top of the other, thus forming the two sections in the terminal moraines.

In some of the sea bluffs the layers of rolled stones under angular blocks are easily to be seen, where the sea has cut into them and exposed a section of their formation. I have heard many theories put forward to account for this stratified appearance, though it is common in all old moraines. Douglas, in his report on the Franz Josef,* written after our visit, mentions the process which is evidently going on at present in the glacier, and assumes rightly, that a similar process went on in ancient times on a larger scale, and would account for the formations in the bluffs, which are, of course, old moraines. He is inclined to put forward a theory based on that assumption, that the old moraines now forming the sea bluffs are not *lateral*, but *terminal* moraines. From what he has told me of his own observations, and from like observations—in a much smaller degree—of my own, I agree with him that they are not lateral moraines; but I cannot go so far as he does, and say they are therefore terminal. There is, I imagine, no reason why the evidence of stratification should be confined to terminal moraines. May it not also exist in lateral moraines, when the ice is pushing its way over level country and not between hillsides? For it would be depositing rolled stones from its lower portion, and dropping them from its upper portion in the form of angular blocks *along its sides*, as well as at its *terminal face*. If this is a sound conclusion, then the inland moraine hills, which contain the two forms of stones, may be either lateral or terminal moraines. If the reasoning is not sound, then all, or

* "New Zealand Lands and Survey Report, 1893-94."

nearly all the old morainic deposits must be terminal moraines; and that I do not think can be admitted.

Some ideas concerning the ancient glaciers and their deposits were put forward in the last chapter, and if they are correct, there would be a field of ice extending over almost the whole of the low country, fed by the numerous glaciers from the ranges. Such an ice field before it broke up would not have either lateral or terminal moraines on the flat country, for the débris would drop into the sea on one side, or form a lateral terrace at the foot of the hills on the other. On the period of retreat beginning, it would gradually divide itself into separate streams, corresponding with the glaciers supplying it, and would leave behind it a confused mass of morainic accumulations which could hardly be classed as terminal or lateral moraines until it had almost retired into the hills. These would be stratified, having layers of glacier drift and angular blocks throughout.

Other glaciers, like the Tasman, Balfour, &c., which are covered with great masses of angular rocks, are not sufficiently broken or crevassed to swallow up a great amount of moraine. Thus the double process does not now go on to such a noticeable extent on these glaciers as on the Franz Josef. It is only during the next few years that it can be seen on the latter, for when the present surface moraine caused by the slip has dropped over the terminal face, there will be no more to come down on the surface, unless another landslip covers the ice with débris.

The ancient Waiho Glacier may, or may not, have been of first-class importance; Douglas thinks that it was not, because he cannot find any of the higher "old ice lines" which he has found in other parts. In the upper valleys of the Karangarua, as will be seen later, I noted several instances of these old ice lines which appeared in the form of distinct terraces in the rocky hillsides, abraded by ancient glaciers. Douglas's remarks on the subject I quote :—

"In valleys containing large glaciers I have always found four tiers of terraces, or old ice lines. These lines keep a wonderfully regular distance from each other, and their inclination is very uniform, from, say, 4,000 ft. to 600 ft. or 700 ft., where the river valley breaks out of the hills. The longer the valley the more gentle the slope. The best places to see these lines are up the Haast, near the Eighteen-mile bluff; and, better still, the wonderful terraces of Mount Caria, up the Arawata River, where the old lines can be seen quite distinctly for 4,000 ft. up, and running for miles down the valley. In the smaller valleys two and three terraces are visible, and in still smaller ones there are none. From this I would conclude that the Franz Josef, although the largest glacier at present, was, during the great ice period, of second, or may be third-rate importance. It must have been far eclipsed by Cook's and the Karangarua."*

It is true that, in the Franz Josef branch of the Waiho there are not four ice lines visible like there are in the two last-named rivers, but I do not think it necessarily proves that this was of second-rate importance. The Cook's, Karangarua and Haast River, to my knowledge, and the Arawata River from Douglas's accounts, flow through harder and more solid country, and therefore would show these old ice lines in a more distinct and lasting form. The Waiho is shattered

* "New Zealand Lands and Survey Report, 1893-94," p. 73.

country, and the lines have probably worn away by the action of the climate and weather generally. The enormous morainic accumulations around Lake Maporika, and even north of that, point to a glacier of considerable importance.

About three miles below the junction of the two branches, or five miles below the terminal face, there is an old terminal moraine almost semicircular, through which the river has cut a channel. This is, perhaps, a hundred feet high, but we had no time to examine it. Comparatively speaking this is a recent deposit, but to which of the ice lines, at present visible, it belongs I will not pretend to say. At no very remote period the Waiho River flowed north into Lake Maporika, and it is quite possible that this old moraine directed the river northwards until it was cut through by the water which again resumed its old course to the sea.

While speaking of moraines, it is worth calling attention to the very ridiculous attempts this glacier has made to form lateral moraines. Below point E (the rocky cape on the eastern bank) there is a line of boulders about two hundred feet above the ice, which have been left balanced in the most insecure manner on the bare rock slope. Just below Camp 2, another small lateral line of stones can be seen in a precarious position. The only real piece of lateral moraine to be found is above Cape Defiance, in the bend by Harper's Creek. The ice has flowed down the valley and meets this obstruction, causing it to eddy into the bend and force its way up in great waves against the Cape. The likeness of a glacier to a river is here most evident, for the ice has done exactly the same as a river would do in a similar case. Having flowed against the Cape, which projects twenty chains across the line of flow, it has banked up behind it and turned round the rocky point in high pinnacles corresponding to the waves in a river. And whereas a river would, in a similar case, deposit large masses of driftwood on a bank, the glacier has thrown up a high lateral moraine of stones which have come down in the ice from above the ice-fall. It has also caused the débris to come to the surface, and the ice in the bend is covered with stones. The absence of all other lateral moraines is due to the solid rock walls which line the glacier on both sides below Cape Defiance, and which are too steep to allow any stones to rest on them, with the two exceptions mentioned by Camp 2; also the broken nature of the glacier has caused all the débris to fall into crevasses, and therefore has left very few, if any, stones for it to deposit on the sides.

When Douglas and I were in the valley during our first visit, we concluded, from various signs at the terminal face and along the sides, that a winter advance of considerable importance took place annually, followed by a large summer retreat. We had ample evidence of the latter, and my visit in September was made in hopes of finding a decided winter advance. We based our conclusions on the fact that in November, 1893, when we arrived at Camp 1, there was a beautiful cone of ice, 110 ft. in height, between the Strauchon and Mueller Rocks. This was covered apparently with riverbed shingle, and seemed to be due to a recent advance during the winter; it touched the latter rock along its base to a height of 25 ft. Other evidence was found in the fresh-dressed surfaces, just beyond the end of the ice, which were of a lighter colour than the rock above; and also there were signs of recent disturbance in the small terminal moraines.

During our stay in the neighbourhood the rapid shrinking, due to the low altitude of the ice, was most marked. The level of the top of the ice, at the terminal face, fell 70 ft.—between November 1st and March 1st—by breaking and melting, and the retreat during the same period was con-

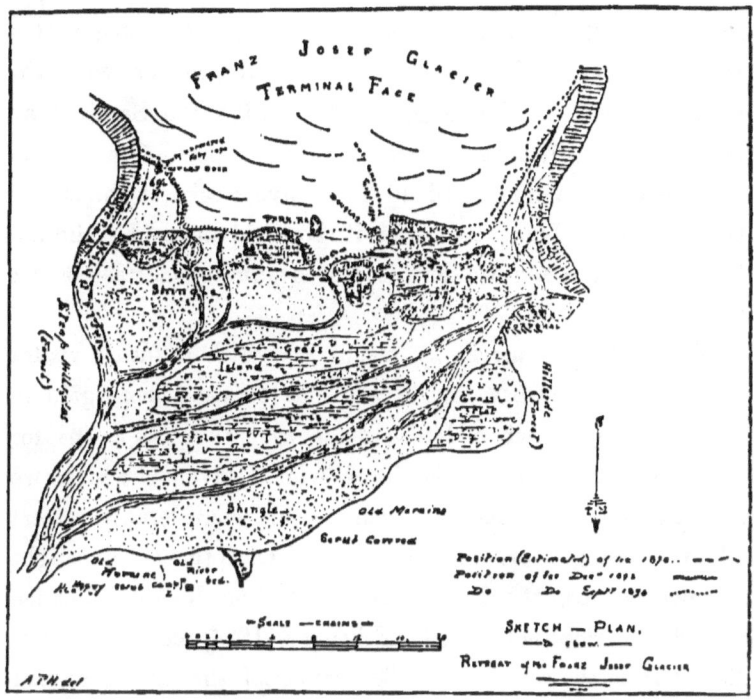

siderable. The most noticeable was at the ice cone; this was, at the beginning of November, quite perfect in shape, and in the position already stated. At the end of February it had lost all shape, and collapsed into a small heap of dirty, broken ice some thirty feet high, besides retreating twenty-two yards in the front, and about ten yards from the rock against which it originally rested. A new rock, which we named the "Outlet" Rock, was uncovered during February, near the outflow of the glacier, to the extent of ten yards. All along the eastern bank a general shrinkage was visible when we left, and, as far as we could see, on the western side as well.

I was not, however, prepared to say that the ice was retreating on the whole, because we fully anticipated that it would recover its lost ground again in the winter, when the melting would not be so great; for behind the Sentinel, an ice cone was thrown up considerably in advance of the rest of the glacier, to a height of 40 ft. in five weeks at the end of the summer. This lifted with it river-bed stones, but did not last long, for when we left it had begun to decrease in size again.

We made two marks by means of which a future visitor might test the retreat, and I was able to use them again in my second visit, when I also made several more cairns for future use. Instead of the large winter advance which we had anticipated, I found a general and considerable retreat all over the glacier, with the single exception of a slight advance between the Barron and Strauchon Rocks. The ice behind the Sentinel had, in February, 1894, been 120 links distant from the rock, and in September of the same year had retired to a distance of 225 links, or a retreat of 1·05 chains. Between Harper and Park Rocks a new rock appeared, which, however, may be part of the former; it was buried in the ice and raked by pieces falling from above. Where the ice cone had stood there was a further retreat of about three chains, and at the outflow the "Outlet" Rock was exposed for one chain—or 50 links more than in February.

On reaching the eastern bank on the route to Camp 2, the general shrinkage was most noticeable. Just below the point at which we left the ice was a creek we named Arch Creek. It descended into a deep gorge, with a rock wall of 200 ft. on the northern bank, and perhaps 100 ft. on the southern. In the mouth of this there was a large, isolated rock, "The Eye Tooth," (estimated) 120 ft. in height; the ice, which flowed past the end of the gorge, was pressing against the outer side of the rock, and in November, 1893, was almost on a level with the top. On our second visit it proved to have retreated on the south bank of the creek for 40 ft.; and continuing along the glacier up the valley, there was a general shrinkage of 10 or 15 ft., while below Camp 2, large holes appeared in the ice, showing the rock and indicating a still further retreat in the future.

On crossing over to Camp 3, at Cape Defiance, we found that though the ice had pushed its way a little further into the mouth of the creek, yet it was not banked up so high as formerly at the cape itself. When pitching Camp 3 the previous summer—it will, perhaps, be remembered—we built a flat platform of large stones in the bottom of the V-shaped valley, formed by the moraine and hillside. This was still there; but, the ice having retired and caused a subsidence of the lateral moraine, the platform had fallen over, or capsized, without breaking, towards the ice, and, instead of being level, was now lying at an angle of 20 degrees. Opposite Cape Defiance, above point E, the ice had banked up higher at another rocky point, but the gain there did not exceed the loss at the cape. This may, perhaps, be merely a temporary upheaval, and in course of a few months the pendulum may swing again, and the ice rise at the cape and fall on the other side. It may be only due to the oscillation or lurching of the glacier in its downward path. The temporary advance behind the Sentinel, observed in February, followed by retreat, and the retreat by the Barron Rock followed by advance in the winter, may also be due to the same cause.

Though all this had taken place in one winter, it is possible that the glacier is only passing through a temporary period of retreat, and that a great part of it is due to a mild season and heavy floods, causing large pieces to break off frequently. If the ice recedes at the same rate every year the glacier will, in a comparatively short time, become of second-rate importance. I anticipate—from the manner in which the Fox Glacier is holding its own—that though no future advance will recover the ground lost by present retreat, yet it will, to some extent, repair the damage, or at least remain stationary. But it is evident that this glacier is slowly but surely losing ground.

There are many interesting problems to solve in this valley, but they would require considerable attention during prolonged and frequent visits; it is little use for a man to go there in the way I have been; he must have leisure, and be able to afford good instruments and plenty of time. Here he would have a glacier at an exceptionally low altitude, obviously flowing at great speed over rocky obstacles, giving good opportunities of solving some of the most interesting questions of glacier motion: such as the comparative rate of the surface and lower ice, its effects on rocks, and the variation in position of the great waves or undulations on the glacier. The speed at which this vast body of ice flows would give more pronounced and satisfactory results than could be obtained on one of the slow-moving glaciers of other districts.

There are also many questions as to the position and extent of the ancient glaciers to be determined, or, at least, the solution is to be looked for in the old moraine hills on the flats, and in the old "ice lines" in the valleys. The fact of there being four distinct "ice lines," or terraces, shows, I presume, that the old glaciers had four separate periods of rest, and possibly advance, during their general retreat. How long these various periods were, and the distances between them, have to be discovered, and the Franz Josef or Fox Glacier may offer evidence on these points to any one who is competent to collect and apply it. The terraces of bare ice-worn rock without vegetation, followed by another with vegetation of a certain age, and yet another with trees of greater age, may go far to help in the solution. I shall always regret that I have not the means at my command to enable me to make a collection of data on the subject of the great ancient glaciers.

The answer to these problems is not to be found only on the low country, but in remote valleys to which as yet no one but Douglas and I have been, and the most interesting one of all, namely, the valley which gives the key to the old glacier which formed the Cascade moraine, was explored by Douglas, and since then only visited by prospectors.

## CHAPTER XII.

### KARANGARUA RIVER.

With Douglas again—Topography—" Futtah " Camp—Floods—Cassell's Flat—Bark Camp—Twain Gorge—Alone—Regina Creek.

ON September 23rd, Mr. Ned Gibb, who has a store on the Waikukupa River, came up to the Waiho on a visit to the diggers, and I returned with him. We had a long talk about golf, for he was a caddie at St. Andrew's before he came to New Zealand, and "hadn't had a good 'pitch' about the old game for nearly thirty years." After staying a night at his house on the beach, I continued my journey to Gillespies on my horse, with my goods and chattles in two saddle-bags strapped one on each side. When a few miles from Gillespies, I discovered that one of my rolls had fallen off, so started back at a gallop to pick it up, because I had been riding close to the surf on the hard sand, and was afraid that it would have gone out to sea. After going about a quarter of a mile I saw it floating 50 yards out, beyond the first line of breakers, and travelling up the coast with the strong current which sets up the beach when the tide is going out. Before I could go in after it the bag sank, and I had to sorrowfully jog on to Gillespies without it. A week later the mailman, coming down the beach, picked up the contents at various places, scattered over the sand some miles north of where I dropped it. As generally happens on these occasions the most precious things were lost, namely, two lbs. of boot nails, tobacco 7 lbs., and two dozen quarter-plates exposed on the Franz Josef Glacier.

On reaching Gillespies I found a note from Douglas, to say that he was at Mr. Scott's farm on the Karangarua River flats; I therefore went on, crossing Cook River and the Salt-water Creek, one of the worst and most treacherous fords on the beach, and reached Scott's that evening. Here I found that Douglas had been suffering greatly from rheumatism all the winter, and though not really fit for it, he was determined to come up the river, at any rate as far as he could.

For some time previous to this, the Government were desirous of finding a pass, by which a road or track for tourists could be taken, from the Hermitage to the West Coast. This pass they require to be "free of snow and ice for three months in the year." It was well known from the eastern side of the Divide that no such pass existed from the head of the Godley to Mount Sefton; and Douglas had been up the Copland River, a branch of the Karangarua, in 1892, and reported no such pass as required up that river. Our work, therefore, in the season of 1893-94, had been the exploration of the Waiho and Cook Rivers, to prove that there was no route such as they required, by those valleys, and also to get Reconnaissance Surveys of this new country completed. Now, however, we had instructions to explore the Karangarua and its branches, and report on the possibility of a track up this river over some saddle into the Landsborough River, and down that valley to a pass found by Mr. T. N. Brodrick from Lake Ohau on the eastern side of the Divide. This would, I pointed out, be a very round-about route; but as it would combine both a report on the route and an exploration of the only district in South Westland still unexplored, the authorities decided to have it inspected.

The Karangarua had been traversed up to Cassell's Flat, a large open basin in the hills, 12 miles from Scott's house, or 16 from the sea. Beyond that point the Twain and the main branch were both unexplored. Six miles above Scott's the Copland River, draining the Divide from Mount Stokes (La Perouse) to Mount Sefton, joins the Karangarua, and on Cassell's Flat the Twain, draining the Divide from Mount Sefton to Mount Maunga, flows into the main stream, which takes its rise from the northern end of the Hooker Range.

The topography of this district is rather puzzling, and somewhat difficult to describe clearly. The Dividing Range, after leaving Stokes (10,101 ft.), runs practically south for four miles, and then circles round in a south-westerly direction for another four miles, passing The Footstool (9,079 ft.), Sefton (10,359 ft.) to Mount Brunner; from there it takes a southerly direction to Mount Maunga, (8,335 ft.), a distance of some two or three miles, and again strikes in a south-westerly direction to the Haast Pass, upwards of 40 miles away. From Stokes the Copland Range branches off, and divides Cook River from the Copland River, and from Mount Sefton, the Karangarua Range runs slightly north of west for 12 miles, dividing the latter river from the Twain River. From Mount Maunga, the Hooker Range runs for 5 miles (to Mount Howitt) due west, separating the McKerrow Glacier from the head of the Twain River, and then turns in a south-westerly direction, continuing for about thirty miles parallel with the Dividing Range, and with it enclosing the Landsborough River, which flows from the McKerrow Glacier. From Mount Howitt, a short pre-

Overlooking Cassell's Flat from near Mount McDonald.

cipitous offshoot runs parallel to the Karangarua Range for about seven miles, and divides the Twain River from the Karangarua main stream, which takes its rise from just under Mount Howitt, and has a saddle leading into the McKerrow Glacier. The Hooker Range, therefore, has cut off the Karangarua valley from the Dividing Range. The so-called main branch is really not the most important, and is, strictly speaking, a tributary of the Twain River, but when the lower part of the valley was traversed, these branches received their names, and they have been retained for convenience; in referring to them I shall consider the Twain River the tributary of the so-called main branch.

On the 1st of October we left Scott's house and camped some four miles above the farm, at the point where the river leaves the hills; we pitched the batwing in some tutu scrub, on a sheltered flat, and remained there for a week. From here we "blazed" or cleared a track up the river for three miles—one mile above the inflow of the Copland River—where we built a "futtah," and made our second camp.

A "futtah" is a small shelter of bark and canvas, raised off the ground, in which to leave provisions and stores sheltered from the weather, wekas, and rats; the one we made here was 4 ft. off the ground, with a floor of 7 ft. by 4 ft., and 5 ft. from floor to roof. It was built of rata bark and saplings, and will in all probability stand for several years; two of us put it up in half a day. On Saturday, the 6th, three horses arrived, by previous arrangement from Scott's, at Camp 1, and we packed enough provisions in the "futtah" to last us for five months, with the help of birds. Above this camp our hard work began, for we had to carry everything up on our shoulders, this being the last point to which a horse could go.

The stores we brought up to the futtah were, flour, soda and acid, side of bacon, rice, sugar, dry figs, chocolate, cocoa, tea, jam, treacle (a splendid thing for this work), oatmeal, a few tins of sardines and meat, two half axes, two bill-hooks, a small frying-pan for baking, three billies of different sizes, three mugs, two plates, a tin prospecting dish, ice-axes, ropes, instruments, cameras, plates, two batwings, three flies, biscuits, soap, candles, matches, tobacco, Alpine climbing lantern, salt and pepper. The provisions were supposed to last for five months with the help of birds. The luxuries—such as cooking utensils and batwing—would only be taken to the head of the Karangarua. Any further work in the Landsborough or Twain we intended to do in "light order," that is with a fly only, and the stores. The half-axes were necessary in case we had to cut a tree down to "spar" the river or a bad creek; the bill-hooks were for blazing a track. By way of amusement I had "Cook's Voyages," "Milton's Poems," and "Pliny's Letters" in pocket editions, also two packs of cards. The latter I found most useful when alone, as I played "Patience" or had a game of Cribbage—right hand against left—by way of a change. It is curious how one generally has a tendency to cheat in favour of the left hand! A blanket each, and one spare one between us, sewing materials and boot nails must be added to the above list, and in order to remind myself that I was a civilised being, and only temporarily a savage, I took a tooth-brush and a comb. For medicinal purposes, Douglas carried "pain-killer" and pills, and I "Eucalyptus," depending on natural medicines for other things.

Since I had last seen Douglas, he had lost "Betsy." She had been with him on a spur of Ryan's peak, and disappeared in a fog on their way down, no doubt having fallen into a fissure in the rocks, or perhaps over a precipice. Douglas had written asking me to bring him down a "various pup"—the greater the variety of breed the better—but curious as it may seem, I could not get one at a reasonable price. It is really remarkable how valuable mongrel pups become when you want one; a dog which the owner was on the point of drowning yesterday, is worth two pounds to-day, when you make inquiries, consequently no sale results. The owner loses a sure half-sovereign, and the puppy probably loses his life in a week or two, by running against a stray bullet which happens to be travelling near him! Douglas, however, had picked up a pretty little dog, and we decided to name him after the first bird he found; soon after we started he discovered a nest of blue duck's eggs, so we dubbed him "Eggs." It was fortunate that we did not wait for him to catch a bird, for he turned out to be quite useless, and only caught one weka, some six months later. Poor dog! It was not his fault even then, because the weka charged him and he had to kill it!

A week of wet weather followed during which we staged three or four loads about two miles up the river, and left them under a piece of canvas. The place we named "Poison Camp," being the scene of one of Douglas's many extraordinary escapes, when working alone as he used to do. A few years before, he had started up the river by himself to explore it, and got as far as this camp with his stores; from here he went on to Cassell's Flat to reconnoitre the route, and returned in the evening, intending to move his camp next day. He had with him a tin or two of sardines, and one of them poisoned him. He was ten days there by himself, very ill, and sometimes delirious—finding himself more than once away in the bush, without any recollection of leaving the batwing. It was also raining a great deal, so, besides sickness, he was nearly all the time wet; no one but Douglas would have survived such an experience. This misfortune of course terminated his exploration of the river, for a time at any rate. On reaching Scott's again, he opened another tin, and gave the cat some of its contents, to see if they were the cause of his illness; the cat only ate one or two of the sardines, and died a few hours afterwards, which was fairly good proof of the exceptional quality of those fish.

The return of his rheumatism compelled Douglas to go back to Scott's on the 17th, and in three days a young fellow arrived at the camp, to go on up the river with me. While alone at the "futtah" camp I had an opportunity of seeing how quickly a Westland river can rise in heavy rain. On the 19th, having been up the river with another load, I turned in early in the evening, and at 9 P.M. the weather was quite clear. I do not know when it clouded over, or began to rain, but at 2 A.M. I woke up, finding the batwing flooded by three or four inches of water, in which I was lying. I got up and drained the camp with my ice-axe, and could hear the river, which was about twenty yards away, coming down in a regular flood. At 5 A.M. I went across to the bank and marked the height of the water, which in the early morning light looked splendid. There was not a boulder to be seen, and branches of trees were careering down in the swirling yellow water; opposite the camp, there were some stones 10 or 15 ft. in height, and they were invisible. Turning in again soon, I slept till 10 o'clock, and on waking, found the sun shining brightly, and the river already lower. I afterwards measured the rise and fall of the water carefully, and found that between the commencement of the rain and 5 A.M. (say five hours) the river had risen 15 ft., and by 4 P.M. had fallen 8 ft., regaining its normal level some time during that night. The great rise is due to the course of the river being narrow at this point.

From the "futtah" to Poison Camp was, for a West Coast river, good going; but beyond there was half a mile of very rough boulder travelling, not nearly so bad as Cook River, but quite rough enough. It is purely a matter of comparison, as to "good" and "bad" travelling on these rivers; I have no doubt whatever, that anyone who had no previous experience of a West Coast river would consider the piece from the "futtah" to Poison Camp decidedly rough going, as the stones are from one to three feet in diameter, and the half-mile above the latter place he would only be able to describe in superlatives, for Cook River would either be left undescribed, or the description would be unparliamentary! When I speak of good travelling I only mean "good" compared with the average river going—it is really quite bad enough.

On the 22nd, my new companion and I went up with heavy loads—I had 80 lbs. and he had 65 lbs.—to Cassell's Flat, and when doing the last half-mile were very sorry we had not made two trips with light loads, instead of one with heavy. At 4 o'clock we reached a knoll, or hillock, covered with rata-trees three-quarters of a mile above the lower end of the flat, and here we camped—about twelve miles from Scott's. Two more days were spent in staging up some of the stores left at Poison Camp, and by the 25th we had made everything snug at Camp 3, putting a bark wall six feet high in a circle of twelve feet in diameter, right round the camp. As we intended to make this our base of operations, and as it would probably be left standing for three months, we made it very substantial, pitching a large 7 by 4 ft. batwing and 10 by 12 ft. fly inside the bark wall. "Bark" Camp, or Camp 3, though airy, was the most palatial residence we ever had the whole time we were out, but of course it was only our head camp, and unless wet weather compelled us to stay in it we should be away for weeks at a time. As it turned out, however, I had nearly two months on this flat, as will be seen later.

Similar flats are to be found on many of the West Coast rivers luckily for the unfortunate explorer. It would be heart-breaking work to toil up narrow, boulder-filled valleys or rock-bound gorges, without some hope of a piece of easy going; and the relief of a mile of flat walking, after several days of crawling and climbing over large boulders, is beyond belief. One feels quite a new man, and, after leaving the flat, ready to attack the inevitable gorge with renewed vigour. One or two rivers, however, are without any easy travelling for their whole length; Cook's, for instance, was more or less all rough, and certainly had no flat; and Douglas speaks of the Turnbull River further south—which he explored—as having 16 miles of gorges out of a total length of 18 miles. A small flat of half a mile on such a river would make the whole difference to the exploration, for instead of being a "grind" it would be a pleasure.

Like most of these basins in the heart of the ranges, Cassell's Flat is the centre of some magnificent scenery; in fact, from the time the low country is left behind until we come back down the rivers, notes of admiration are necessary so far as scenery is concerned. It is a level patch of ground surrounded on all sides by high rocky mountains, which form an oval basin, one and a-half mile long, and one mile wide. About the middle of this basin was Queen's Knoll, at the foot of which we made " Bark " Camp.

It is a matter for scientific men to decide how these flats are formed, but here I believe a lake existed at one time. The surrounding mountains are steep and bare, with rocky slopes, incapable of holding any glacial deposits, rising for some thousands of feet very abruptly out of the flat. At the Southern end—or " The Corner," as I named it—the main branch of the Karangarua comes in, through a rocky gorge and over high cataracts. On the eastern side the Twain River and Regina Creek flow through similar great gorges and cataracts, divided by a high conical hill of rock, and join the main river about the middle of the flat—the former about a quarter of a mile above " Bark " Camp and the latter immediately opposite, across the stream. At the northern or lower end of the basin is a large bar of glacial deposit, augmented possibly by slips from the hills.

This bar has, perhaps, caused the river to flow more slowly, and consequently to deposit a large amount of small gravel, gradually filling up the valley to its present level, and at the same time spreading out to a greater breadth. But I think that it is more probable that a lake has existed here in the past. For there are numerous terraces on the flat, showing that it was once considerably higher, and has since been cut down by the river. The bar of old moraine at the lower end would have caused the river to back up, and form a lake ; while the constant denudation of the hills in the upper valley, and the numerous slips of which there is evidence, would by slow degrees have filled up the valley, until the lake ceased to exist.

The channel through the bar has then, in course of time, become lower, and allowed the river to reach its present level, leaving the flat high and dry, and also the above-mentioned terraces. In the middle of the river opposite " Bark " Camp, was an island, which, with Queen's Knoll, is nearly all that remains of an old terminal moraine. They are both composed of great boulders, heaped up promiscuously, amongst which large rata-trees are growing. The island had a single kiwi on it, so I named it Crusoe's Island. The rest of the flat was lightly timbered, and covered with very dense scrub of 10 to 20 ft. in height, until some of the higher terraces were reached, and these had older and larger trees on them. There were also three or four small "pakihis," or spaces of open grass, perfectly useless for pastoral purposes, but pleasant to walk over, after emerging from the scrub. The general level of the flat was 680 ft. above the sea.

My present plan was to follow the Twain to its source, and cross over a saddle into the McKerrow Glacier, and Landsborough River; follow that valley down to Brodrick's Pass—some 25 miles or more—and then, returning to the McKerrow Glacier, find my way over into the Karangarua main branch and follow it down to Cassell's Flat again. This would probably have taken two months if the weather was not unusually bad.

On the 25th we forded the main branch just above the in-

Mount McGloin and Gordon Falls, from Cassell's Flat.

*To face page* 188.

flow of the Twain River, and "blazed" our way with bill-hooks along on the south bank of the latter stream, hoping to find a route through the decidedly ugly-looking gorge. In this we were disappointed, for after a day's hard cutting we emerged from the stunted vegetation on to a sheer smooth face of rock rising hundreds of feet out of the water, without any chance of a route. As we got further into the gorge, the hillsides became steeper and the vegetation more stunted, and at last it was evident that we should hardly be able to traverse this side with heavy loads, though we might do it in our present unburdened condition. Telling my mate to await my return, I went on to see what the place looked like round a rocky point ahead.

The sides now were practically sheer precipices, and I was clinging on to the scrub entirely. Having at last come to the end of the vegetation and reached the bare rock, I could see that no man could get along on this bank, for the rock was smooth and perpendicular, throwing out short buttresses of rounded water or ice-worn rock, affording no more hold than the side of a house. Hearing the water a long way below, I caught hold of a shrub above with one hand, and leant out to look at the river, and it proved to be two or three hundred feet below me.

To show how precarious a hold the vegetation has in such places, my weight caused the whole mass of scrub for 20 ft. above me to leave the rock and stand out a foot or two a perfect network of roots, with apparently no hold on the cliff for 20 ft., where there was evidently a crevice or a ledge. It can be imagined that I did not waste many minutes getting back to where the side was sloping less steeply, having no wish to further test the strength of the roots! I believe, if the roots were cut along the ledge above, that the whole network of vegetation would fall outwards like a curtain for 20 or 30 feet.

The gorge, now that we could see into it, was truly magnificent. The south bank rose nearly sheer, that is precipice after precipice, with ledges here and there, for some 3,000 ft., straight out of the water. In places, great overhanging rocks frowned down at us from above, and seemed to be ready to topple forward as we climbed along beneath them; at one point the rocks leaned over to such an extent that a stone would have fallen 1,000 ft. without touching the cliff once on its descent. The opposite side sloped back at an angle of nearly 40 degrees, and was covered with luxuriant bush. Through this gorge the river descends some 500 ft. in about 300 yards over large boulders, up to and over 40 ft. in diameter, which are jammed in magnificent confusion into the narrow rock-walled channel, forming a cataract to which I have never seen an equal. Above the cataract the gorge continues with its stupendous walls for over a mile and a-half, and then the valley takes a bend away southwards, toward the glaciers of Mount Sefton. This river descends 2,500 ft. in $3\frac{1}{4}$ miles through two gorges. It was quite evident that the north side would be the best to attempt, for it was not by any means so precipitous, and had trees growing on it which would afford shelter and firewood.

The Twain was without doubt going to give us some trouble, and it would be by no means easy to take our loads through so bad a gorge. My companion thought it very grand, and was surprised when I told him that of course we should take our camp through if possible—he seemed to have some idea that we should make no further attempt to get up the river. The next day, sending him down to the "futtah" for a load, I traversed some of the larger creeks below the flat, and brought up a "fifty" of flour in the evening. And on the 27th we both went to Poison Camp for the rest of our stores there, spending the afternoon in completing our shelter and bathing in a fine pool close to camp.

During these two days my mate was somewhat silent, and occasionally sounding me as to the idea of going on into such bad-looking country; he couldn't understand how we were to find our way if no one had been in front of us, nor could I excite his enthusiasm by saying we were the first two in that country. I was hardly surprised therefore, on Sunday morning the 28th, to find that he was going back to Scott's, before it was too late. I remonstrated with him, but all to no purpose.

"It is too lonesome," he said, "up here. I'm going back."

"As long as we are together," I suggested, "it would not be lonesome."

"Oh, well," he answered, "I'm not the sort that likes being stuck away up here anyhow—*I* like seeing life."

I admit the idea of anyone "seeing life" in South Westland, or anywhere else on the coast, amused me somewhat, and, as I knew he had never been away from the district, I said, "Good heavens, man! where can you see life?"

"At Gillespies, of course," was the answer, given with considerable surprise at my ignorance.

A somewhat feeble description of Gillespies has already been given, so it may be imagined the idea of "seeing life" there was rather too funny to be taken seriously; and I fear that the guffaw which greeted his answer hurt his feelings. He left me alone in my glory that morning, taking down a message to

Douglas to try and send some one else, and also some letters to post. The fact of the matter is, that he was frightened of the rough work, like most other young fellows of the district, for, except south of the Haast River, it is hardly possible to induce a man to go into the ranges. This has been Douglas's experience in the past, and is the reason why he did so much of his work alone.

The weather up to this point had been rather finer than usual, but on the 28th it began to rain, and continued for a week without interruption, confining me to my shelter, with little to do. Luckily I had brought up a flute, but something went wrong with the works, and the lower three notes refused to make any sound! There are not many tunes which one can play on three notes only, so beyond several hours of vigorous puffing to get more than a wheeze out of the low notes, the instrument afforded little amusement—but a great deal of hard work!

Heavy rain has its advantages in the ranges, as well as its drawbacks, for, when amongst the great rock peaks, the waterfalls are wonderfully fine. One day, during this week, I counted no less than eighty-six good falls within half a mile of camp, varying from 2,000 to 300 ft. in height, those coming down the great rock slopes of Mount McGloin being magnificent. This peak is situated on the southern side of the flat, and its bare rock slopes rise to a very steep angle—and in places sheer precipices—to a height of over 5,000 ft. above the flat.

The weather cleared on Guy Fawkes' day, but as the rain had been cold and snow had fallen on the tops, the river was not high. Deciding, therefore, to explore the creek I had named

MOUNT McGLOIN, FROM REGINA CREEK.

*To face page 192.*

"Regina," I forded across from the camp to Crusoe's Island, a distance of eighty yards, and again from there to the other side, another fifty yards, finding the stream just strong and deep enough to necessitate the use of a pole. Regina Creek joined the river at this point—after descending through a boulder-filled gorge, and over a grand cataract of 700 ft. in a quarter of a mile. Not only is the course of the creek filled with large stones, but the hillsides, far up into the bush, present as rough a piece of travelling as I have seen since Cook's River the year before. It took no less than an hour to go the last six chains at the top of the cataract, through large forest trees, growing on and amongst boulders of all sizes up to 60 ft. in height, and 200 ft. in girth. Sometimes deep gaps between these would be spanned by an old tree trunk, over which was the only way to cross—and very uncanny it was; one never could be sure that the bridge would bear, and the hole in most cases had water at the bottom, in semi-darkness, in which I could see my reflection as I passed over. At the top of the cataract the valley, as usual, opened out into a broad basin lined with bold precipitous mountains, at the bottom of which the stream flowed through a small flat. A mile above the great cataract a smaller one was met with, beyond which the valley again opened out and showed another rock-bound basin, with a small secondary glacier at its head, which supplies the creek. Though Regina Creek is on a smaller scale than the Twain Gorge, it has very grand scenery and would eclipse many favourite resorts in Europe with its attractions. I should, however, prefer not to be the unfortunate man who has to engineer a track or road through those terrible boulders, which have to be negotiated before the upper valley is reached.

At the foot of the cataract there was another instance of that "reasoning power of trees" already referred to. On an isolated boulder in the stream, two large rata-trees were growing, and evidently found their rocky home too small to give sufficient nourishment. No doubt when young saplings they had quite a good time, but now they were full-grown trees, and had to find better means of support. The rock was ten yards from the bank, and one of the trees had sent out a sucker, or arm, across the intervening river-bed to the richer soil of the terrace. The sucker was about the thickness of a man's arm, and had twined round two stones, about one and two ft. in diameter, on its way to the bank. On reaching the terrace it had lifted itself from the river-bed, and raised with it the two stones, which were to be seen quite 4 ft. from the ground, firmly held in its clutches.

The 6th and 7th were again wet, and the river rose too high to allow me to ford it safely; so, instead of going to the Twain Gorge, I carried the traverse up to the foot of the Karangarua Cataracts, and went, for a quarter of a mile, along a very bad and precipitous hillside, into the gorge. It is not so fine as that of the Twain, but—if the latter was not so close—the Karangarua Cataract and Gorge would strike anyone as a very grand piece of scenery. The only result of this day's work is summed up in my diary, "The gorge will give us some trouble"—and it did.

I now had nine more wet days, during which the river rose 8 ft., even on the flat—a real "old man" flood; it must have been very high in the narrow valley by the "futtah" and in the gorge. It was, of course, impossible to go up to see the cataracts, but they must have been a wonderful sight: I could see great jets of water shooting up, now and then, above the high trees, from the Regina Gorge. On Sunday, 18th, it cleared up again, so I took a "day off" and hung everything out to dry, and had a general washing of clothes. I do not mean to convey the impression that this was the first time I had washed clothes since leaving Scott's! That very tiresome operation was carried out every week when possible, and as we never took a change, except an extra shirt and pair of socks, we had to sit in our blankets while washing and drying the garments. On the 19th, I went down to the futtah for a "fifty" of flour, and some odds and ends.

The long spells of wet weather had been rather dismal for me by myself, for it had put all the creeks in flood and prevented any work. It also cut me off from Scott's, because no one could have come up in the present state of the rivers. However, the last three notes of the flute had not yet given forth any music, therefore, until they did, I had some employment; and if by any chance I had made them sound, then there were reasonable hopes of a tune sooner or later. Stores also were plentiful, and so far there had been no lack of birds, so I was able to spend considerable time in preparing meals of several courses, and more time in discussing them, for I generally had to cook the next course while eating the one just cooked!

The *menu* on a wet evening when there was plenty of food and time to cook it, may be interesting:—

POTAGE.
Weka-Kiwi, and Piki-Piki Fern.
POISSONS.
Sardines à l'huile.

**ENTREES.**
Sardines à la Karangarua.

**RELEVES.**
Boiled Kiwi.

**LEGUMES.**
Boiled Piki-Piki Fern.

**ROTI.**
Roast Weka.

**ENTREMETS.**
Flap-Jack and Jam.

**SAVOURY.**
Sardines on Toast.

**DESSERT.**
One Dry Fig.

Sometimes the birds would be roasted on the end of a stick, and on Sundays we allowed ourselves one onion—if we had any—by way of a treat. We tried, on these swell occasions, to imagine our tea was brown sherry! Of course, only in wet weather did I try to raise a smile on my own face by going through the formality of a long dinner; in fine weather there was too much work to do, and when anyone was with me, time did not pass quite so slowly.

Sardine à la Karangarua is rather a good dish. Cut a thin strip of bacon, roll a sardine in it, fry for a few minutes, and—as the cookery books say—"serve hot" on toast.

## CHAPTER XIII.

### KARANGARUA RIVER (*continued*).

Bad Weather—Twain Gorge—A Maori arrives—Douglas returns—Karangarua Gorge—Lame Duck Camp—Douglas again Ill—Head of the River—A Lonely Christmas.

ALLOWING the river another day to reach its proper level, I left camp on the 21st, and, fording just opposite, went up the north bank of the Twain, to see if a route was practicable on that side. These rivers are glacier streams and very cold indeed to ford; after a long crossing like the one opposite camp, which was about eighty yards of actual wading, the cold made one's legs sting painfully. Though we had to ford creeks or river four days in a week during the work in the lower part of the valley, we never got really used to it, and always found the stinging cold very disagreeable for a few minutes. The weather, at this period of our work, was so bad that it would be monotonous to record my daily experiences. The 20th to 24th were wet days, but very cold, so the river did not rise enough to prevent a certain amount of work; on the 21st and 23rd I made trips into the Twain Gorge, trying first a high level, and then a low level route, along the north bank, and, in each case, was stopped by a bluff or terrace of smooth ice-worn rock, some 200 ft. high, facing up the valley, and running obliquely from the top of the range down to the water's edge. A party of three could no doubt find a route through the gorge with help of a rope, but for one man it proved too difficult to make it practicable.

About seven miles along the Karangarua Range from Mount Sefton, is Mount Glorious, which sends off a spur, in a south-westerly direction, for about four miles. The spur divides the Twain Gorge from the valley of Regina Creek, and is the only offshoot worth mentioning from the Karangarua Range on either side. The slopes of the range and the spur are smooth, and lie at an angle of 35 degrees, showing here and there large patches of ice-worn rock and high bluffs. The soil all along this slope is very thin, and has in many places slipped away, leaving the bare rock. On the north bank of the Twain Gorge, the vegetation, consisting of large trees, has only a foot or two of soil in which to grow. In several places in the bush, there are large bare faces of rock, and the trees seem to have formed a network of roots to help one another to stand. The high-level route took me a mile into the gorge, at a height of 1,700 ft. above the water, and the lower one I could only follow a very short distance, as the above-mentioned rocky terraces, which ran down obliquely to the course of the river, kept forcing me up, before a way over them could be found.

The view of the gorge, from the furthest point I reached, was very imposing. The opposite side, which had proved too much for us, before my companion left me, showed a bare face of perpendicular grey rock of hundreds—nay, thousands—of feet, with a ledge or shelf, here and there, on which some trees found a precarious foothold. Several springs of water were to be seen, shooting out from the rock face for a foot or two, and then, dropping downwards, would be lost in space, only reaching

the bottom as spray. During the second attempt, I was fortunate enough to witness the effect of a thunderstorm, while in the gorge, an experience I should have been sorry to miss. The echo and re-echo of the thunder from those vast precipices, combined with the mists swirling across their faces, can never be forgotten, and the effect was intensified, and appeared far grander, because I was alone.

How feeble one's pen feels when attempting to describe such wondrous scenery as this! The Twain Gorge, with its awful grandeur, Regina Creek, with its beauty of a quieter sort, and the Karangarua Gorge, with its fantastic surroundings, require a form of word painting entirely beyond my powers. Again, the charm of a quiet evening after a storm, in the midst of such wet and boisterous weather as we had at Bark Camp, has to be experienced before it can be realised. When sitting out on the river-bed below the camp, listening to the murmur of the river, the weird cry of the ka-kas flying across the valley, the clear note of the tui, and more familiar sound of the English blackbird—which has found his way into these solitudes—and when looking at the picture of blue ice-water flowing round a dark bush-covered island, backed up by a gloomy gorge, through which the ice-capped summits of the higher mountains could be seen, lighted up with a warm glow by the last rays of the sun, I used to feel that in spite of my loneliness I was to be envied.

The absolute peace and restfulness of such an evening is better appreciated after a hard day of climbing and rough work —alone—forcing one's way into an unknown gorge; or after a long spell of stormy weather such as there had been lately, when the very elements seemed determined to hinder one's attempt to push ahead. While smoking in quiet contentment, and looking at the magnificent surroundings, one would mentally picture other similar evenings, by no means uncommon, in other localities, and wonder why one never got tired of such things. I suppose a true lover of nature never does tire.

On the evening of the 26th, I was sitting in my ragged clothes over the fire, and, having been unable to make those three lower notes sound on the flute, I decided to have some songs. While singing—as a man only can sing when he knows there is no one within miles of him—I was startled, in the middle of a verse, by seeing a yellow three-legged dog, and then a Maori, emerge from the darkness into the firelight.

Both were evidently very much amused at the picture they had seen before I noticed them. This proved to be "Ruerate-maihi," or "Bill," as he is more commonly called, and he told me that "Tarlie (Charlie Douglas) he say you fell' go up find Harper." Having given him some cocoa, which he said "Make pery good tea," I asked him if he had any letters or papers for me, to which he replied, like all Maoris, "Oh yes, plenty time."

However, I was not prepared to wait so long, having been without news for nearly six weeks, so I unrolled his load, and, to my delight, found a great roll of papers, *Graphic*, *Detroit Free Press*, *Strand Magazine*, *Weekly Times*, *Pall Mall Budget*, and *Sketch*, &c., also letters, and some fresh meat and onions. Douglas was coming up in a day or two as he was better, and Bill was to go on with us in order to help him with his load, as he was determined to reach the head of the river.

On the 29th, Douglas arrived, not yet really fit for work,

but as plucky as usual, and we had seven days of uninterrupted rain by way of showing him what it had been doing for the past month! However, the budget of papers gave us plenty to read, and the time did not hang heavily on our hands. At last, on the 6th of December, the weather cleared, having been exceptionally bad for six weeks, and raining on thirty-three days out of forty. From this date, till the end of summer, the season was as good as we could wish, and fully made up for the previous long spell of rain.

Since it was not possible to take our impedimenta through the Twain Gorge, from Cassell's Flat, it was quite evident that, in order to explore its head waters, we should have to find a route into the valley by some saddle higher up the Karangarua Valley. In 1893, Messrs. Fyfe and Graham had crossed from the Mueller Glacier into the Landsborough Valley, and, finding that river too rough to follow, had gone up the McKerrow Glacier and dropped over a saddle on to a small flat, but had not gone any further, returning to the Mueller Glacier again. From photographs, and their description, we knew that they had reached the head of the Twain Valley, but had not attempted to follow it down. We therefore decided to push on up the Karangarua River, and get into the Landsborough Valley, and from thence into the Twain River, and coming down it, join on the traverse at, or near, the point I had reached from Bark Camp. Another route, equally good, would have been up Regina Creek, and over the spur into the Twain Valley, but there was no advantage in taking that line.

Sending the Maori down to Scott's with a mail and to get a few odds and ends, I went up the river and, crossing Niblick and Tui Creeks, cleared a track through the gorge. It was a difficult and rough piece of work, taking three days to reach the more open valley above, a distance of three miles, of which only one and a-half mile required a track, and was responsible for the whole three days' work. The route, after mounting a steep broken slope, overgrown with tangled vegetation, had to be taken along above the walls of the gorge, some 200 ft. above the river, and below high overhanging cliffs of black rock. The two or three creeks which flowed into the river here, dropped over the precipices in fine cascades, having pools between each fall, and wherever the water flowed the bare rock had been exposed, showing only two feet of soil on the surface. There will be terribly large landslips some day in this district, because the hillsides are very steep and the soil has little hold.

In the pools between the waterfalls, we found some "Cock-a-bullies," a small fish of three or four inches in length—unhealthy, black-looking beasts, with bullet heads. One pool had five or six in it, and was between two waterfalls of about fifty feet, so that it was rather hard to understand how they had got there. Douglas tells me he has seen these fish climbing up the wet moss at the edge of a waterfall, evidently finding sufficient moisture from the spray; they are also to be seen on the move in very heavy rain. Some of these same fish have been found in the water at the bottom of a deep shaft on the Ross goldfield.

The river descends 1,100 ft. in this gorge over two large cataracts, which have been formed in the same manner as those in the other branches, by great boulders filling up the narrow rock-bound channel, and preventing the water from cutting the valley floor down to a lower level. Above the upper

DOVETAIL GORGE.

cataract, the valley opens out and has, on one bank (the south), a terrace of hard gneiss rock, 300 ft. high, at the top of the cataract, which gradually becomes lower as the floor of the valley rises, until it ceases altogether some two miles further up the river. The opposite bank has a series of rocky bluffs with good shingle beaches, and small grass flats between them, and affords good travelling.

On December 11th, the Maori and I took a light camp up to a spot I had chosen a quarter of a mile above the gorge. On the 12th I sent him back to Bark Camp to bring another load and help Douglas over the track, while I pushed on up the river to reconnoitre. The camp we were now in was rather an awkward place to be caught without stores in bad weather; for, in order to return to our head camp, it was necessary to ford the river which ran deep against the rocky side, and cross two large creeks. Had the river risen a foot it would have been impossible to cross, and one's retreat would be cut off. We therefore called this camp the "Rat-Trap."

About a mile and a-half above here, the river has cut a most fantastic gorge through the rock. The sides are some 40 ft. high, and in places approach to within three feet of one another, while the water has worn a very tortuous channel for itself. The banks resemble two pieces of rock which have been roughly dovetailed and not placed quite into position; between these walls the water is 20 ft. deep in places and very clear. On emerging from the gorge there is a small flat 2,083 ft. above sea-level, which seemed a good place for the next camp, and was surrounded as usual with high rock peaks; from one of these a fine waterfall (Theodore Falls) descended in four leaps over rocky precipices from a height of 1,700 ft.

This flat I named "Lame Duck Flat," because "Jack," the Maori's dog, pursued a duck which had young ones and nearly killed himself by going over a waterfall into the gorge.

When a pair of ducks have a brood and danger threatens, the female goes away, with the young ones, and the drake draws the pursuer after him, in the opposite direction, by pretending to have a broken wing. Most dogs know that it is only pretence, and make no attempt to follow, but poor "Jack" gave chase and, for nearly half an hour, was now swimming and now running on his three legs on the river bed, while the drake kept just five yards ahead of him. At last the bird drew him towards the gorge and, before I could prevent it, Jack was over a waterfall between the rocky walls. However, I believe that dog had nine lives, for he reappeared lower down, grinning as usual, but looking very foolish!

Next day I went down through the big gorge to Bark Camp, and on the following morning (the 14th) we all returned up to the Rat-Trap Camp—Bill and I with heavy loads. On the 15th we moved camp again to Lame Duck Flat, and, while the Maori made two or three trips down to Bark Camp for stores, I went on up the river alone with a fly, leaving Douglas at Lame Duck Camp with the batwing. Passing through another troublesome, but beautiful, rocky gorge, I put up my shelter a mile and a quarter further up the river, at the point where a large tributary, which I named "Troyte" River, joins the main stream. This drains Mount Fettes (8,092 ft.) and flows through an imposing gorge between towering mountains. Half a mile after the Troyte stream joins the river, it flows through a short gorge of twenty chains. At the lower end the rock sides form a great arch over the water—which is 20 yards wide at this place—and approach to within 6 ft. of one another at a height of 40 ft. from the river—an almost complete arch—and 60 yards above this the two sides actually touch from below the water to 15 ft. above. The river here goes down in a whirlpool, on the upper side, and bursts up with a furious seething and bubbling on the lower side, evidently having only a narrow passage below the water-line. This must be a wonderful sight in a flood.

Starting from Troyte River Camp early on the morning of the 18th of December, I pushed on through some bad travelling to the head of the river and, climbing 2,800 ft., reached the saddle (5,641 ft.) leading into the McKerrow Glacier about noon; a short climb down a snow-filled *couloir* of 300 ft. brought me on to the glacier, about a mile above the terminal face.

Having thus proved that a practical route could be found into the Landsborough Valley, I decided to return at once down the river to see how Douglas was getting on, and by dint of some pretty fast going, reached Lame Duck Camp at dark, after a day of fifteen hours. Here I found poor Douglas quite unable to attempt further work, and reluctantly making up his mind to return to Scott's. It was very hard luck, because he had explored—or shared in the exploration of—every river on the West Coast, from the Wataroa to the Sounds, and had set his heart on reaching the head of this, the last unexplored valley. However, he showed his usual pluck by swallowing his disappointment without grumbling, and the next morning began the return journey. Sending the Maori down to Scott's—two days' journey—Douglas and I made a long day, and were able to reach Bark Camp at dark, as we had nothing to carry. Douglas was to wait here till Scott sent up some men (and a horse to the futtah), in order to help him down, for he was really not able to walk much, having had to be carried over the creeks and river by me the day before. Leaving him, therefore, in good quarters, with instructions to the Maori to bring up a load after me, I returned to Lame Duck Camp, with a load of four days' stores to leave at the Rat-Trap, for use on our return after finishing the Twain and Landsborough Valleys.

Having to fix a station on the north side of the valley, the next morning I went down to Coleridge Creek, a large tributary flowing into the river just below the Dovetail Gorge, and draining a small patch of ice on the top of the range. The hillside here is bare rock for some 2,500 ft. above the river—varying from 32 to 36 degrees—off which the whole surface of soil and scrub has slipped.

The slope was too steep and smooth to attempt in my boots, so I dispensed with them and found that bare feet made the walking quite easy, though the slope was rather steep in places. On reaching 1,300 ft. above the river I sat down to take bearings, and was greatly amused at poor "Jack," who had accompanied me; he was looking at me in a very reproachful manner, and trying his best to sit down, first with his head up hill and then down, but of course a slope at such an angle is not an easy seat for a quadruped, though he could walk up it well enough. However, 500 ft. higher there was a small tarn ten yards in diameter, on a shelf in the rock, and here he was happy while I was making further observations. Going down

"OLD MAN" FALLS—250 FEET—KARANGARUA RIVER.

*To face page 206.*

again was rather difficult, but beyond one approach to an involuntary *glissade* of some 900 ft. the descent was uneventful. Leaving two pounds of oatmeal, a tin of hare soup, and one of jam, under a stone at the camp, for use on our return, I made my way to Troyte River Camp, taking all the things up in one load.

While passing through some bad boulders, which at two places completely bridged the river, I nearly came to grief by trying to get through a hole formed by two of these monsters lying against one another on the top of a third stone. The opening roughly resembled a single oriel window about four feet from the ground, and narrow, therefore I put one leg through, and lifting my arms over my head got my shoulders through, but the load proved too large, and became firmly jammed. Owing to the position of my arms, I was unable to get back, or to reach the sheath knife in my belt to cut the shoulder straps, and I could not use my legs, for they were both off the ground. After some three or four minutes of pulling and straining—which seemed more like an hour—I began to fear that I should never get out, but one more desperate effort was successful, and I extricated myself with numb arms and pretty well exhausted by the brief struggle. There is no excuse for this mishap, it was gross carelessness on my part to risk the chance of sticking in a place like this— when alone; the proper plan, and the one which I generally adopted, was to get through the opening first, and pull the load after me, instead of endeavouring to pass with the load strapped on my back. Like all other dangers, it was a case of "familiarity breeds contempt."

From Troyte River Camp I tried to follow the Troyte stream

through the gorge, but without success, as it was rock-walled with cliffs of 300 and 400 ft. in height, and full of waterfalls. To go up this branch would require a climb through the scrub over the spur forming one side of the gorge, I therefore made a climb on the north bank of the Karangarua and was able to overlook, and make all necessary observations for mapping, the Troyte basin. Mount Fettes (8,092 ft.), with a small hanging glacier, lies at the head of this stream, and shows a magnificent rock face of some 4,800 ft., cut up in ridges, buttresses and *couloirs*. To the right, about two miles up from the junction, a low saddle shows where Jacob's (Makawiho) River takes its rise, which flows behind Mount McGloin, and reaches the sea eight miles south of the Karangarua.

On Christmas Eve I took half my impedimenta up to a small flat (2,803 ft.), under the saddle at the head of the river—a journey of a mile and a half, taking a good three hours—and leaving them in shelter returned to camp that evening, where I had some observations to make.

Not particularly relishing the idea of spending Christmas under a sixty-lb. load, and over bad travelling, I decided not to begin festivities until my shelter was rigged up on "Christmas" Flat. Leaving Troyte River, therefore, at 5 A.M., I reached that flat at 8 o'clock, and had the camp pitched two hours later; and having brought up a small piece of suet and a few raisins, on purpose for Christmas, I made a pudding and had it boiling by noon.

When everything was snug, I shook hands with myself, wished myself a "happy Christmas," and offered my congratulations on reaching the head of the river. I then produced the flute, and, sitting on a stone near the fire—so that I could

A LONELY CHRISTMAS.

To face page 208.

watch the pudding—struck up a Christmas tune or two; but, as the three lower notes were still silent, the only part of the tune that my audience could hear was the part that happened to wander amongst the upper three notes! My audience—which, by the way, consisted of two wekas—I killed after the concert was over and prepared them for my evening meal. It has since been insinuated, by kind friends, that the audience probably died from the effect of the performance!

The best mode of roasting a weka is to make an opening at the back of his neck and clean him, then get a stone, about an inch in diameter, and, having made it red-hot, put it inside the bird, and, passing a stick through his body, stand him in front of the fire to roast. When the bird is cooked—in about half an hour—we plant the stick in the ground and proceed to carve slices off as it stands up in front of us.

My Christmas dinner consisted of five courses, namely—Weka's liver and heart on toast—Roast weka—One onion—Devilled weka's leg—Plum duff—Three dry figs; and I venture to say that, though I had no brandy for the pudding, and the suet was too old and made it taste tallowy, I spent as happy a Christmas as most people. But I confess that a man must have succeeded in reaching the head of his river, after some pretty rough work, before he can really appreciate a "duff" made of bad suet! After a short smoking concert in the evening, I hung the remains of my socks on a branch over my head and turned in, but I suppose there were too many holes in them, for in the morning the contents "panned out" very poorly—a little hoar frost only. It must be admitted that a man must be rather a maniac, before he can enjoy these sort of discomforts. Bill, one day after he had rejoined me, put on my cap by mistake, and found it too large, so he said, "You fell' got pery tick (thick) head"! Possibly he was right, and that may account for my enjoying this solitary Christmas!

Just after I had hung up my socks and turned in, I heard a shout down the flat, and on going out, found that the Maori had arrived, having slept at Lame Duck Camp the previous night. We, therefore, put up a shelter for him by the light of the fire, near my own quarters, and made another brew of tea before finally turning into our blankets. He had a good load of stores, and a grand budget of papers and letters for me, which I spent the next day in reading; for, owing to my custom of going about bare-footed when anywhere near camp, I had burnt my instep and was unable to put on a boot or do any work.

A most tantalising invitation was amongst the letters, from Mannering, who, writing in November, stated that a large party were to be at the Hermitage for Christmas, and were anxious for me to find some pass over and join them. This would probably be easy to do, had my companion been any good on hills, but he proved to be of little use, so I dared not attempt a high pass with him, and had to give up the idea. The newspapers contained news of the Czar's death, by cable, and were more than six weeks old when they reached me.

The Maori made a first-rate companion, and his English was amusing—it was rather like Chinese pigeon English; he always said "I me" for "I," and "you fell'" for "you"; he could not pronounce the letter "R," but always substituted "L," and many other little peculiarities. For getting birds he was capital, and, if any were near, he and his dog "Jack" always found them. The only drawback was that he was painfully slow, and no good on hills or rocks, so I had always to leave him, in or about camp, and do the high work alone—sometimes a risky performance. One thing which interested me greatly, when he arrived, was that he said, "You fell' son of white man?" I asked him what white man he meant? "Oh, de white man long time (ago) he come down with Terapuhi." By this, of course, I knew he was referring to my father, who was the first white man to cross from the East Coast to the West.

In 1857, he went over at the head of the Hurunui River, with a few Maoris, and explored the coast down to the Haast River, as it is now called, but having written very little about it, the expedition has been practically forgotten. Bill, however, told me he was a little boy, and that his father took him up to Okarito to see "the white man," and the old chief, now living at Jacob's River, told him, when hé was coming up to join me, that I had the same name, and might be the son of "the white man."

On the 27th I sent the Maori up to a rock on the saddle, to leave a load of stores under it, and leaving camp at 4.30 A.M. myself, I made an ascent of Mount Howitt, and another peak, "Cairn IV." between the Karangarua and Twain Rivers. By 6 A.M. I had topped the range some 3,000 ft. above camp, and after spending an hour or more observing and photographing, I went along the *arête* between the McKerrow Glacier and Twain River, to the latter point, 7,400 ft. above sea-level.

The climb was uninteresting from a gymnastic point of view, but, being alone, I had to be careful of the large snow cornice on the *arête*, and of some rather steep ice; also on the return in the usual fog about noon, it was difficult to see my way down the steep and rotten rocks for a short distance. But, topographically, the view was grand. The Twain Valley could be seen over 3,500 ft. below, walled in on the left by immense cliffs which extended from the source down to the gorge by Cassell's Flat. Across the valley the Karangarua Range, with Mount Sefton at its head, could be followed down to the junction of the Copland River; on it is the large ice-field of the Douglas Glacier, coming off Mount Sefton, and then a high offshoot, which I named Pioneer Peak, divides the Douglas from the *névé* of another fine primary glacier, the snout of which was seen sweeping down a tributary valley into the Twain. This, which I christened the "Horace Walker," with some smaller glaciers—which I named Wicks, Pilkington, Morse, Fitzgerald, and Fyfe—drains into the Twain River, and accounted for the volume of water seen at Cassell's Flat. To the south, the Landsborough Valley could be traced from the McKerrow for some thirty miles, and peak after peak of the Dividing Range towered up, like the teeth of a huge saw, carrying little snow and ice, but forming some fine rocky summits.

The 28th we spent on the saddle, completing the observations for the Karangarua Valley, and also bringing stores to place under shelter of a rock up there, in order that, on our return from the Landsborough to the Twain, we could replenish our supplies as we passed up the McKerrow Glacier under the saddle, thus avoiding a descent to Christmas Flat. The ascent to the saddle was an easy one, up an open rough creek for 1,200 ft., and then 1,600 ft. or so over open grass slopes covered with large erratic blocks. The creek ran at the foot of a huge

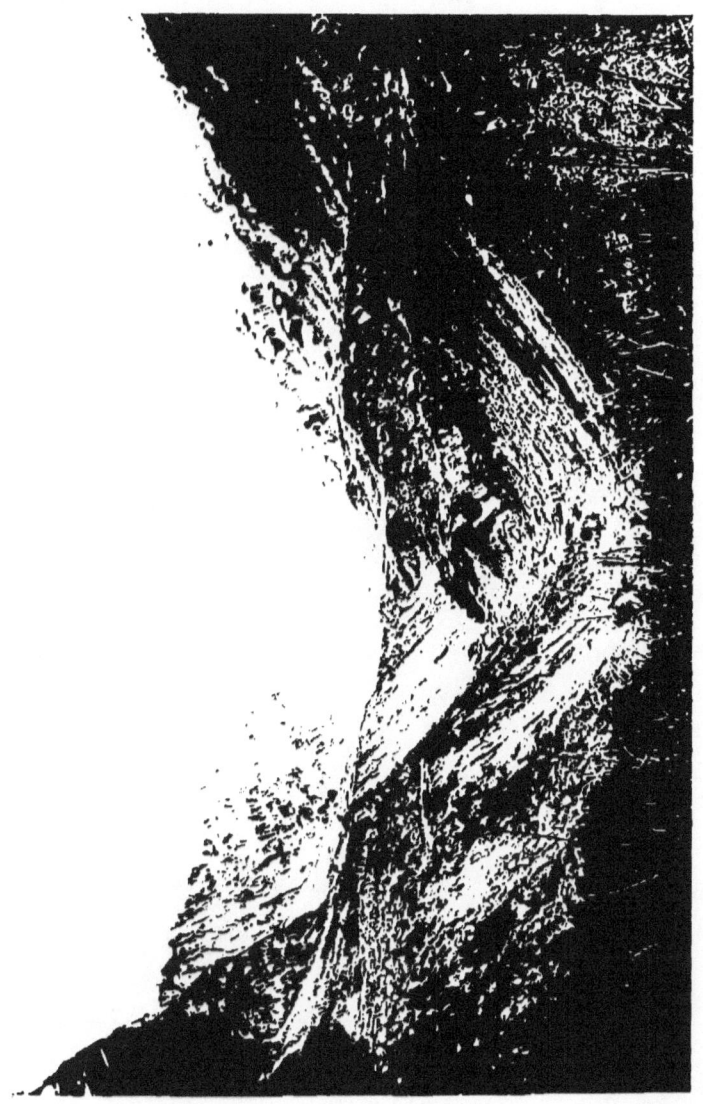

The Head of the Landsborough River.

precipice of ice-worn rock, the top of which was rather higher than the actual saddle. Beginning at nothing just above the saddle, this cliff became higher, as the ground sloped down to the flat, until it was 1,500 ft. high; a waterfall, "The Sisters," came over this in one leap of 800 ft. half-way up the slope to the saddle, and formed one of the sources of the Karangarua. Four other creeks flowed down in various directions and joined on Christmas Flat, draining small snow-fields on the hill-tops.

Very stunted and thick mountain vegetation grows for 600 ft. on the lower slopes of the hills, and in places on the flat itself the scrub was fairly thick and grew to a height of 10 or 15 feet. The greater part was, however, open grass and young scrub, which we burnt; we also fired one or two spurs. At the head of a valley, if the weather was dry enough, we generally fired the scrub, but rarely got a good burn; it never grows again when burnt, and thus, in the future, a few open spaces may delight the heart of any other maniac who tempts Providence by following in our footsteps.

## CHAPTER XIV.

### LANDSBOROUGH RIVER.

Into Landsborough Valley—New Year's Day—No Birds—Starvation Rations—
A Forced March—Haast Pass Track—Return up River—Brodrick's Pass—
Back at Christmas Flat.

It is always best to camp, if possible, near some scrub, in case of bad weather, for it would be very wretched to be without a fire for two or three days. From the Karangarua saddle it seemed that four hours' good travelling would be necessary before the first scrub was reached, which meant about seven hours from Christmas Flat. Accordingly, on the morning of December 29th, I sent Bill away at 6 o'clock, and followed three hours later with light loads. Unfortunately, instead of two hours to the top of the pass he took nearly seven, finding the climb "too teepy (steep) pery lough"; consequently, instead of leaving the pass at 11 A.M. for our descent into the Landsborough, we did not leave till 2 P.M.

On looking over the stores on the saddle, I saw that we should be running very close to short rations unless we had luck, for there was a distance of at least twenty-five miles to go down this valley, and after the return there was the Twain Valley to do. The trip down the Landsborough and back I calculated would take at least eight, and perhaps ten, days; but as no one had been into the valley since it was first explored some years ago by Douglas, we expected to find an unlimited supply of kakapos ; it would not, therefore, be necessary to take much food. These birds, as stated previously, live only in districts covered with birch forests, and the whole of the country from the Landsborough to Jackson's Bay, and even further, is birch country.

About five years before, a party—of which Mr. Mueller, then chief surveyor of Westland, was a member—led by Douglas, made the first exploration of the Landsborough River by the north bank. During that trip the whole party of six had only carried a little flour, and lived entirely on kakapos, which were so plentiful that Douglas says they "had to tie the dog up, she caught too many."

The river is unfordable from the moment it leaves the glacier, and hitherto no one had traversed the south bank, so I had every reason to anticipate no trouble in finding birds, for we should be the first to travel down that side. Accordingly I decided to leave as much food as possible under the rock on the pass for our two days' work on the Twain River. We therefore took seven or eight pounds of flour, some tea, sugar, a little chocolate, cocoa, and treacle—enough to last us, with luck in birds, for ten days; in fact, so certain was I that we should have no lack of birds, that I almost decided to take nothing but tea and sugar. In addition to the food we had camera, instruments, a blanket each, field-books, ice-axe, 8 by 10 fly, and a small axe in case it was necessary to cut a tree for "sparring" a creek; the whole made light loads of about 35 lbs.

The Maori "no likee" the climb down the snow *couloir*, but the rope eased his mind greatly, and when he got on to the glacier below, down which we had to go for nearly a mile, the poor old fellow was very unhappy. He pushed one foot gingerly along in front, and brought the other up to it, and so on, having grave doubts whether the ice would bear his weight! However, in a quarter of an hour he felt happier, and when we got on to the surface moraine he "likee more," and stepped out like a man, being quite convinced that he was off the glacier. I here unroped, and was pushing ahead when I heard an exclamation behind me, and found that the Maori had stepped on a piece of thinly covered ice, with the usual result of sitting down with more speed than grace. On turning round to get up, he saw that he was still on ice, and with the most ludicrous expression of surprise said, "Golly, I me tink no more ice." When we ultimately reached the lateral moraine he was still very doubtful, and fully expected to find ice cropping up somewhere. I do not know if any one has had a Maori on a glacier before, but imagine this is the first time that one has been on Alpine rope, and, considering all the superstitions concerning the ranges that Maoris have, I consider Bill showed uncommon pluck in facing it as he did. I could see he was in a regular "funk," but he showed his courage by setting his teeth and not betraying it—except by his colour, which was yellow!

Below the glacier, for two miles, the river runs between high terraces, in a channel cut down through old morainic and other deposits, there being a large grassy plateau (4,300 ft. above sea-level) on each side of and 300 ft. above the river. This is covered with large erratic blocks, and is cut through by the Spence Creek at one mile and Le Blanc at two miles, which flow from the glaciers of those names between high terraces. These two glaciers are both near the river, and the streams from them are black with slaty silt, and rush down over large boulders, at a great pace. Both gave us considerable trouble to ford, and the latter especially being really dangerous enough to be unpleasant; for we had to step on to large stones a foot under water, between which the stream was deep, and owing to the dirtiness of the water we could only find the next stone by feeling with the ice-axe. The stream was running like a mill-race, which made it the more difficult to make a sure step.

Here, at 3,520 ft., we found the first burnable scrub, and made a rough shelter with a piece of canvas under a rock, about sunset, having taken thirteen hours over a journey which could have been done in seven hours had my companion been any good in rough country. The Maori worked like a man and did his best, but owing to short-sightedness was painfully slow.

It was fortunate that I had made a point of reaching a place where we could have a fire, for it rained for two days; but we were not at all happy, as there was only room for one of us to sit up at a time! However, Bill was "pery tiffy" (stiff), so he was not sorry to lie down most of the day. The reason of this discomfort was that we could not find any poles to pitch our fly properly; had we been in a better place for timber we should have been happy enough. On the moraine of the McKerrow I had killed a kea with a stone, but had seen no other birds, consequently our flour began to dwindle rapidly, and by the end of the second day we had little left, though limiting ourselves to a small slice of bread per meal, and a stick of chocolate.

On the last day of 1894, my diary states that "This

is a poor game when caught in bad weather, under a stone where only one can sit upright at a time. We can neither return, nor go on; everything is in flood. When limited to two small slices of bread a day, and no birds, the fun begins! Bill and I have been talking of our first kakapo all day, and are beginning to doubt if any birds exist. Menu for the last dinner of 1894 :—

<blockquote>
"A conversation about Kakapo and Wekas.

DESSERT.

A slice of bread and cup of cocoa."
</blockquote>

This shelter we named "Musk Camp," because here our only fire-wood was mountain musk, as it is generally called. It is a shrub of the myrtle species, of a sage green colour, and grows to a height of four feet. The leaves, when burnt, smell very like incense, and are not unpleasant to mix with tobacco. It only grows above the 2,500 ft. level—a pure Alpine shrub. There is another kind, of which I have only found two specimens, with a large leaf and slightly different scent when burnt; this I call the "Incense plant," and found it in the Douglas River, near the Marchant Glacier, also one specimen in the Waiho country. To burn a little of either shrub in a room has a delightful effect, and is much liked by those who have had it brought to them from the ranges. The former is found on both sides of the Divide.

January 1st, 1895, was dull, but the rain had stopped, therefore we pushed on down the valley. A few miles below Musk Camp—on the northern side—a fine glacier sweeps down off Fettes Peak right into the valley to 2,950 ft. above the sea, having its terminal face for a quarter of a mile washed by the

Looking for "Tucker."

To face page 218.

Landsborough River. About four miles from the camp, a very large creek from the Arthur Glacier, on the Dividing Range, descends in a series of cascades through a fine gorge, and then bursts out over great stones into the river. We arrived here at 3 P.M. and found it uncrossable, so built a shelter for the night, hoping it would be lower next morning. We dined off one skinny kea, and a quarter of a scone each. Bill felt "pery sore inside, makee knee pery weak,"—but it could not be helped. A rough day after breakfasting off a conversation concerning wekas is not easy work, and to have to finish it with only a mouthful or two of kea and bread, is trying to say the least of it!

About sunset we heard wekas, kiwis, and kakapos within fifty yards of us—across the river. The Landsborough has a mighty volume of water in it, and rushes down at a great pace in its rapid descent; it is unfordable from the glacier for thirty miles of its course; it spreads out on to large flats at that point, and could be forded by a horse—if such an animal could by any chance be brought to the spot. Consequently, unable to cross the river, we had to sit and listen to birds quite close to us, and hunger in silence like Tantalus:—

"Egens benignae semper dapis."

On the morning of the 2nd, thanks to a hard frost in the night, the creek was four inches lower, and enabled us to cross by jumping from boulder to boulder—most risky work, but accomplished without accident. A mile or so below camp I saw a weasel in the bush close to the river, which explained the absence of birds on this bank. Weasels have been turned out over the Haast Pass by some officious person, and have found their way all along the south bank of the valley, but so far have not been able to cross to the other side. Soon after mid-day we reached the first piece of flat travelling, and continued to meet with small flats, between a mile or two of rough travelling, until the evening, when we camped opposite Mount Dechen, some eight miles from, and 1,283 ft. below, the last camp. We got no birds, and were pretty well done up for want of food, having to breakfast and dine off the same conversation and a small slice of bread about 4 by 3 inches!

Next day we again moved on, and travelled till 6 P.M. over extensive flats of open "pakihi" land, in the birch forest, with short stretches of bad travelling in between, and one or two nasty creeks to cross. At 5 P.M. we found three wekas, and as soon as we came to a good place to camp—in about an hour—we kindled a fire, and had the three birds roasting on three sticks, and with three hot stones inside them. In half an hour they were standing up in the ground in front of us, while we cut, sliced, and devoured them, and in another half hour three sticks were all that remained, "Jack," the Maori and myself having given a very good account of ourselves! A weka is equal to a "common, or garden, fowl," so three birds between two men is a fair meal!

I had very little to guide me, as to the whereabouts of the pass I was to report on, and did not know where it would be on this side of the range; but from instructions received before starting up the Karangarua, I imagined that it would be near this camp. However, Bill's boots were quite worn out, and even had we plenty of stores it would be folly—if not cruelty—to make him attempt a return journey in such foot gear. I therefore decided to push on down the river next day.

About fifteen miles below here, the Haast River joins the Landsborough flowing from the Haast Pass (1,800 ft.), over which a transinsular horse track has been formed for some years from the West Coast to Otago. On the beach at the mouth of the river—25 miles from the junction of the Haast—is a store, and the same distance up the valley track from the junction would take us to Stewart's sheep station in Otago. Mr. Stewart had been the first to cross the pass (on which Sir Julius von Haast afterwards placed his own name) in the early sixties, and put cattle on the very extensive flats which are found at the junction of the two rivers (300 ft.). To reach these flats and the track which skirts them, involved fifteen miles of rough travelling interspersed with long stretches of level going. I decided to go on as far as this track, and then either go over to Stewart's station, or down to the store on the beach, in order to get Bill a pair of boots. I had heard, however, that part of the track was to be repaired during the summer, and was in hopes that we should find a road party at work, who could perhaps satisfy our wants, and save the extra twenty-five miles.

I intended to go alone, but Bill did not care about being left in these solitudes, so we both set out on the following morning, leaving everything in our shelter. The travelling seemed easy—unburdened as we were—but a climb of 1,100 ft. over a bluff was trying to us after our long fast. This is a good illustration of the trouble caused by bluffs on the rivers, where a spur descends towards the stream, and ends abruptly in a cliff, at the foot of which the river flows deep and swift. After ascending and descending 1,100 ft. through bush, we emerged 500 or 600 yards only from the point at which the climb commenced, or two hours' work and little over a quarter of a mile gained. It was dark before we reached the great flats, at the junction of the two branches, but we managed to find an old hut near the track—the remains of one of Stewart's mustering "whares"—in which to pass the night. At 8 o'clock next morning we were wakened by a blast of dynamite about two miles away, and knew that for the present our spell of short commons was over, for a road party was at work on the track.

Leaving Bill to follow, I hurried across the wide flats and river-bed, forded the Haast stream, and in an hour was near the road camp. Here I met one of the men, and he would not believe that I had come down the Landsborough—*terra incognita* to them—but thought I had come over the pass from Otago. However, he soon saw something was wrong when he took me along to his tent, and saw me sampling a cold stew, for I could not wait until he had cooked a meal. When I explained that two of us had travelled forty miles down the river, and had only two keas, three wekas and a little flour between us, in eight days, he said that accounted for my eating a "cold, greasy, old stew." It also accounted for a good hot meal which he had ready for me when the stew was finished! I knew Mr. Nightingale, the overseer, so went on and found him, but he did not know me at first, in my rags, with the four months' growth of hair and beard, nor did I recognise myself when he gave me a looking-glass! The Maori turned up in due course, and ate twelve large cold dough-boys (suet dumplings) while waiting for something to be cooked, and like me he "feel pery gland, quite full." We spent four days in this hospitable camp, and were fed up like two turkeys being prepared for Christmas!

It will perhaps be remembered that Bill brought me some old newspapers, when he rejoined me at Christmas Camp, after having taken word down to Scott's about Douglas. Consequently, as there were then rumours of complications in Europe resulting from the Czar's death, I was anxious to know whether I belonged to Russia or England. The men at this camp, being on the track, were able to get a mail every fortnight, so they were only two weeks behindhand in their news, and had papers of more than a month later date than those the Maori had brought me. During our first evening, sitting round the camp fire, I asked what news there was, and was told by one man that Jackson and Corbett—or some such names —had decided not to fight. So I said, "Is there no other news?" and was informed that there had been no news for months. However, on looking at the papers, I found them full of the mail reports of the Czar's death—not short cable messages—and reassuring cables that the general peace was not likely to be broken. This had apparently not been worthy to be called "news," as compared with a possible prize fight!

This, however, is the same all the world over, for I recollect, when quite a small boy, going to England *viâ* San Francisco, in 1878; the last news from Europe, as we left Aukland, said that "War inevitable between England and Russia." On arriving at Honolulu, then the only port of call, a Russian man-of-war lay near the entrance of the harbour, and my parents were most anxious to have the latest news. When the pilot came on board, there was such a rush that my father could not get near to him, so waiting until he got an opportunity, he said to one of the passengers, "Well, what news?" to which the passenger replied, "Confound it, his name begins with a

P!" The rush had not been to ascertain whether war was declared, or whether the man-of-war was going to cut off the mails—but only to settle a sweepstake on the pilot's name!

It was most amusing to see "Jack's" behaviour here. When we arrived he was as well-behaved as possible, and did not attempt to steal, but he was only waiting to find out which camp we were going to patronise. As soon as we had established ourselves in Mr. Nightingale's camp, he began to thieve right and left from the other tents; it is owing to this failing that he lost his leg some months previously. Bill caught us plenty of eels and wekas, which were plentiful here, and prevented the double strain of our presence from affecting the stores of our hosts to any extent, before the packer came up from the beach with more provisions.

The Maori's boots were quite worn out by the time he reached Nightingale's camp, and we had a good deal of trouble to get another pair. The packer arrived in due course, and returned to the beach for a few stores for us, but could get no boots, so Bill had to content himself with two old odd ones belonging to some of the men; having got these, we started on our return up the river on January 11th with a few pounds of rice and flour. The Maori took two days over the journey, as I wanted him to catch some birds on one of the lower flats, but I pushed on and reached camp the same evening, doing the fifteen miles in eleven hours, which is pretty fast going. The camp was 1,003 ft. above sea-level and 750 above the junction of the Haast.

In 1890, Messrs. T. N. Brodrick and Sladden crossed from Lake Ohau, in Canterbury, over a low saddle of 4,300 ft., and descending to the Landsborough River, stayed a night in the valley and returned to the Canterbury side of the range. As already stated, I did not quite know where to look for this saddle, but on going up the river to the camp I crossed three open grass flats absolutely alive with rabbits, and then a fourth and fifth without any of these vermin. The small flat on which we were camping was the sixth, and this had literally thousands of rabbits, the ground being as bare as a barrack yard. When we reached this open space and came out of the trees on to the grass, it seemed as if the whole surface of the ground turned a somersault in sections—in such countless numbers were the rabbits diving into their burrows. The ground looked honeycombed. The fact that there were two grassy flats free of bunnies between this point and No. 3 flat, showed that they had not come up the river; therefore they must have come from the eastern side of the Range *via* some low pass—probably Brodrick's. Having left the pea-rifle at Christmas Camp, and owing to the extreme shyness of the rabbits, we could not have got any had we wanted them, and the three wekas, caught on our arrival here on the way down, had saved us the trouble of a possibly useless hunt. There were none on the smaller flats above this point.

The next day was too foggy to attempt an examination of the high country, so I hunted wekas and snared two or three, while the Maori, who arrived in the afternoon, brought four kakapos and two wekas—a heavy load. The 13th was a wet day, but we got nine more wekas a little further down the river, and spent the 14th, which was again wet, in smoking them for future use—having lost our salt we had to depend on smoke. We had now enough birds to last us till we reached the stores on the pass.

The 15th I spent in ascending Brodrick's Saddle, which, as I anticipated, was above the camp, and the rabbits must have come over by that route. I also looked at another low pass more to the east, but neither was of much use for a road, being too precipitous. The view into Canterbury was very extensive, and I gloated over the grand, open, grassy hills for some time, before descending again to the terrible West Coast scrub and forest.

There was, however, no reason to complain of the bush in the Landsborough Valley, because, like all other country covered with birch forest, it is fairly easy to travel in. The bush is fairly open, with fine timber—clean-limbed trees of five and six feet in diameter—and little undergrowth, and when the grass-line is reached at 3,500 ft., there is none of the usual mountain scrub; the trees merely become smaller until they cease. From near Brodrick's Pass I took several photographs, which were unfortunately spoilt by damp, like so many others this year. I had to leave the boxes of exposed plates sometimes for weeks under a stone or other shelter to be picked up on our final return to habitation, and the damp marked several rather badly.

A grand view of the Hooker Range was to be seen from this spur. Mount Hooker (8,644 ft.) across the valley, with its great horn of rock rising out of fine ice-fields, looked as if it would give some trouble to ascend; the pure white ice dome of Dechen (8,500 ft.), some ten miles up the river, has a snow-line of under 5,000 ft., and, except for innumerable *bergschrunds*, would make an easy climb. Dechen is, I think, one of the most beautiful snow-domes, or cones, I have seen. It rises at a gentle angle which gradually becomes steeper at the top, and in its perfect symmetry almost reminded one of the volcanic cone of Taranaki (8,260 ft.) in the North Island, though the actual cone only began at 4,000 ft. Beyond Dechen the rocky pinnacles of Strauchon (8,359 ft.) rose out of sundry fine secondary glaciers, and a little further away Fettes' Peak (8,092 ft.) showed his fine rock peak, an equally hard nut to crack as his neighbour, from a climbing point of view. Miles away to the north-east I picked up the Footstool, Sefton, and Dwarf, which lie at the head of this and the

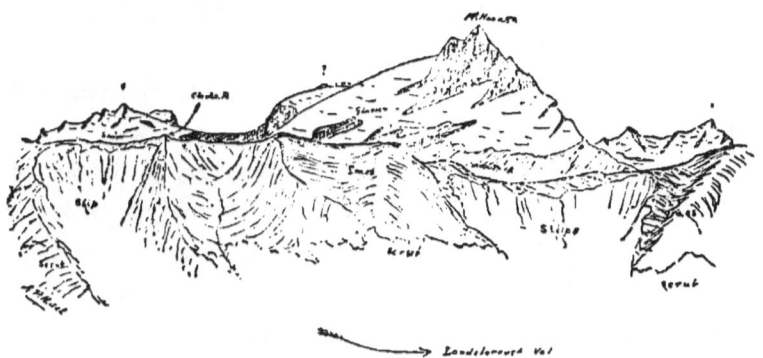

*Mt. Hooker from near Brodrick's Pass. From Field-book.*

Karangarua River. Four thousand feet below, the valley could be followed for twenty miles, the first few miles having a broad flat bottom with many large "pakihis," or grass flats, through which the river twisted here and there, flowing close against the base of a spur, dividing the different flats. Gradually, however, as the eye wandered up, the valley became narrower, till at last no flat places appeared, but each spur descended right into the river, and formed difficult and rough travelling. On the immediate right hand Mount

McKenzie (over 8,000 ft.) raised his rocky summit, with hardly a vestige of snow or ice, a miniature Matterhorn, which, with his shattered rocks, would be a troublesome fellow to climb on this side.

At 3 P.M. a storm of rain wetted me to the skin, and compelled me to descend to camp. On the way down "Jack" caught me two kakapos, but the climbing being beyond his powers, by the route I took, he went home by the line we ascended, so no further birds could be found. On the 16th we went up to our third camp on the down journey, and had reached a point half-way to Arthur Creek the next day when more rain compelled us to camp. Here I made another ascent, on the 18th, but beyond obtaining some observations and photographs there was little worth mentioning.

We had two empty treacle tins which we brought in case of necessity, and these we filled with the oil of the kakapo. This liquid is of a light straw colour, and, though not as good as weka oil, is very nourishing. As I knew we should find ourselves short of flour till we reached the Rat Trap, on our return down the Karangarua, I saved all the oil I could, to mix with the flour—it is a good, though not very palatable way to economise. The Maori was very happy now, for we had unlimited food, having not yet finished the smoked wekas, and because I got one, or sometimes two, kakapo on each ascent; they seemed to have been all above the bush line at this time of year, which accounted to some extent for our bad luck on the way down the river.

One evening, sitting over the fire, Bill mentioned a man whom we had seen at the road camp, and said "he never pore."

"Never poor," I replied; "what do you mean?"

"He always fat, never pore."

"Of course he's always fat, you old fool," I said. "When once a man is fat he generally remains so."

"De Maori," said Bill, "he sometimes pore, sometimes fat; he no tucker he pery pore—but belly full he pery fat—same as de hen."

He meant by this that a Maori gets in good and bad condition in the same way as a weka does, according to his food. I laughed at the notion, at the moment, but on looking at my companion next day, I saw that his dusky old face was now shining like a copper kettle, and he looked like a well-groomed horse—in a ragged cover, certainly, but still well groomed. A fortnight previously he cut a sorrowful figure, and looked in wretchedly poor condition after the short spell of starvation. I have since been told that the change is quite noticeable amongst Maoris, according to their food.

The 19th was cold and wet, the snow was quite low down, but we pushed on in order to cross Arthur Creek before a warm wind came and caused it to flood; and getting over far more easily than before, we made a rough shelter opposite Fettes' Glacier, in a storm of sleet and rain. On the following morning there was a little improvement, and we travelled on and crossed the Le Blanc stream—also very low, owing to the cold—and bivouacked out on the grassy plateau (3,993 ft.), about a mile and a-half below the McKerrow Glacier, reaching there about 5 o'clock. The day had cleared during the afternoon, and the peaks began to show, as the clouds slowly dispersed, and by sunset they were all visible, looking glorious in their coating of fresh snow.

This was a wild-looking site for a bivouac, a great grassy basin of two miles by one, with great erratic blocks scattered over it, surrounded on three sides by towering rock and ice-capped peaks, down which avalanches would thunder every half-hour, making poor Bill start and look nervously round, over his shoulder—for he never got over his fear of the avalanche thunder. While from a hillock behind, we could see miles down the gradually darkening valley of the Landsborough, in descending which, three weeks before, we had had such a bad time. As the darkness closed in, we gathered some stunted vegetation which grew in tufts here and there a few inches high, and coaxed the billy until it boiled, and, sitting down, watched the last three of the smoked wekas being cooked.

They had to be all cooked that evening, as Bill informed me they were a "bit long"—*i.e.* high—but they were none the worse for that, luckily, as we always had good appetites. As usual, when we trusted to the weather being fine, and put up no shelter, it began to rain as soon as we had rolled into our blankets; and with equal cussedness, no sooner had we put the fly up on a rope between the ice axes, than it stopped again, and the stars shone out!

The Maori explained this by saying, "He com'—he see over de hill—he say, 'Golly, two men no camp,' he lain; he see again, he say, 'Dem fell' have camp,'—he stop." We were, therefore, able to use the canvas as an extra blanket after all.

Bill's boots were again nearly done for, so instead of going direct into the Twain River, we returned on the 21st over the Karangarua Pass to Christmas Flat, taking some of the stores from the depôt on the saddle. It was hardly worth while spending three or four days in going down to Cassell's Flat for more stores, though we only had bare provision for a week left. It may have been foolish to risk another starve in the Twain Valley, but I venture to say that most persons would have acted as I did—and risked it—instead of going down and up that awful river again.

This is one of the occasions on which I cursed my fate at having to do such hard work with only one man, and I am afraid I sometimes wished those who were responsible could have had a few of our experiences before refusing us a third member of our party. However, the Twain was still in front of us, so we could not afford to waste time; accordingly we only spent a day and a-half at Christmas Flat, to allow Bill to make himself some Maori sandals, or "parara" out of flax. These do not last long, but are capital foot gear for ordinary river-bed or other travelling, one pair a day being about the average; on sharp stones, however—as will be seen—they are soon cut to pieces, and three pairs will only do a day's work. Bill was convinced that three pairs would be sufficient for the Twain River, so he made five, and left two at the camp when we started on the following day. I spent my "day off" in washing, and generally mending my rags, which hardly resembled clothes, and making a few extra observations in order that no time need be wasted when we came back out of the Twain River.

The geology of this district forms an interesting study, and I greatly regretted my ignorance on that subject. Of course we brought in hand specimens every day, which we looked upon with little favour when they increased to several pounds in weight; for though a 50-lb. load weighs 50 lbs., I am sure it is heavier if there are 20 lbs. of stones in place of 20 lbs. of food! These specimens which have been collected for years by Douglas, and during the last two years by me, are from every valley, and almost every range of the Southern Alps on the western slopes—from the Waiho River to Jackson's Bay. They are all in the Hokitika Survey Office, labelled and classified according to their locality, with the dip and strike of the rocks noted on each one. A most valuable collection, which should enable a geologist to do good work. When these will be made use of I do not know, but only hope they will not die the death of most things which find their way into a public office.

Generally speaking, the main Dividing Range of the Southern Alps is composed of a reddish sandstone, and a great deal of slate—in fact, the prevailing rock is slate, at most of the places I have crossed. The outer ranges are schist and gneiss, the junction of the two formations is generally near the Divide. In the district at the south of Mount Sefton, however, the slate formation appears to extend from the Dwarf across to the Hooker Range, and to continue along it for some 20 miles, where it again crosses on to the Dividing Range. The latter seems to be of schist formation from the Dwarf to near Brodrick's Pass, and then again runs into the slate formation. The Landsborough River, down to this point, follows the junction of the two formations, the valley having schist on the east and slate on the west side. About Brodrick's Pass the river, however, leaves the schist formation, and has cut through the slate, and, sweeping round, has found its way to the sea on the West Coast. This would lead one to suppose that the Hooker Range is the original Dividing Range, and that the water of the ancient glacier found its way eastwards. Of course it requires a geologist to decide this point, and many other interesting points, but at present no geologist has been into the West Coast Ranges; a great deal that has been written on the subject is pure guesswork and in some cases quite incorrect.

## CHAPTER XV.

### TWAIN RIVER (KARANGARUA).

Douglas Pass—Head Basin of Twain River—Douglas Glacier—Camp—Horace Walker Glacier—Moraines—Lower Valley—Hasty Retreat—Bivouac—A Night with the "Taipo"—Return to Habitation.

FROM Cairn IV., on December 27th, I had been able to examine the Twain Valley, from Douglas Glacier to the great Gorge, and could see that we should have a long day's work, with the Maori's slow travelling, before a suitable camping-place could be found in that valley; I therefore decided to sleep near the saddle on the night of the 23rd of January. Leaving one day's food on Christmas Flat, and taking the remainder of our stores, now reduced to sufficient for four days—with reasonable luck in birds—we ascended the slopes towards the saddle, and having found a fairly level place, 1,298 ft. above camp, slept out on the grass. At 5.45 A.M. on the 24th we again moved off, and dropping over into the McKerrow Glacier went about a mile and a quarter up the ice to a saddle (the Douglas Pass, 6,115 ft.) on the north side, reaching it at 10 A.M. Here I had to spend two hours making observations, and continuing a short distance further up the glacier. The formation of the country is most peculiar here, and needs a word or two of explanation.

As already stated, the Hooker Range branches off from

MOUNT SEFTON—THOMSON AND FITZGERALD GLACIER, FROM DOUGLAS PASS.

Mount Maunga, and runs to Mount Howitt before turning in a southerly direction. The Douglas Pass is a high saddle over this part of the range, but lies only 20 or 30 ft. above the McKerrow ice. On the Twain side of the Pass, however, there is a steep slope cut up into ice-worn, rocky terraces, descending for 1,550 ft. on to a small gravel flat half a mile wide by one mile long. Thus, this offshoot of Mount Maunga seems to be an imposing range from the Twain, but from the McKerrow Glacier appears merely a low rocky ridge rising out of the ice. From the Pass the view is weird and magnificent—as, indeed, is the whole of the Twain valley—though very limited in extent.

Looking northwards we had on our right and left a ridge rising sharply from us towards Mount Maunga and Cairn IV. respectively, and forming the saddle. To the right front a deep short ravine, surrounded on three sides by overhanging black cliffs, on the top of which several small ice-fields are scattered and keep up a running fire of avalanches, forming in the bottom a moraine-covered glacier which I called after Mr. FitzGerald, who was in New Zealand at the time, with his guide Zurbriggen. Forming the eastern end of the ravine in which this glacier lies, is the Dividing Range, well over 8,000 ft., Mount Maunga, a very graceful two-horned peak, rising at its head. The glacier flows for a mile between the enormous cliffs to the edge of the small gravel flat (4,562 ft.) across which the stream flows to the foot of some immense terraced precipices, which form the left of the picture, and flowing along their base, finds its way out of the flat at the northern end, under the moraine-covered ice of the Douglas Glacier, which flows past the opening of the basin on the north.

Straight in front of us lay the grand *névé* of the Douglas Glacier, coming off Mount Sefton, which stood in all its white majestic grandeur, framed by these dark and gloomy precipices. This great ice-field lies on the sloping rock "roof" of the Karangarua Range, and is bounded on the east by Mount Sefton and the west by some precipices 500 ft. high, rising up to the summit I named Pioneer Peak when on Cairn IV. It is nearly four miles long and slopes down to the top of a long, sheer, black precipice, varying from 200 ft. at the west end to 1,000 ft. at the eastern end, over which ice avalanches constantly fall and have formed the trunk of the glacier in the valley, nearly four miles in length. Consequently we have the peculiar picture of a *névé* running along *parallel with the trunk of the glacier,* supplying it with avalanches over great cliffs, and *not at any single point having direct connection with it.* The simplest way to form some idea of it would be to imagine an ordinary "lean-to" with a roof about three and a-half miles by one, and the back wall averaging 500 ft.; the *névé* lies on the roof and drops its ice over the back wall, forming the glacier which flows along the base of the wall and for half a mile beyond it. The approximate area of the ice-field lying on the roof is 2,500 acres.

It is probable that a body of water, like the Märjelen See by the Aletsch Glacier, was at one time in possession of this basin, fed by the FitzGerald Glacier, and upheld by the Douglas as it flowed past the northern outlet of the flat. When I met FitzGerald and Zurbriggen later in the season I could not help regretting that they too had not seen this wonderful sight, which of its kind is the finest scene in our Alps, and I doubt if it can be surpassed anywhere.

Looking to the south the view was cut off by the spurs of the Dwarf, but the fine sweep of the McKerrow Glacier, as it curved past under the great precipice from the Karangarua Pass and Mount Townsend, was beautiful. Beyond the Pass, Fettes, as usual, showed prominently, his fine peak reminding me very much of the Weisshorn.

At noon we began the descent into the Twain, and I had the most trying bit of work of the season, for not only had the loads to be lowered down on the rope over the rocky faces, but the Maori and his dog also. Poor old Bill did his best, but is not a mountaineer; he is only an honest Maori who was never built to do Alpine work! We had the pea-rifle with us and managed to shoot two keas on the way down. A short, quick tramp took us across to the northern end of the flat, and four hours—three of which were occupied in going two miles over the worst moraine I know—brought us at 7 P.M. to a small flat a quarter of a mile below the Douglas Glacier, where we rigged up a rough shelter near some stunted scrub, 3,600 ft. above sea-level.

The Maori's sandals of course made him very slow, and were cut up quickly by the sharp stones of the moraine, and the last of the three pairs he had brought with him came to pieces on his arrival at camp. While making our shelter of scrub we got four wekas, and though without salt or sugar—indeed, we were getting used to it now—we had a good meal, the first since 6 A.M., and were soon asleep in our blankets.

On the 25th I went down the valley to the terminal of the Horace Walker Glacier (3,511 ft.)—about a mile below camp—and skirting along its great lateral moraine, traversed the grassy and rocky slopes until I could see through the great

Gorge into Cassell's Flat. Having completed the lower portion of the valley, I descended to a most interesting system of lateral moraines near the Horace Walker. This glacier flows from a basin formed by Pioneer Peak and the Karangarua Range, and descends in a westerly direction for nearly two miles, and then sweeps round until at its terminal face it is almost flowing in an easterly direction, the whole roughly forming a large horseshoe. At the point where it comes out of its valley it has formed a very fine lateral moraine on the outer side of the curve, and behind this moraine is the peculiar series of smaller moraines mentioned above. From the

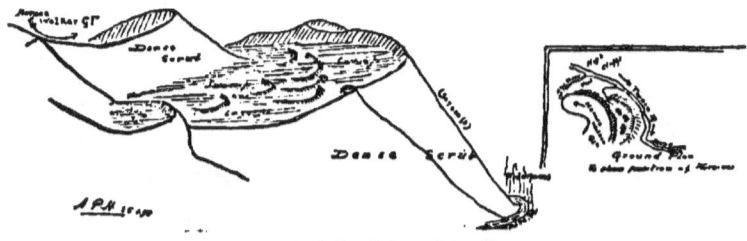

*Field-book Sketch from Point H.*

top of the present lateral moraine on one side to the ice is over 100 ft., and on the other to the river, there is about 450 ft. descent.

About the middle of the curve, on the river side of this lateral moraine, and 60 ft. below it, there is a series of semicircular moraines, with great gaps or openings in their sides, like gates in an old Roman fortification; and in front of each such opening a small moraine has been thrown up, as if to cover the entrance to the fortress. These smaller terraces are 10 to 20 ft. high, and extend in curve after curve for 200 or

300 yards in the widest part, until there is a large unbroken semicircular moraine which falls away nearly 400 ft. on the river side, but is only 30 ft. high on the inner side of the fortress. It would have been an ideal place to defend in ancient days, and really seems to have been built by human hands, each earthwork being thrown up with great accuracy.

I find some difficulty in accounting for these old moraines, for they are lower than the present lateral; had they been higher there would be good reason to suppose that the glacier at one period of its existence took a wider sweep before turning up the valley. There may have been a large terminal moraine thrown across the valley by the ancient ice-flow of the Douglas Glacier, and the Horace Walker being unable to cut its way through has been turned in its course. I am not, however, prepared to allow that these great moraine deposits belong to the Douglas Glacier, but am of opinion that the Horace Walker has been responsible for them entirely. It is more than probable that the ice originally flowed directly down its valley and came out at right angles to the Twain, forming in the first place an outer moraine across about two-thirds of its terminal face, and having its outflow at the other side, where the moraine did not exist; and then, retreating a little way, deposited another great moraine, partly terminal and partly lateral, which now forms the high lateral moraine. This was followed by a considerable shrinkage, until the glacier was smaller than it now is, and then a period of advance set in, causing the ice to flow down against the old terminal moraine, and being unable to push it aside turned along its base and flowed down to its present position. Had this been the case, the glacier would have the old terminal moraine along its side, and make it appear to be a lateral moraine. Otherwise I am at a loss to account for the easterly curve of the glacier *up* the valley, unless some such old morainic deposit caused it to do so; the natural course would appear to be down the rapidly descending main valley of the Twain River.

From Point H, above this lateral moraine, a general view of the valley can be obtained, and the wonderful precipices bound-

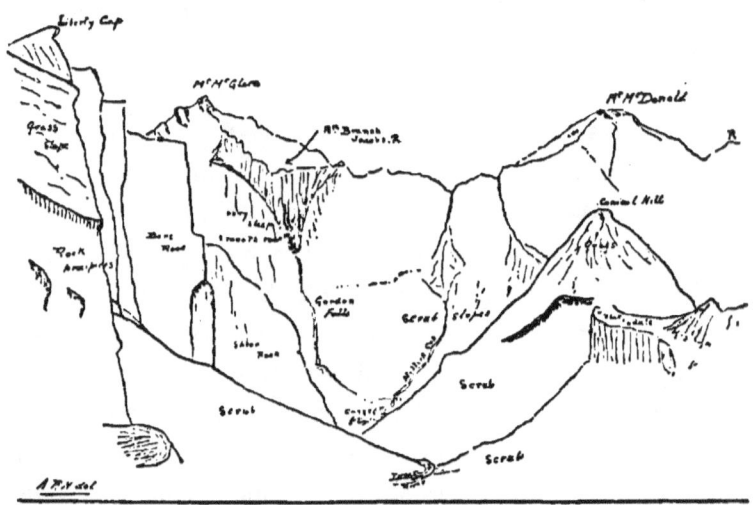

Looking down Twain River from 'H.' Taken from Field-book.

ing it on the south are seen to advantage. From the Douglas Glacier to Cassell's Flat the whole of the southern side is walled in by rocky precipices descending from terrace to terrace for 2,000 and even 3,000 ft. At the base of these the river flows, having formed here and there a small flat of an acre or less behind the short buttresses—they can hardly be called spurs—of the range. About a mile and a-half after it leaves the Douglas

Glacier, the river is joined by the short, but deep stream from the Horace Walker ice, and a mile further, having passed along the foot of the moraines of that glacier, it descends rapidly through a narrow and deep gorge. Apparently it has here encountered a rocky bar across the valley, and has cut a narrow, black-looking channel of over 200 ft. in depth at the lower end, while at the upper end, where it first encounters the bar, it has only been able to wear away a shallow channel of a few feet. On each side of the gorge is a level floor of water-worn rock, and at the lower end the walls cannot be many feet apart. I had not time to go down and inspect this place closely.

Lower down the valley, after another deep but short gorge between two picturesque rocky bluffs has been passed, the precipices, as it were, retire back from the river, and rise out of a gentle slope of débris which lies at their base for three or four hundred feet, and is covered with vegetation. Above this slope the cliffs are more sheer than before, and in places look as if they had been rough-hewn by human hands for hundreds of feet. After flowing along the foot of the short slopes for a mile, the river turns to the left, and descends rapidly over the great cataracts, through the gorge, to Cassell's Flat.

On the northern side of the valley the Karangarua Range rises gently at an angle of about 30 degrees, broken here and there by terraces of rock, and its grassy slopes evidently having little hold on the rock underneath, for spaces of smooth rock can be seen where the soil has slipped or been washed away. Above the Horace Walker stream is a grassy flat of about twenty acres, on which numerous heaps of old moraine are to be seen, and after passing along at the foot of a terrace, another flat is found higher up the valley of smaller size, at the edge of which we were camping. For a quarter of a mile between the camp and the glacier there was a confused mass of moraine hillocks and large erratic blocks, more or less covered with stunted scrub; and beyond this again, filling the upper portion of the valley, is the moraine-covered trunk of Douglas Glacier (3,663 ft.), flowing at the foot of black cliffs, parallel with its grand *névé*, which descends like a great white mantle from Mount Sefton's mighty shoulders.

During the day I had been rather anxiously looking out for some flax to take back to Bill, with which he could make some more "parara," and at one time I feared there was none growing in the valley. If there had not been any, it would have been very exceptional, for it grows as high as any other mountain scrub; it would also have been most awkward, because Bill could not have gone back barefooted. However, on the Horace Walker moraines I found some, and cut enough for all purposes, for I wanted some for the bread also. This year, when away from Cassell's Flat, I used to knead the flour on a flax mat, and bake the bread on a flat stone over the fire, which turned out, perhaps, better bread than the frying-pan. Having cut all the flax that we were likely to require, I set fire to the scrub on the old moraines, little thinking that I was starting more than an ordinary conflagration; the scrub, however, was dry, owing to a prolonged spell of fine weather, and burnt for three whole days, filling the valley with a dense cloud of smoke, which was seen—so I heard afterwards—over Mount Sefton at the Hermitage. This burning of scrub will benefit any future expeditions, for it never grows again, and will leave a few open patches in unexpected places.

On the way down from camp in the morning I had avoided

the Horace Walker stream by crossing on the ice, but as I was now traversing the main river up along the side, I had to ford the stream near where it joined the river. It has a very rapid descent, and was dirty and fairly high after the hot day, so I found it rather awkward to cross, and when just in the centre I trod on a large loose stone and fell over. Luckily, my hands came on to another stone near the surface of the water, so I was able quickly to recover my footing; but had they gone into deeper water, nothing could have saved me from being washed out into the main stream, which was rushing along towards its rapid descent into the gorge. The Twain is unfordable in the summer from the glacier to Cassell's Flat, and, like all other such mountain torrents, it would kill a man by dashing his head against a boulder before it drowned him. The cold of the water is, of course, intense; even where it joins the Karangarua, miles below the glacier, the temperature was just under 40° Fahr.

When at Bark Camp, on my return, I measured the daily rise and fall of the river—in fine weather—due to the melting of the ice up the Twain. The stream at that point was about 80 yards broad and the rise and fall varied from 3 to 6 inches in the twenty-four hours, according to the temperature of the day. No doubt, if such measurements could be extended over a long period, some interesting figures could be recorded as to the melting caused by the sun in summer and winter. My measurements only extended over three days, and were therefore of little value.

Arriving at camp about 7 P.M., I found that Bill had cooked the rest of the birds which we found the evening before, but had failed to find any more. On the 26th I was again working in the lower part of the valley for nearly ten hours. These long days of heavy climbing were hard work, as the Maori was no good on the hills and had to be left in camp, also I had to carry 25 lbs. of instruments, camera, and books all day—a constant handicap. In fact, ever since the beginning of December all the high work had to be done alone, and I had no companion on any expedition from camp on the mountains. Bill spent this day in making sandals and looking for birds, but had no luck, so we were again reduced to small rations.

We had only brought enough stores into the Twain to last us for four days, if we had got plenty of birds; in fact we were practically depending on the latter entirely, and the little flour, &c., was not equal to more than one or two fair meals. No one had been into the valley before, therefore birds should have been plentiful, as they were in the Karangarua Valley, but not only did we get none except the four above mentioned, but also those four were too poor to be of much use. There was still work for two days to be done, and I dared not risk being caught in bad weather here, because our retreat would have been cut off, so instead of taking a "day off" on Sunday, the 26th, I went up the Horace Walker Glacier to the foot of the ice-fall.

Though of no great size, this glacier is very fine, and has only one small patch of surface moraine on it, about a mile from the terminal face. Before it reaches the Twain Valley it is bounded on the north-western side by fine precipices of 900 to 300 ft. in height, on the top of which a large secondary glacier lies, and drops frequent avalanches on to the trunk of the Horace Walker. This upper ice-field I named the "Pilkington Glacier," and it comes from a nice-looking peak,

Mount Glorious, and forms a snow saddle between the Twain and Regina Creek Valleys, draining partly into the latter. The *névé* of the Horace Walker is of considerable extent and lies in a basin formed by the Karangarua Range and the short high spur on which is Pioneer Peak; a fine ice-fall between high cliffs connects it with the trunk. Had there not been several photographic plates and some note-books left in various parts of the Upper Karangarua Valley, I should have endeavoured to pilot the Maori over the Pilkington snow-field into the Regina Creek Valley, making an ascent of Mount Glorious on the way. From that peak a view into the Copland Valley could be obtained and much useful work done, but it was not a fit climb for one man, and my companion was not equal to it; he was willing but utterly unable to do these things. How I regretted that Douglas, or some good man, was not with me here, and wondered why this work was not considered worth the additional slight expense of a third member to our party.

On returning to camp I was aware that had the Maori found no birds our meal would only consist of a small slice of bread; and I could see by Bill's face that he had found nothing, so did not ask any questions. When the billy had boiled, and tea been made, I took the last scone but one out of the bag and quartered it—one piece each for tea and one piece each for next morning. These scones were round, and six inches in diameter by nearly an inch thick, so it can be seen that a quarter is not a sumptuous repast! To my intense surprise Bill said, "I me no hungry," and refused his quarter; I knew he had not eaten anything all day any more than I had, because there had been two scones in the bag that morning.

I therefore exclaimed, "Not hungry? that's all humbug!"

"I me big feed to-day," said Bill; "belly full, me feel gland."

"What did you have?" I asked.

"Oh, plenty food—you fell' have blead," he replied. "I me had Maori hen (weka) pery good."

I knew this was not true, because there were no feathers round the camp, so I said, "You old sinner, where are the feathers?"

But he stuck to his point and replied, "You fell' work all day—I me lie down all day and have good tleep (sleep) and no hungry. You fell' have bread."

It was evident then that the old boy wanted me to have all the food because I had been working, and go without it himself, having tried to tell a lie about the weka; but protesting was no use, he still held out and said he was not hungry.

At last I said, "All right, old man; if you can't eat that bread now put it aside till to-morrow; you are not going to starve yourself for me; we are both in the same boat."

This did not satisfy him, but after half an hour I saw him take the bread and eat it quietly, as there was evidently no chance of my taking it. I could not help being touched by his unselfishness, which fully corroborated the many stories we hear of what fine characters some of the old Maoris have— quite different to the younger generation of natives, I fear.

So far the weather had been cloudless and perfect, but a great change appeared on the following morning; instead of the beautiful clear blue of the New Zealand sky, there were high, black, windy-looking clouds drifting from the north-west, the forerunners of bad weather. The effect of an approaching north-west storm is very grand in the high ranges of the West Coast. It first shows in the shape of high, light, filmy clouds, which drift slowly over and far above the Dividing Range, gradually thickening and closing together, until they appear like a coal-black curtain, against which the eternal snows of the great peaks stand out with weird distinctness. A few hours after this black-looking pall has passed behind the range, ragged and torn clouds roll in from the sea at a level of from 4,000 to 6,000 ft. and cover everything, bringing with them the rain. Accordingly I could see that we should be fortunate if the weather remained fine for even twenty-four hours.

Hastily swallowing our quarter scone and cup of tea at 6 A.M., we rolled everything up preparatory to a quick retreat out of the valley. I gave the Maori most of the things to carry and sent him on up the moraine-covered glacier to the small gravel flat under Douglas Pass, and followed with the instruments and camera, making rapid observations, and carrying the traverse up the trunk of the glacier. On reaching the flat about 2 P.M., I spent two hours traversing it round, fixing more stations, and going a little way on to FitzGerald Glacier, and at 4 P.M. returned to the large rock at the northern end of the flat near the moraine of the Douglas, under which we intended to bivouac if necessary. By this time, however, the rain clouds had obscured the main peaks, and I was unable to fix the point from which my base line was to start, so reluctantly decided to make the best of a bad job and stay here in spite of the storm and no food. From this flat we could retire to Christmas Flat at a pinch in any weather, but at the camp below the Douglas two hours' rain would have cut us off completely by flooding two creeks which we had to cross. Rather than go away, leaving the work incomplete, I determined to stay on this flat for another day at least, though there was only enough grass to boil the billy with difficulty.

By sunset we had chained a base-line and turned into our blankets, having eaten a quarter of the last remaining scone. I shall never forget the grandeur of that night—and I do not think the Maori will either, though for a different reason. Within fifty yards of us the hillside rose sheer for nearly 1,000 ft., and then in tiers and ledges for the same height above to near Cairn IV., and looked as if it might at any moment fall forward and annihilate us. Half a mile away the Douglas *névé* sent down its ice avalanches all through the night—sometimes twenty-five, sometimes thirty in the hour. These crashed down with a sharp report, like a great gun, echoing and re-echoing from cliff to cliff surrounding that great basin; the thunder of one had hardly died away before the next began. Then at midnight the storm burst on us, with its peals of thunder and its vivid lightning, adding to the noise of the avalanches, and causing an indescribable din, as the crash of the thunder and roar of the avalanches echoed from the surrounding precipices, sounding as if all the demons of ancient and modern times were loose. Poor old Bill "no likee," and during the hour or two after midnight while this overwhelming noise was going on, I believe he was calling all the gods to witness that he would never come into such a place again! Every now and then with a nervous laugh he would say, "I me tinkee Taipo (devil) here!"

Fortunately at 3 A.M. it had calmed down, so I got up and saw that the mists were lifting, giving me an opportunity at four o'clock to fix my base-line. At 7 A.M. we ate the

Mount Sefton and Névé of Douglas Glacier, from the Trunk.

last quarter of the remaining scone, and rolling up our loads, went over to the foot of the ascent to the Pass. The mist, however, would not give me a chance of seeing the proper route till we had waited for an hour or more, but at last an opening gave me the line to take, and we began our climb. The rope was necessary three or four times to give my companion and his dog a help over the rocks, but he travelled well, and needed much less nursing than on our descent. After reaching the Pass, descending the McKerrow Glacier, and dropping over the Karangarua Pass in a thick wet mist, we made Christmas Flat in the afternoon, having got three keas on the way. Here a glorious stew and a large feed of porridge soon made us less hungry and helped us to enjoy the luxury of even a batwing, after our long spell of a month in makeshift shelters.

The three days of starvation in the Twain was my fault entirely, for I deliberately took the risk, instead of going down to our depôt for more provisions. However, I believe that anyone in my place would have done the same—that is, taken the risk—rather than going down the river and "punching" up more stores over that rough ground.

The 30th of January was very cold and wet, snow falling round the camp, so we stayed in our batwing by a good fire all day. On the following morning we went down to Lame Duck Camp, as there was nothing to eat at Christmas Flat, having given up waiting for the few additional observations I had hoped to obtain, for the weather was still bad. Here we were again amongst our friends the birds, catching three ducks and two wekas. On the 1st of February we again moved on, reaching the Rat-trap in the afternoon, where I stayed for four days, having to make a climb on each side of the valley. I sent the

Maori down with part of our impedimenta to Bark Camp on Cassell's Flat, telling him to bring back some sugar, flour, and salt.

It may be remembered that we left four days' provisions at the Rat-trap on our way up the river, but of these the flour had turned black with damp, and the jam was fermenting in the tin. On the Maori's return he stated that there was no sugar at Cassell's Flat—a great disappointment, as it was now more than two weeks since we had any. Consequently I was tempted to eat the jam, which owing to fermentation in a tin may have become poisoned; on turning the pot round in my hand, however, I saw a guarantee by the maker—Kirkpatrick, of Nelson, N.Z.—that his tins were especially prepared, and no chemical action could be produced by fermentation; so I decided to take the risk, for we were hungering for something sweet. I suggested to Bill that we should toss up as to who was to try it first, but he laughed and said, "You me both eat!" We therefore each took some, and between us finished the whole of it. Next morning I had forgotten all about the jam, when Bill suddenly said, "You me no dead, jam no bad!"

This reminds me of an occasion, some weeks before, on which the Maori lost his footing and fell over a sheer drop of 15 ft. on to some rocks below; I did not hear him fall, but was astonished by a shout from below, "I me no dead, I me right"; and on making investigations we found he had fallen on to his load, which, as is usually the case, had turned him over on to his back, and he was practically unhurt.

On the 4th of February we went down to Bark Camp, and spent two or three days generally washing up, patching our rags, bathing, and posting up the field-books. The Maori had a complete change of good clothes here, but mine were at Scott's, so I had to do the best with my present rags. It was little use trying to mend my nether garments, for they consisted of canvas patches fastened together by other patches, very little of the original stuff remaining, but care enabled me to make them sufficiently decent to appear at Scott's, by binding them round my legs with flax. When Bill put on his good clothes he looked a "terrific swell" beside me, and I told him so, saying, "Well, Bill, old man, they'll think you are my master." But he would not admit it. "Oh no," he said, "you fell' de boss still!"

On the 7th we wended our way down to the low country, and calling at the futtah for a pair of boots which I had left here in November—those I had on having completely come to an end—we arrived at Scott's farm in the evening, just a day or two over nineteen weeks since I last saw habitation; for I had been in the ranges ever since we originally left on October 1st, 1894, and never been nearer to it than the futtah during that period.

## CHAPTER XVI.

### KARANGARUA DISTRICT.

Pleasures of Habitation—My New Companion—A Climb on Scott's Hill—General Features of the Country—Ancient Glaciers—Roto te Koeti—Alpine Vegetation—Insect Life at High Altitudes.

THE pleasure of such homely food as potatoes, cabbages, and other vegetables, with mutton and bread, cannot be realised until one has been without them for months. Since October, the previous year, I had not had any vegetable except ferns and a few onions, and our bread had been either ordinary damper—flour and water—or soda bread. The cream and milk too seemed far better than any I had ever tasted. Again, a man must spend a long period away from habitation before he can thoroughly appreciate a chair and table, for we had with us absolutely no luxury, nor had we an army of porters to carry tents, bedsteads, mattresses, &c., but had to content ourselves with some scrub branches or ferns to lie on, and a log in front of the "bedding," about four or five inches in height, to sit upon when in our shelter. It may, therefore, be easily understood that a chair and table for our meals were very welcome, after months with the plate—when we had one—balanced on our knees, while sitting on a log.

It must not be supposed that I am bemoaning the discomfort of the work, because, though it might be rough and uncomfort-

able to the average man, I did not find it either the one or the other; but the comfort of even a rough farmhouse in South Westland is welcome for a change. It is also worth while to have hair and beard several inches long, in order to have the pleasure of a good crop, even with a pair of sheep shears! When we arrived at Scott's in February, I could tuck my hair under the collar of my shirt, and my beard was long and tangled!

I found Douglas very little better, and only able to walk a few yards; he had been confined to his bed for some weeks after he had returned. It was perfectly useless for him to attempt further work, so we got a young fellow—Dick Fiddian, recently out from England, and digging at Hunt's Beach—to accompany me. I regretted afterwards that he had not been sent up to me when first Douglas came back in October, for he was a capital mate and plucky, which is more than can be said of the man who left me at Cassell's Flat; he was also a good walker and had the makings of a climber, so would have been, on the whole, preferable to poor old Bill.

The Maori evidently had an exaggerated opinion of my powers, because not only did he give the road party on the Haast Pass track, an extraordinary account of my climbing, but he went to see Dick, and warned him that the work was "pery lough" (rough), also saying, "You fell' no follow Harper in de hills, too 'teepy, taight up."

"Oh yes," said Dick, "I can manage if he helps me with the rope."

"Well, you fell' see I me light, you no follow. See de monkey climb de pole?" asked Bill, working his hands and feet to indicate one of those toys that run up and down a stick.

"Yes, often," said Dick.

"Well, Harper, he just same as de monkey!"

However, Dick decided to come in spite of the Maori's wonderful yarns, and I could not have had a better companion than he proved to be.

Instructions came from Hokitika to say that they had decided to try a saddle at the head of the Copland River for a track to the Hermitage, in spite of the fact that it carried perpetual ice. I was to send in my map, &c., of the Karangarua country first, and then go over to the Hermitage *viâ* the Copland River, and report. This is the line I and others had wanted the authorities to examine for some two or three years past, so these instructions were very welcome. Accordingly Dick and I went up to Bark Camp, and brought the stores and other things which were there to the futtah; and then sent up horses from Scott's to bring everything down to the flats, and, crossing the river, move them up to a mile below the inflow of the Copland, or further if possible. Here Dick was to camp and blaze a track up a spur to the grass line on Ryan's Peak—which we had to ascend later for some observations—while I plotted and sent in the map.

Mr. Scott has a few sheep on the hill on the south of the river, where it flows out of the ranges, and finds the snow grass above the bush line very good pasturage in the summer. He had, however, left the animals there too long the previous season, and was unable to muster, owing to the winter snow having driven the sheep down into the thick scrub. Hearing that he was going up again I decided to accompany him, and go back along the ridge to get a good view over Cassell's Flat and other parts of the river, for a few more observations and photographs. Leaving Dick, therefore, to continue the track up Ryan's Spur, I went with Scott up the sheep hill, and, pushing back, we camped at the head of the Mana-kai-au Creek, which flows out near Jacob's River. One of the party was a young Maori—Dan Koeti, who is an excellent man on the hills—and he told me that, a month previously, he had followed some sheep back further than anyone had been, and found a large lake. Doubting his story somewhat, I went with him next day to a place where we could see, not only the lake — which did exist after all — but also an extensive panorama of the ranges. While Dan went down to the water and back to our bivouac by another route, I spent my time in completing the observations, &c.

From this point (R.) a view of all three branches could be obtained, and an accurate idea formed of the size and direction of the vast ancient glaciers which evidently filled these valleys. The country appeared more weird than it did when we were up the river, the gigantic rock precipices and smooth slopes showed to advantage, and the very narrow ridges in evidence everywhere, proved how hard and solid the rock was. The peculiar conformation of this district was also plainly visible, but it was no easier to account for than when up the valley.

Every divergent range and every spur on such ranges in this district have a sloping side and a precipitous side, thus—

In all the branches of the Karangarua this is most evident; for instance, on the range between the Twain and main branch I was able, on the Karangarua side, to walk up a bare slope of smooth rock, only interrupted in places by a bluff or low cliff, running across or down it; but the vast precipices on the Twain side not only appear to be impossible to scale, but are equally hard to describe. Again, in the Twain we have the slope of the Douglas *névé* to the summit of the range on the southern side, but in the Copland Valley, the same range drops in enormous cliffs on to Welcome Flats. Between the Copland River and Cook's, we find on the southern side of the Copland Range comparatively long spurs, but on the northern are the inaccessible cliffs of Copland Peak, which I attempted to describe in a former chapter. Take one example of the spurs of these divergent ranges, namely, the ridge between Regina Creek and Twain Gorge; here we find a slope varying from 32 deg. to 36 deg., and in a few places a trifle more on the Twain side, but Regina Creek is walled in on that bank by steep precipices.

The slope on the Karangarua Range is the same as the dip of the rock, and it is probable that the great precipices are due to the fracture of the formation. Unfortunately, however, I am not sufficiently well grounded in geology to attempt a solution or explanation of this peculiarity, therefore, having described it to the best of my ability, I shall leave it for others to explain.

For studying the action of ancient glaciers on mountains and valleys, this river and its branches give as good opportunities as any district I know. From the inflow of the Copland River to Cassell's Flat, the valley is, roughly speaking, a mile wide, filled with glacial deposit, which descends in gentle slopes from the lower part of the hills to the centre of the valley. Through this morainic drift the river has cut a channel, leaving terraces on each side from 20 ft. to nearly 100 ft. high, while its course is full of large erratic blocks, in some places completely blocking the valley. The top of the terrace is chiefly flat for some chains back, cut through here and there by deep channels, and generally covered with large boulders. At the end of the spur, opposite the inflow of the Copland River, the glacial drift is piled up for some 400 ft., while the spur itself, above and behind the drift, shows in places ice-smoothed rock.

The slopes of Mount McGloin, and other mountains, into Cassell's Flat have been described in a former chapter. Above the flat the valley narrows to half its original width, and the whole floor rises abruptly for 1,200 ft., the ancient ice having evidently come down in an ice-fall at this point. The faces of the abrupt "step" in the valley are rounded and smooth, forming what might be called "whale backs." From this point to the saddle the valley has been cut out of hard gneiss rock, and has high bare cliffs on the south and smooth rocky slopes on the left, while the floor is of the same rock, and slopes gently down on the south from the foot of the precipices to the river, broken here and there by terraces.

In the upper portion of the valley, from Lame Duck Flat to the saddle, the rock floor has been covered with morainic drift as the ancient glacier retreated up the valley, and débris from the hill sides—in places the whole surface of soil and boulders has slipped away, leaving naked rock slopes. At Lame Duck Flat the river runs on a smooth rocky bottom, and from here to the bar below Cassell's Flat it has evidently met with less obstruction, and, flowing over rock unprotected by débris, has gradually cut the floor down to its present level. After leaving this flat, the river descends gradually through the Dovetail Gorge to the great cataracts, leaving behind it on the left a rock terrace, which gradually grows in height as the river descends, until at the cataract it is upwards of 300 ft. high.

From the top of this terrace there is a gentle slope, for a few hundred yards back, of smooth rock interrupted by two or three terraces, to the foot of the great solid precipices which rise from one to two thousand feet above. This was evidently the old valley bottom, abraded by the ice. In places where a creek comes down to join the river, broad roads of bare rock have been cleared by the water through the trees, interrupted by a few waterfalls, and, on reaching the terrace, drop over into the river making picturesque cascades—picturesque because the rock is worn into fantastic grooves and channels.

The actual cataracts are, I imagine, due to the large erratic blocks, left behind by the ice in its retreat, forming a bar across the valley, and the hills being too steep to hold them they have fallen and accumulated at the bottom. These have gradually collected in the gorge as the water has cut away the ground underneath, and having collected, are now preventing the water from further deepening the gorge. The stones in the cataracts of the three branches meeting in Cassell's are of immense size. It is possible that large blocks of rock have broken away and come down from the hill on the right bank, and also slips may have helped to form Karangarua Cataract, but the other two—Twain River and Regina Creek—are solely due to large boulders left by the old glacier.

There is a curious freak of nature, which I have not mentioned before, on the main branch. In the gorge by the great cataract, the bush, as in all other valleys, is composed of large rata, kamahi, totara, and miro trees, but suddenly on the south bank this class of timber ceases, and the mountain birch begins. The line of demarcation is very marked, and neither class of tree encroaches on the other. On the north bank the usual rata forest continues, with only two, or perhaps three, birch-trees on that side; but on the south bank, the latter have absolute possession till the Theodore Falls and Creek are reached just above Lame Duck Flat; here they cease as suddenly as they began, and the usual mountain vegetation continues on both sides to the head of the river. On Christmas Flat, however, a clump of about a dozen large birch-trees can be seen towering above the low mountain scrub. It is a curious freak of nature, and I can see no reason for it; the real birch forest country does not commence for some distance south of this river, and this isolated patch of birch forest is the only one I know in this district.

Judging from the general appearance and formation of this part of the country, I believe that in the remote past an immense ice-field existed south of Mount Sefton, and discharged itself in three main streams seawards. The low saddle of the Douglas Pass would form no obstacle to the junction of the ice-fields off Sefton and those further south. Even assuming that the limit of the ice-smoothed surfaces coincides with the level of the ancient glaciers, and that they were no higher than these marks are now found, the streams of ice flowing from this central field must have been of great depth, for they have left their marks with great distinctness in the Twain and Karangarua valleys. The spur from Mount Glorious, which divides the Twain and Regina Creek valleys, has a high rocky hill of conical shape rising at its extremity, some 2,700 ft. above Cassell's Flat. Behind this is a low flat-topped depression, and it seems evident that the most northern stream of ice flowed down the Twain valley and covered the lower end of this spur, being joined by a small glacier from the north down Regina Valley. The central stream came over the Karangarua Pass, and down the main valley, joining the

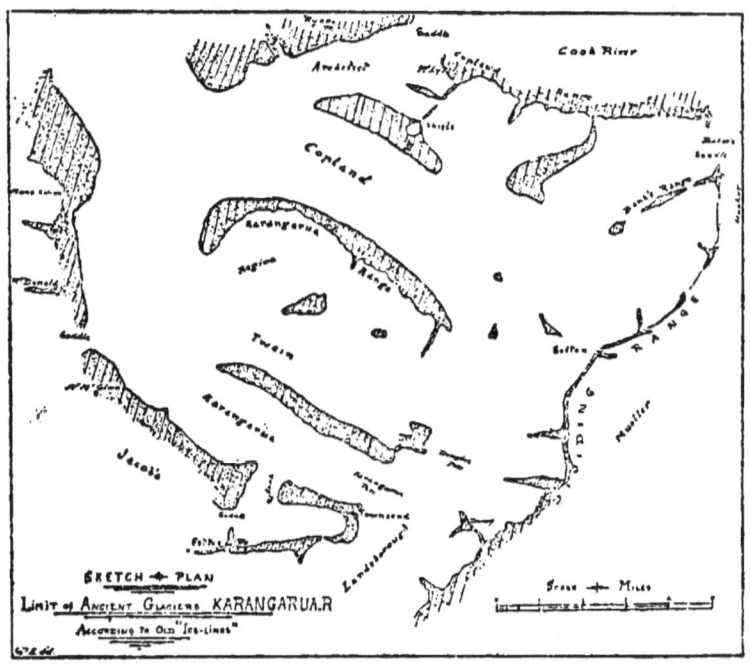

northern stream in Cassell's Flat. It then flowed against the hill on which we are now supposed to be—close to Mount McDonald—and has, I think, left its mark in the number of large blocks which lie on the side in places. Then, turning in a northerly direction, it would join forces with the great glacier which filled the valley of the Copland River, and came over Baker's Saddle from the central *névé*, or the Mount Cook of that day. The combined ice flow would by this time have assumed enormous proportions—far exceeding the ancient Waiho Glacier, and larger than the old Cook River Glacier—and, flowing out on to the flats, would no doubt augment the great ice-field at the base of the hills.

These glaciers must all have been of considerable thickness, and it is perhaps possible that the Twain and Karangarua ice streams overflowed the ridge below point R., on the map, to a slight extent before turning towards the lower country. There is a depression in that ridge, in a direct line with the depression behind the conical hill; a line drawn from the present Douglas Glacier down the Mana-kai-au River would pass through both depressions. That ice has been at work in the head of the latter river, in the past, there is ample evidence; but the most interesting and weird *roches moutonnées* at the source of that river may only be due to a smaller local glacier having no direct connection with the larger one. I am inclined to think that the above-mentioned depression here is accidental, and has no connection with the one behind the conical hill, being rather too high above sea-level.

Further evidence, however, is forthcoming of the great depth of ice on Ryan's Peak, which Dick and I ascended later in the season. There were two distinct lines of boulders lying on the Copland side of the peak at a height of over 4,000 ft. above the sea, which had every appearance of a lateral moraine. The "ice-lines" in the upper valleys of the Karangarua and Twain, which are to be seen as high as 5,800 ft. above sea-level, and fully 3,000 ft. above the present floor of the valley, all point to the same fact.

On the period of retreat beginning, the glaciers would shrink and leave behind them the great mass of morainic accumulations in the valley below Cassell's Flat, and by the inflow of the Copland River. Also in the latter river there are large erratic blocks scattered on the hillsides by the retreating ice. Having gradually retired up the valley, and separated from the Copland Glacier, the Twain ice would probably find its way over the low depression into Regina Creek, and, at the same time, send another stream down the gorge. Douglas, however, from what he saw at Bark Camp, is not inclined to believe that ice ever came through this gorge, but thinks it is due to a fissure in the rock formation. This I cannot agree with, for the Western side has been most certainly abraded by ice, and there is a large loose boulder lying on a ledge some way up the precipice on the eastern side of the gorge. My opinion is that the Twain Glacier found its way to Cassell's Flat through this opening, long after the Karangarua had retreated above the cataracts, and is responsible for the bar of moraine which I found on the flat. I have mentioned already Crusoe's Island and Queen's Knoll, which are evidently remains of a moraine, for on following the line back towards Mount McGloin I found other small heaps of boulders.

There is, in my mind, no doubt that an ice stream came over the Karangarua Pass, for the rock is ice-worn, and large blocks scattered on its slopes. There are also three very distinct "ice lines" in the valley, especially noticeable between the Pass and Troyte River. I believe that this glacier would not be cut off from the central ice-field until it had retired up the valley to Cassell's Flat. But as the period of shrinkage progressed, there is no doubt that it would suddenly be separated from the main source of supply at the Karangarua Pass, which is upwards of 5,600 ft. above sea-level, and, having no high peaks near it from which to draw fresh supplies, it would suddenly and rapidly retreat up the valley from Cassell's Flat to the head: for I presume the fact of so little morainic deposit in the upper portion of this valley is due to a sudden retreat such as this.

The idea of a stream of ice flowing over Baker's Saddle (6,300 ft.) is supported by the presence of sandstone blocks in the Copland valley of the same formation as Mount Cook. But as the main range near the Footstool has some of the same rock, it is possible that these stones came from the Divide between Stokes and that peak—yet, as it has not been closely examined along there, it is hard to say. However, such a low depression as Baker's Saddle must, I think, have been an outlet for the ice of the central *névé* lying near the Mount Cook of that day.

The third stream of ice from the supposed ice-field went down the Landsborough, helped by glaciers from the Hooker and present Dividing Range, but whether it discharged its water westwards or eastwards I will not presume to offer an opinion. There seem, however, good reasons for supposing that the former range at one time formed the watershed between the two coasts.

The lake of which Dan Koeti informed me is a most interesting and picturesque little Alpine tarn. It lies under Mount McDonald, on the seaward side of the ridge, and is half-a-mile long by 200 yards across, draining into Jacob's River. I named it Roto (lake) te Koeti after the finder. There is no bar of morainic accumulations at the lower end, but it is one of those rock basins which is difficult to explain, except on the theory that it was excavated by a glacier. The rocks, smooth and ice-worn, descend precipitously into the water, which is apparently of great depth. Unfortunately, avalanche débris and a stream from McDonald are gradually filling it up.

The vegetation, flowers, grass and scrub, in this district, is the same as elsewhere in our Alps. The mountain\* scrub on the eastern side of the Dividing Range is—where it grows—as dense as that of the West Coast, but is found in such small quantities that it gives little trouble. The shrubs of which it is composed are all found on the West Coast, and, so far as I could discover, there are only three mountain plants which do not grow on both sides of the range. The thorny Wild Irishman (*Discaria toumatou*) I have never seen on the West Coast Alps, while in the Tasman valley it grows with great luxuriance; the Nei-nei—said to be a heath, and "Incense" plant—a myrtle of which I have only found two specimens, are both peculiar to the Westland Alps. The latter has a larger leaf, and the shrub is much smaller in size than the "mountain musk" which flourishes on both sides of the Alps. The former I have already described in Chapter V. While talking of plants there is a very awkward sword grass (*Aciphylla colensii*) which we call the "Spaniard," it has bayonet-shaped leaves, two ft., or more, long, which will sometimes pierce the leather of a boot, and at all times, when one is going through the long snow grass, it will make its presence known in a most unpleasant and unmistakable manner.

Without having made a complete collection of the numerous Alpine flowers, it is of course impossible to say whether there

\* See Appendix, Note IV.

are any peculiar to either side of the Divide, but I am inclined to think that there is no difference in this respect. There are many flowering plants found on the Alps in Westland, which are not found—or, at least, are not common—in the Tasman district; but they flourish in other localities on the eastern side. The great majority of New Zealand Alpine flowers are white, in fact there are comparatively very few coloured ones. The most beautiful is the now well-known Mountain Lily (*Ranunculus Lyalli*) which is the finest Alpine flower I have seen in any country. Besides this there are three or four other kinds of *ranunculus*, some of which are bright yellow and more plentiful on the western ranges than the eastern. Three or four kinds of daisies or *Celmisias* are met with in great luxuriance, above 3,500 ft., in Westland. The finest of these has a white flower with a yellow centre, and grows to three inches in diameter; their broad silvery green leaves are over a foot in length, and are pure white underneath.

This white underleaf can be stripped off and resembles thin white kid; and if it is twisted and knotted into a short string, it is almost unbreakable. I have found the stripping of one leaf strong enough when rolled between my fingers to stand the strain of as hard a pull as either Dick or I could give. The grass which grows on the Alps is coarse and long, but makes good pasturage after it has been once burnt, though care has to be taken that it is not burnt in the wrong season, or it will never grow again; it only seeds once in three years, so far as I have observed. We call this snow grass the "climbers' friend," because it is absolutely safe to catch hold of, when going over the Alp, and no ordinary weight or pull will uproot it. "*Edelweiss*" of a different kind to that growing in

Switzerland, but very pretty, is to be found in great profusion from 3,000 to 6,000 ft. above sea-level, and several varieties of gentians are to be met with on the lower Alps.

Douglas talks of an *anemone* which he once saw, but we have never found any in flower while together; it is a brilliant yellow and, he says, as beautiful a plant as he has ever seen; however, not having myself found a specimen it is difficult to say what it is, or whether it is peculiar to one locality only. I do not consider the sub-Alpine flora of New Zealand equal, as a whole, to that of Switzerland, for though the *Ranunculaceæ* and *Celmisias* are perhaps finer than anything on the Alps of Europe, the smaller plants are not so varied, plentiful or brilliant. We never see an Alp, here, showing such a blaze of colour as those in some parts of the European mountains.

Taking the central portion of the Southern Alps as a whole, I should say that vegetation ceases at 6,200 ft. above sea-level; isolated instances are found of its reaching 6,600 ft., or even more. I have found a small patch of edelweiss at 6,800 ft., and Douglas reports that he once found a " single pale yellow anemone growing on a bare patch surrounded by snow at an altitude of nearly 8,000 ft." This, I think, must be considered too exceptional to take into account, and is probably only a seedling growing for that one season. However, it was not in the district now under consideration.

Birds and insects are fairly plentiful in the high Alps, and, I believe, in every case are common to both sides of the range. The highest life that I have found—except the blow fly (*Calliphora*) which follows one everywhere—is a black weta (*Hemideina*), and a black butterfly (*Perenodaimon pluto*); the former has a body nearly an inch long, and delicate *antennæ* an inch and a half in length. I have found them walking or hopping over a snow-field some 8,500 ft. above sea-level on Mount De la Bêche, and Mannering reports that he has found them still higher, on rocks where even lichens have ceased to exist. The black butterfly has a slow lazy flight at a high altitude, but when found on the lower glaciers it is as lively as most of its kind. Grasshoppers are plentiful on the grass, and also green lizards (*Naultinus*), which grow to a considerable size.

The commonest of all insects is the moraine spider. They are large black fellows, and are seen in hundreds on lateral moraines, and I have rarely found a patch of surface moraine —however isolated—without one spider living like a Robinson Crusoe on his desert island. How a spider could have found its way to a patch of moraine, surrounded by a mile at least of broken and crevassed ice, is difficult to say; and what he lives on when he has reached it, is a still more difficult question. On the Franz Josef, broken and crevassed as it is, we found numbers of these insects on the middle of the glacier far away from moraine. Douglas acknowledges the same difficulty in attempting to explain their presence in the midst of all these crevasses, but puts forward a few suggestions :—

"Perhaps," he says, " they have lost themselves. Perhaps they are practising for a polar expedition, a sort of a *arachnidæ Nansenii*, but the puzzle is, How do they cross these crevasses? Why do they not get their feet frozen? I dare say while the sun is shining they are comfortable enough, quietly freezing towards evening, and thawing out again next day proceed on their journey. We saw no dead ones. When chased they go tumbling down a deep crevasse, as if it was a haven of refuge for oppressed spiders. Whether they ever come back I cannot say."

While on this glacier we found some small insects in the pools on the ice—near the ice-fall—which were black, and about an eighth of an inch long; they took refuge in the minute cells in the ice. No doubt they were the *larvæ* of some insect, but the pools would freeze solid every night, so I do not quite understand why their parents chose such cold quarters for them!

Besides the kea, the only bird found in localities surrounded by ice and snow, is the little mountain wren (*Xenicus gilviventris*), a peculiar, inquisitive little fellow, with no tail, and thin, comparatively long legs, on which he hops from stone to stone, or hummock to hummock on the ice, coming quite close to one, bowing and bobbing like a little machine. I have never seen him quiet for a moment. This bird always reminds me of a feathered walnut on two thin white sticks about two inches long, which have a spring in them, worked by clock-work. They are found everywhere in the high Alps, and on the West Coast; for some hours before rain they collect in flocks and descend to the bush line, where they flutter about in company with the canaries, keeping up a bewildering chirping.

When on Cassell's Flat, I saw a pretty little owl, from three to four inches in height; it had strayed from its hole in the daylight and was so dazzled that it made no attempt to escape. Rather foolishly I did not shoot it, for it seemed a pity to kill so harmless and pretty a bird. Since returning to Christchurch, I have ascertained that though reports of such an owl have been made before, no specimen has ever been obtained. This, however, is not a dweller in high country.

Owing to the very small allowance made by Government for the work of exploration, we were unable to carry proper appliances and materials for collecting flowers and insects. Had we been allowed a larger party, there is no doubt that a most exhaustive collection could have been made during our wanderings over the Alps, and a most satisfactory description given of vegetable and insect life. I have only here attempted to put forward a general idea of the most interesting features in this direction.

## CHAPTER XVII.

### A PASS TO THE HERMITAGE.

Instructions to go to Hermitage—Forestalled—Meet Fitzgerald and Zurbriggen at last—Saltwater Creek—Pass to Tasman Glacier—A Memorable Meeting at the Hermitage—Solitary Journey back to Copland River—West Coast Work discussed—Complete the Exploration of Copland River.

RETURNING from the hill to Scott's farm, I spent a few more days completing my map before sending it to head-quarters, intending to start in a few days to inspect the range west of the Footstool with a view to taking a direct track to the Hermitage. This, as I have already stated, was the line I and one or two others had for some time past held to be the only likely route. It was direct, and possessed grand scenery; but the Government had required a route which should be "free of snow and ice for three months every year," and therefore this was not acceptable. However, now that Douglas and I had proved—what many of us have known for years—that no such pass as required existed without going an unreasonable distance to the south, they at last made the best of a bad job and decided to inspect the Copland again—Douglas having already reported on it in 1892.

The evening before I was to leave Scott's house for the Hermitage, Dick—who had been at the camp—arrived with two strangers, whom I at once recognised as Fitzgerald and Zurbriggen. They had just come over from the Hermitage by the very pass I was going to cross, and had forestalled me in the first passage by a few days. However, I was glad they had come, and congratulated them on finding the pass, for though we had known of its existence, no one had crossed it.* They seemed to have considered the river a very bad one to descend. This opinion of the character of the travelling is rather useful by way of comparison, because Douglas and I look on the Copland River as an easy one—for the West Coast—to descend, *if taken the right way.* And it fully bears out what I have already stated, namely, that what we call "fair" travelling is, to those unaccustomed to the work, really very bad. Fitzgerald said he made use of *five* languages to properly express his opinion of the rough going, I therefore calculate that he would have had to use at least *ten* if he had come down some of the other rivers—or else kept silence!

It can well be imagined what a treat it was to spend a day or two with Fitzgerald, who was elected member of the Alpine Club on the same day as I was, and knew many of my friends in England. We had a long talk about Switzerland, England, and affairs in general. I was also anxious to have a talk with him about the good work he and his guide had been doing in New Zealand this season, and was pleased to hear that his enterprise had met with such well-deserved success. They had intended to go back by the Franz Josef Glacier, but I dissuaded them, for I felt sure that so late in the year it would be impassable, also it would take two days to reach it. After some discussion I suggested the route I had planned last year while on the Fox Glacier as an interesting one—

* See Appendix, Note V.

namely, over the Bismarck Range to the Franz Josef *névé*, and thence over Graham's Saddle to the Tasman.

Fitzgerald kindly pressed me to be his guest, and return with him, an invitation I most gladly accepted, chiefly for the pleasure of a week with them, and partly because it enabled me to share the first transinsular pass *viâ* Graham's Saddle. I had a desire to cross this, for I had already been within an hour of it from both east and west, the actual pass having been left unfinished in the latter case, when easily in our reach, for reasons stated in Chapter XI.

Sending Dick, therefore, up the Copland River to Welcome Flats—some eight miles above its junction with the Karangarua—with a light camp, and four weeks' stores, I left Scott's for the Fox Glacier with Fitzgerald and Zurbriggen. My plan was to cross with them to the Tasman, perhaps ascend Mount Cook, and then return alone, *viâ* the pass they came by—which I named Fitzgerald's Pass—to the Copland River, joining Dick, who was to meet me at Welcome Flat, in a fortnight, with all the stores.

We rode to Gillespies' beach, crossing the Saltwater Creek and Cook River Ferry, and thence went up to Ryan's lower hut on Cook River, situated two miles nearer the sea than the hut which Douglas and I had made our base of operations the previous summer. There was no trouble in crossing the Saltwater, luckily, as the tide was out. This creek is one of the most dangerous to ford on the coast; it has since been bridged above the lagoon. Like most other streams its course is at times blocked by a bar of gravel thrown up by the sea, and is easily crossable; but it generally runs out amongst large stones and very deep, giving considerable trouble.

The Maoris call it "Ohinutamatea." This was the name of a woman, who, according to the legend, was going with her two sons up on the outer range of hills for some purpose, when she fell ill and died on the grassy alp above the bush line. The two sons, being unable to bury her, made a heap of dry grass and burned her where she died. They then went over a ridge, following some tuis which flew in front and guided them to a splendid valley full of wekas, where they lived in plenty for some time. On returning by the route they had gone, they discovered a spring of water rising on the spot where their mother had been burnt, and flowing down to the low country formed the creek named "Ohinutamatea" (or sometimes spelt Oinetamatea). It is possible that these two natives crossed a spur of Ryan's Peak, and dropping into the Copland River, reached Welcome Flats, for the Saltwater Creek flows from near this peak.

As we had some 30 lbs. each to carry, Fitzgerald brought Dan Koeti to carry his load, and we all rode up to a point a mile below the terminal face of the Fox Glacier, arriving there in somewhat heavy rain, and I was able to amuse my host and Zurbriggen by a little bit of "bush craft." We had no tent, and when it began to rain they were for returning to the hut, which would waste a day, but I showed them how to build a "mai-mai," or shelter of ferns and bark—like those I generally use—in which, with the help of a piece of mackintosh and a blanket, we spent two wet nights in perfect comfort.

On Sunday, March 3rd, we reached the Chancellor Ridge, following my route of last year, and chose a stone at the lower end under which to camp. It was raining most of the

T

evening and snow set in at sundown, but we had a good though small shelter. Luckily, however, there was plenty of scrub, which burns green or dry, and I was able to boil the billy I had brought in my load, and we had a good hot brew of cocoa before we turned in. Douglas had given us a blanket, and I brought two of my own, which allowed us one apiece, and right glad we were of their warmth, when the sky cleared and frost set in. About 2.30 A.M. we got up and kindled a fire, which enabled us to have two hot drinks of cocoa before starting; I was amused at Zurbriggen, because he did not know whether to praise the steaming cocoa, or blame the delay caused by letting it cool! I suppose guides are always a little hard to please. Dan, by the way, had only brought up his load to the foot of the Chancellor Ridge and then Fitzgerald sent him back to take the horses back to Scott's on the previous evening.

As I had to return down the Copland River, and might be stuck by the floods, I carried one of my blankets over the pass with us, the others we left at the bivouac with the billy and half a flask of whisky—they are still there. Leaving the sleeping place about 4 o'clock in the morning, we went up the Victoria Glacier towards the saddle into the Fritz Glacier, which I had found on the previous year, and on reaching the foot of the rise, we roped. The ascent to the *col* gave no trouble, and from there Zurbriggen, who still rather underrated the broken nature of our glaciers, led us up the middle of the Fritz *névé*. We soon found the *bergschrunds* too bad, and had to return and ascend a ridge which bounded the Victoria Glacier. From this we crossed the top of the Fritz, and reached a *col* leading into the head of the Blumenthal, a tributary of the Franz Josef Glacier. This saddle we named after Zurbriggen.

From here we could see the great *névé* of the latter glacier, and in front of us the spurs of the Bismarck range stood out, separating the Melchior and Agassiz Glaciers, also tributaries of the Franz Josef. Behind us the Waikukupa River, which drains the Fritz ice, was visible to the sea; it has no special features about it, being merely a straight, narrow valley, which would probably be a difficult one to ascend. Below, on the left, the fearfully broken ice of the Franz Josef gave Zurbriggen something to examine through the glasses; he acknowledged that it looked impassable, but would not commit himself from that height. On our right, Tasman's mighty shoulders and vast brown cliffs rose in all their glory from the Fox *névé*, and to the south we could see over the country which Douglas and I explored in 1894.

Leaving the *col* after a short spell, we rounded the head of the Blumenthal Glacier, and reached the spur dividing it from the Melchoir. This had appeared to present no difficulty when I passed under it in September, 1894, but now we found some little trouble in descending to the glacier below. No doubt the shortest way would have been round the base of the spur which ended in a steep face of rock, but I had strongly opposed that route, as the lower ice of the Melchior is always very broken. Zurbriggen, however, soon found a feasible route down the rocks, and we descended to the Melchior Glacier. Everything was in our favour—clear day, hard snow, and easy walking—so it was fairly early when we reached the point to turn up to Graham's Saddle. Had the snow been in the good order it now was, when I was on the *névé* in September, we should have been on Graham's Saddle in less than half an hour from where we had turned back. Unfortunately we now made the mistake of spending an hour here melting some snow over a candle, for we were rather thirsty, so that it was well after 5 P.M. when we mounted the ridge and overlooked the Tasman Glacier.

What a glorious panorama of ice can be seen from here! I have twice before—in 1891—seen the same view when on De la Bêche, and should never tire of seeing it again. The fog over the low country prevented a clear view westwards, but the Tasman could be seen sweeping down mile after mile to the terminal face nearly fourteen miles away, drawing its supplies from innumerable ice-falls and glaciers off the main range. De la Bêche rose 1,000 ft. above us on the left, and the Rudolph Glacier flowed away from the saddle on which we were, to join the Tasman four thousand feet below.

Time, however, was precious if we intended to reach the Ball hut that night, so we could not delay on the pass. Hitherto I had been last on the rope, but knowing this slope of De la Bêche only too well, we swung round and I took the lead, travelling as fast as the very hard snow would allow, down to and across the *névé* of the Rudolph Glacier. A short ascent of 200 ft. was here necessary up a slope rather open to falling stones, but previous experience had showed me it was the only way, so we scrambled up the snow to some rocks, down which the descent was easy. Here we unroped, and after a short traverse to the left got into an open *couloir* and hurried down to some steeper rocks below. How different from the last occasions I had gone over these same rocks and snow slopes!—then I had twice a sick companion, and once a terrific storm—now we had a clear still evening and were all as fit as the proverbial fiddles. On nearing the bottom we found the rocks coated with ice as it rapidly became dark; my poor old boots were not up to such slippery work at any speed, therefore before we knew where we were, it was dark, and we had to sit down on a ledge five feet by two, and wait for dawn. Zurbriggen and I took the outside, so were unable to sleep, but Fitzgerald towards midnight had a little quiet, though uncomfortable dozing, as he sat between us with his knees under his chin. My two companions had dry socks and boots, but I had nothing, so put my feet into Zurbriggen's spare gloves and rück-sack.

We managed to make the latter angry, during the night, and it took an hour to calm him down; they then tried to "put my back up" so as to pass the time, but being prepared for it I did not lose my temper; however, we spent another hour over the futile attempt. At midnight we sang some songs, ending up with the most appropriate one we could find, namely, "We won't go home till morning!"

It was now rather cold and my thermometer had fallen to 25° Fahr., which I endeavoured to explain to Zurbriggen was the cause of the cold. However, he seemed to have some settled notion in his head that the weather and temperature affected the instruments, and all my eloquence could not convince him that in New Zealand the instruments affect the weather! This occupied another hour, and then the cold was becoming troublesome, so I unpicked my blanket bag, which we had over our knees, and opened it to the full size of the blanket; this we put over our heads, and tucked down behind us, making a rough tent; each taking a candle we held it between our feet and produced quite a warm current of air.

It was very amusing to watch Fitzgerald; he would hold his candle and drop off to sleep; in a short time the candle would burn down and wake him up with a start, as it scorched his fingers; muttering some "foreign lingo" he would lower his hand another two inches, and again doze off, with the same result!

At last the light of dawn appeared on the top of Cook, and we slowly untied ourselves from the various knots and twists which invariably result from a long night on a small ledge—nothing will persuade any of us that the sun did not for once in his life oversleep himself, and rise an hour or two late! My boots were too hard frozen to put on, so I cut them open and made sandals of them, trusting that Adamson, at the Hermitage, would have an old pair to give me for my return to the West Coast. Three hours' easy walking took us to the Ball hut, where we had breakfast and waited for Adamson, who was to meet Fitzgerald there by previous arrangement. About midday he arrived, and I returned with him in the evening to the Hermitage, where I spent the night, and obtaining from him two old boots, went back to the hut with a heavy load of provisions. For four days we stayed in that hut waiting for a good day to ascend Cook, but it rained one day and snowed the next, until Fitzgerald decided to give it up, and go down to the Hermitage. I could not help contrasting the comfort of this hut, and convenience of the track, with our difficulties in the past years. Yet from the way my two friends expressed themselves, I suppose it must even now be considered more than ordinarily rough. I know that, as compared with Zermatt and Grindelwald, it is very uncivilised work even at the Hermitage.

But is not the luxury at those two places rather too great?

The pleasantest surprise of the whole trip awaited me at the Hermitage. When coming up to the hotel I saw a visitor coming from the house, and said to Fitzgerald, "Why, that must be Tuckett, but he is not out here." However, on getting nearer I found that it was Mr. F. F. Tuckett, with whom I had spent some pleasant days in England in 1892. It appears he had come up for two days to the Hermitage, and having heard I was on the West Coast never expected to see me, but curiously enough we both arrived on the same day. Nothing could have given me greater pleasure, and having introduced Fitzgerald to him, we three members of the Alpine Club sat down with a Swiss guide in the smoking-room of the little Hermitage, and were soon over the seas to the other side of the world. It was a memorable occasion—for me, at any rate—and the second pleasant ray of sunshine on my uncivilised life in the ranges. But it only lasted for one night, as he left for Christchurch next morning with Fitzgerald—driving his "buggy" to Fairlie Creek, where the road meets the railway.

Zurbriggen and I spent the 12th in going for a short walk up the Hooker Glacier, and he showed me the whole of his and Fitzgerald's fine climb up Sefton. The evening was chiefly spent in discussing Mount Cook, for Zurbriggen was bent on the ascent, and I was anxious to accompany him. However, "duty before pleasure" is an universal rule, and I felt that my absence had already been too long, and that if I did not at once return, Dick might go down to Scott's and raise an alarm, justified by my non-appearance; for no one had ever crossed the range alone as I proposed to do now. Zurbriggen's very enticing proposal had therefore to be refused.

On the 13th I left the Hermitage—alone—for the West Coast, taking a loaf of bread, a bill-hook, and blanket, the same moment that Zurbriggen left with Adamson for Green's bivouac—namely, at 6 A.M. The route lay up the Hooker Glacier for a mile or two, and then I crossed, and took a spur about a mile further west than Fitzgerald and Zurbriggen ascended when they crossed. After some interesting climbing along a broken *arête* I reached a small ice-field which was steep and covered with fresh snow. It took me forty-five minutes to traverse, an awkward *bergschrund* having to be crossed before I reached the topmost rocks of the range. At 1 P.M. I topped the Divide at a point about a mile west of Fitzgerald's Saddle, and dropping down an ice-filled *couloir* on the Copland side, I traversed round to inspect the pass. Leaving there at 2 P.M., I descended through the clouds to the valley of the Marchant Glacier and Douglas River.

Though my route was to this point different to Fitzgerald's and Zurbriggen's, it presented, as far as I can gather, about the same amount of difficulty, excepting the fresh snow on the rocks and ice which I found, and the disadvantage naturally consequent on a man travelling alone. The two journeys, however, afford such good examples of the wrong and right mode of descending a West Coast river, that I venture to quote the times taken on each occasion; and to describe shortly the best way of attacking this country, in hopes that it may be of service to climbers making a similar expedition. In future these rivers must be attacked by others than Douglas and myself, so it is as well that the best mode of procedure should be known, for the work is quite unlike anything found in Switzerland, or on the eastern side of our Alps.

Fitzgerald and Zurbriggen told me that they left the Hermitage at 5 A.M., an earlier hour than I did, and bivouacked later, and on the second day again started earlier, and at 4.30 P.M. reached Welcome Flats; and on the third day they made my camp below the junction of Copland and Karangarua about 6 P.M., reaching Scott's house after 9 P.M. that evening.

I left the Hermitage, as stated, one hour later than they did, and travelled half an hour less, but managed to bivouac half a mile lower down the river on the first day than they; and on the second, though starting half an hour later, arrived at Welcome Flats by 8.45 A.M. instead of 4.30 P.M.—or ten hours in advance of their time at this point. Judging by our trip down from here to Scott's, three weeks later, I could have reached his house by 10 P.M. on the second evening, that is in *two* days, instead of *three*, from the Hermitage.

The reason of their longer times is to be found after reaching the grass line on the Copland, for up to this point they were ahead of me, the natural result when two men are together above the snow line. On arriving at the grass they descended straight down to the river and began to clamber over the great boulders, here and there meeting one which compelled them to go into the scrub. The scrub, in this valley, is not bad, for the West Coast—that is to say, worse is to be found elsewhere. Here they would meet the usual tangle of stiff, unbreakable, and stunted vegetation which would alone account for the use of the five languages they found necessary! In a short time they would again take to the river bed, and have more hoisting on one another's shoulders, crawling under stones, and sliding down slippery boulders, followed by another deviation into scrub—and so on *ad libitum* for—let us say— three or four miles. This would be succeeded by open travelling and long stretches of still more boulders, involving feats which would, to quote Fitzgerald, "turn a gymnast climber's hair grey."

Considering that they took these difficulties "on a face"— as the diggers say—the times made by these two are good; but the pity of it is that *it was all a waste of energy, owing to their having no means of ascertaining how to tackle this country.* It is to prevent such waste of time in the future that I am contrasting our experiences.

On reaching the grass, the first thing to do was to have a good look at the valley. It was evident that there was no spur, or ridge, to follow above the scrub; but it was also evident that on reaching the second large creek, flowing down on the left, I could go up it for some 200 ft., and reaching a piece of open grass could skirt the scrub till another large open creek was reached, thus avoiding an evil-looking part of the river, which to a West Coaster's eye meant mischief. The result was some fairly rough-and-tumble work in the river, a stiff but short ascent up an open creek bed and good travelling for a short distance to the next open creek from which a view could be obtained round a bend in the river. There was, however, nothing to be done here, but descend and follow the river, for nearly a mile, yet the time saved by the above deviation was probably more nearly two hours than one. From here I had to follow the same tactics as they pursued,

NEAR THE FORKS OF THE COPLAND RIVER.

*To face page 283.*

and made the best of a bad job, until the inflow of the Strauchon River—half a mile below my bivouac—was reached. Here it was at once evident, that as the bush was composed of large rata-trees, it would afford fairly open going; therefore by ascending 100 ft. from the river, and traversing along the hillside, I avoided endless work amongst large stones, and reached Welcome Flats in ten hours shorter time than they did. Below the flats the same course has to be pursued, namely, go back from the river, because the valley is, here—for a short distance—as bad as Cook River for large boulders.

The Copland is not, as I have already said, a bad river to descend, for there is no bluff necessitating a high climb, like that described on the Landsborough and Cook Rivers, nor is there a bad gorge like the Karangarua and Callery Rivers. None of those rivers can be descended without high climbs. I do not think the route I took down the Copland would account altogether for the shorter time; it was probably due, to some extent, to my being generally more accustomed to rough work than Fitzgerald and Zurbriggen; but the method would be answerable for at least two-thirds of the difference in time.

On arriving at Welcome Flat, I saw some footmarks, which showed me that Dick had been there, and a little bit of tracking along the gravel soon discovered the camp. Dick arrived in the evening, having been down for the last load of provisions which he had left at a rock where he slept on his way up. I now had to traverse the Douglas River from the forks of the Copland to the Marchant Glacier, as Douglas had not followed it to the head in 1892, because it was evident that no pass absolutely free of snow existed here. Thinking it possible that some party might come over the pass during the following summer, we spent some days blazing narrow tracks through the scrub, wherever the river compelled one to leave the open. These we marked* most plainly with cross sticks.

It was the 29th of March before we explored the Marchant Glacier, as there had been some very stormy and cold weather; a biting wind blew, and the thermometer never rose above 50° Fahr., and was constantly below 32°—a low temperature for us, in our tattered and draughty clothes.

The Copland River has two main branches: the Douglas on the south from the Marchant Glacier, and the main branch from the north, draining the Strauchon Glacier. Douglas had visited the latter glacier in 1892, and as I wanted some photographs of it, we returned and camped on the 31st half a mile below the forks. Here we "sparred" the river, in order to get to the northern bank.

This operation is generally fairly easy, but here it gave us considerable trouble. We found two large stones, 10 ft. apart, between which the whole river had to pass, and hoisted a 15-foot spar of totara on to the top of one of them, intending to launch it over the gap. This, however, was difficult, for the stone we were on was narrow, and did not allow room to manipulate so large a piece of timber comfortably. Accordingly we went 200 yds. down the river to a place where a boulder of 30 ft. in height overhung the river, and nearly met the branches of a tree on the opposite bank. After some slippery, bare-footed work, we got to the top of this stone, and

---

* Owing to my report that a track *viâ* this pass would be most expensive, I fear there is no immediate prospect of the Government undertaking its formation. A considerable portion of such a track would have to be built up with solid masonry, as the rock is very rotten.

REDUCED TO A PETTICOAT.

*To face page* 285.

a gap of a few feet separated us from the branches, the river boiling and foaming past 30 feet below. Dick went back down the stone on the side away from the river, and there he secured himself, with the rope ready in case I fell; and I, with rope round my waist, made a spring of a few feet on to the branches of the tree, and succeeded in reaching the opposite shore safely. We then adjourned to our spar, and with a rope and man at each end, launched it with ease, and were able to cross in comfort.

Having agreed to "bar fooling in camp," as my diary says, we went up the Strauchon Glacier on All Fools' Day, but had bad luck with the fog, which only gave us isolated glimpses of the views of Cook and Stokes to the north, and Sefton to the east. After waiting three or four hours for the clouds to lift, we gave it up and returned to camp. On the 2nd and 3rd we journeyed down the river, completing some observations, and repitched our camp below the junction of the Copland and Karangarua Rivers, at the point where Dick had "blazed" a track up the spur of Ryan's Peak, which I had to ascend before returning to civilisation.

## CHAPTER XVIII.

#### COPLAND RIVER AND GENERAL WORK.

Welcome Flats—Douglas River—Ruareka—Strauchon Glacier—Decrease of Native Birds—First Ascent of Ryan's Peak—Return to Hokitika—Conditions of our Work—Topographical Knowledge.

BEFORE describing our ascent of Ryan's Peak, I shall give an account of the Copland Valley, which, like all others on this side of the Divide, is of wonderful grandeur, and bears many interesting traces of ancient glaciers. It does not equal the Twain and Karangarua in the latter respect, but for scenery it is in every way on a par with them. Before reaching Welcome Flats, for a short distance some really bad and large boulders obstruct the valley, and amongst these giants, some beautiful glimpses of Mount Sefton and the Footstool can be seen, with the great rata-trees making an effective frame to the picture. Welcome Flats—some 7 or 8 miles up—form an ideal spot for a hotel; the surroundings would delight the heart of the most discontented tourist—provided of course that the cooking was good, for that seems to be a matter of greater importance to many than the scenery!

Imagine for a moment an open flat-bottomed basin (one mile by half a mile) in the high ranges, at each end of which the valley narrows to such an extent that it appears to cease. The river flows down over a grey shingle bed, 100 yards wide, and

THE DOUGLAS RIVER AND THE FOOTSTOOL.

*To face page* 286.

has grassy flats on each side for 200 yards at the broadest place, with a terrace or two to vary the monotony of the level. Between the grass and the hillsides another 200 yards or so of flat ground is covered with luxuriant forest, which on the north bank grows up the spurs to a height of 3,500 ft. above sea-level—or 2,000 ft. above the flat—and on the south side stops abruptly at the foot of towering grey precipices, which rise for 3,000 and 4,000 ft. These grand cliffs are cut into *couloirs* and gullies with wonderful effect, and their summit is serrated to a marvellous degree. Douglas waxes eloquent over this scene, and that should be good proof that it is of surpassing grandeur, because he has spent twenty years in traversing untrodden valleys containing glorious scenery. He likens the "Sierras," as he named these cliffs, to a badly made saw; "it looks as if some giant with little skill, and a very bad file, had attempted to make a saw out of the mountains. . . . . . Other countries may show fine glaciers and higher mountains, but I doubt if anything finer than the 'Sierra' exists out of the moon."[*] I should not venture so far as this latter statement, for it is rather broad; but this part of the Karangarua Range will some day attract much attention. Between the various peaks a glimpse can be caught of snow, which is the upper portion of the Douglas *névé*, and bears out what I stated in the last chapter of the slope on the south and precipice on the north sides of the ranges here.

To the north Mount Lyttle towers up, with a fine ice-field of the second order on its slopes, looking higher than it really is owing to its isolated position. The view of the peak is flanked by high, dark green bush-covered hills, which enclose a dark

[*] "New Zealand Land and Survey Report, 1892-93," p. 43.

and gloomy valley, down which the Ruera River flows, draining the glaciers off Lyttle and Copland Peaks. The snow-line on these peaks must be only 5,000 ft. It is difficult to attempt a description of such scenery, and Welcome Flat includes all kinds—on the one side, beautiful alpine and snow-covered peaks, on the other, weird and awesome rock precipices, and in the midst, a peaceful valley, in which pigeons may be seen rocketing in the evenings, and the few birds left by the weasels and cats are as tame as usual.

The Douglas River is more like the upper Twain in its surroundings, not perhaps so fine in some respects, but still far grander than most places accessible to the ordinary traveller. Mount Sefton rises over 7,000 ft. above the river in bare rocky slopes and precipices, so steep that no glacier of any size can find a place. The Marchant Glacier at the head of the valley has fine surroundings, and owes part of its existence to avalanches from the cliffs above. Two good rock peaks on the north, which I named Unicorn and Dilemma, have one of those peculiar little glaciers perched on a narrow ledge so common in Westland, and due to a portion of the avalanche ice being caught in its downward career.

The short, divergent Banks Range branches to the west, separating the Strauchon and Marchant Glacier, from near Ruareka Peak, which lies at the head of the valley. This peak we named after a Maori woman, who was said to have found her way over to the East Coast many years before New Zealand was colonised. She had some ornaments and tools made of greenstone, which is found largely on the West Coast. The Ngaitahu tribe, by whom she was found, made her lead a party of warriors back over the range by her route. The invaders

MOUNT SEFTON, FROM MARCHANT GLACIER.

*To face page 289.*

seized all the greenstone they could find, and many fights between them and the Ngatimamoe tribe took place, in which the latter were generally defeated. Te Uira, the Chief of the defeated tribe, however, made a final stand at Teihoka, and endeavoured to drive the invaders back, but was again compelled to give way. He then retired further south with a few faithful followers, taking his sacred *mere*—the badge of office—into the inaccessible mountains between the Otago Sounds and Lakes, and there disappeared. Rumours of recent date point to the existence of this lost tribe even now, for fires are said to have been seen in the hills from the sea-coast; but no reliable evidence of their survival has been found. Some of the Ngaitahu tribe settled on the West Coast, and were in their turn defeated by invaders from the North Island, who also left some of their number behind to intermarry with the vanquished tribe. My old friend Bill was descended from one of these North Island men, and had a South Island mother.

The Marchant Glacier has five well-formed lateral moraines on the north side, one of which is very fine, having about 200 ft. slope to the glacier on the south, and nearly 150 ft. descent on the northern side, with an unbroken ridge of grass for some distance along the top. The whole of the trunk is covered with heavy débris, which gives the head of the valley a desolate appearance. Looking back, however, from a mile up the glacier, the cliffs of Mount Sefton, with slopes of scrub-covered débris at their base, look very imposing, and I very much doubt if such a great series of rock precipices is to be found elsewhere in New Zealand.

The southern end of the Strauchon Valley is entirely blocked by a high moraine of 500 ft., through which the river has cut a deep channel. Whether this bar has been formed by the present Strauchon Glacier alone, or by the old Marchant ice, is not clear; I am inclined to think that to some extent both are responsible for it. The ancient glacier in the Douglas Valley was once the largest and most important, and it is only because the surrounding hills are so steep, and face the north, that such a small remnant now remains. From the point we reached about two miles up the Strauchon ice, which is completely moraine-covered, the view of Mount Cook over Baker's Saddle is as good as any I have seen of the peak. It is framed, as it were, by the 1,500 ft. precipices of the Unicorn and 4,000 ft. of sheer cliffs from Mount Stokes. I believe, from the glimpse I had of Stokes in the fog, that at one place a stone thrown out, say, eighty yards, would fall 4,000 ft. without touching anything. The bluff was at the end of a short spur, which seemed to have been sliced down with a knife at the end and the lower part of two sides, looking not unlike the buttressed and gabled end of a great cathedral, 4,000 ft. from roof to base. The avalanches off the western face of Stokes appeared to me, as to Douglas, to be swallowed up in their downward career by some gap in the mountain side. This we were able to account for after our visit up Cook's River, as already related.

West of the Ruera River, which flows into Welcome Flat, Mount Lyttle sends off a high spur, which encloses a large valley with Ryan's Peak. This valley is Architect Creek, and was evidently in the past occupied by a glacier. From the signs of ice-action on the spur of Ryan's Peak, where I found two rows of boulders suspiciously like old lateral moraines, it is possible that the Cook River Glacier sent a stream over the low saddle of 3,890 ft. at the head of this valley. There are, however, few signs of ice action on this saddle, and I am inclined to disagree with Douglas on this point, and consider that the saddle has formed by constant denudation since the great glacier period. The valley of Architect Creek, however, has at one time, no doubt, been filled to a great depth with ice: either a glacier originating from the peaks around, or from an overflow of Cook Glacier. The valley, however, must have been very much shallower at the time.

Before leaving the Copland River, let me give an example of the decrease of native birds in some of the valleys, due to weasels and cats. In Douglas's report, already quoted, he speaks of the gradual disappearance of birds in all valleys during the last few years, and continues to say that " Welcome Flats put one in mind of other days. It was swarming with birds. The kiwis were of larger size than usual . . . the wekas were large-sized, more like Otago or Canterbury birds. . . . The robins ate out of one's hand; the bell-bird sang its chorus in a style only now to be heard south of Jackson's Bay; while the blue-ducks were as tame as of yore. . . . With the exception of the kakapo (which I did not expect to see, as I never saw one outside the mountain birch), every bush-bird was represented on the flats."

It is hard to believe that birds could disappear so quickly as they have in this valley. Compare Douglas's picture of peace and plenty with mine three years later. I should say that never, with the exception of Cook River and the Twain Valley, have I seen such a dearth of birds—of kiwis we neither saw nor heard a trace, of wekas we caught two and saw one. Dick says he heard one robin, which is more than I did—bell-birds were either non-existent or silent—of blue-ducks we saw one pair, so wild that we could not get near them. Whereas Douglas caught and shot some thirty wekas and between twenty and thirty ducks for food on the river generally, and left hundreds, we only got three kakas, two pigeons, and two wekas; and instead of, like Douglas, finding too much to eat, and having to leave stores behind rather than bring them out, we took more with us than he did, and yet were on short rations for two days. Douglas was the first man in this valley, and between his visit and ours (except Fitzgerald, who did not attempt to catch any) *no man had been into these solitudes. The decrease must be entirely due to cats, and to a greater extent to weasels.*

From our camp at the foot of Ryan's Peak we ascended by the track Dick had blazed, and at nearly 4,000 ft. reached the open grass. The scrub here grew to a higher altitude as the hill faces the sea, and on the north-western spurs I found scrub at 4,500 ft., while on the south-eastern side it did not reach more than 3,500 ft. above sea-level. After travelling some hours we reached a fair place for a bivouac, overlooking the Architect and Copland Valleys. Close to us was a remarkable rock, "The Spike," which is a feature in this view from just below the Futtah Camp on the Karangarua, and lies on the southern end of Ryan's Spur, just in the mountain scrub. It is a solitary column of rock which has become detached from the rocky spur behind its present position, and, falling outwards, is now poised over the precipice into the Copland Valley. This rock has a clear reach of 58 ft. overhanging the precipice, and is 15 ft. thick by 16 ft. in breadth, and has the appearance of a

"The Spike," Ryan's Spur.

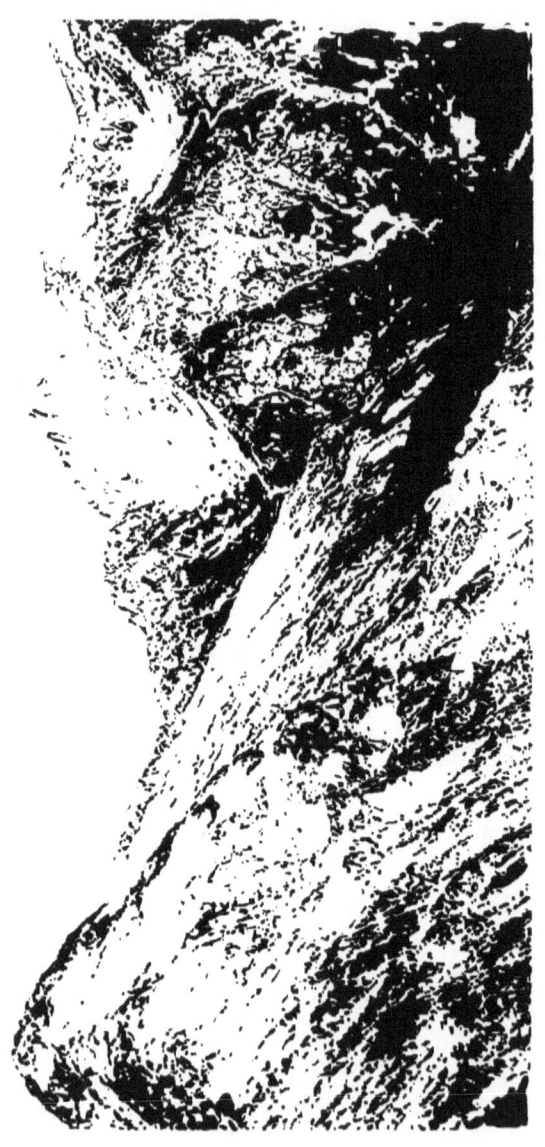

great gun mounted to command Regina Creek Valley, slightly elevated to drop a shell over the Karangarua Range. How far it goes back into the hill, or why it retains its position, is not clear, for it is on the brink of the precipice.

Leaving our bivouac at 4 A.M., we travelled along a gently rising grass spur for two hours by the light of a good moon, being able to see the mountains on our right like great spectres in the moonlight, while on our left the flat country was under a low mist. The sun rose clear and bright about an hour before we reached the first or lower peak of the range, some 5,000 ft. above sea-level. Between this and the main peak a narrow rock *arête* ran for a mile or more, too rotten and steep to tackle on the seaward side, and having too many awkward *gens-d'armes* to allow us to travel along the top. The side towards Architect Creek was smooth and sprinkled with snow, giving us some little trouble, for we only had one ice-axe between us. Having traversed this slope—somewhat difficult in its present condition—for an hour, we reached a small glacier, and found the snow in good order. Half an hour of steep walking over this brought us to the last rock, up which we scrambled without trouble. The peak is just under 7,000 ft., and easy, but with the early winter snow on the steep rocks, and only one ice-axe, it gave us an interesting climb. The last hour over the rocks and snow, combined with the most extensive panorama I have ever obtained of the great ranges, made Dick wish he had been with me the whole summer; he was convinced that there could hardly be a finer sport than exploring new country and putting in a climb at intervals.

I can only say what we saw generally, for the effect of such a panorama of snow-clad peaks and glaciers, combined with deep valleys, flat country and sea, is difficult to describe even roughly. Alpine climbers who read this will sympathise with me, and at the same time picture the view to themselves. Those readers who have not climbed a peak above the snow-line could never realise the glory of such a sight, even if described by the pen of a Ruskin.

We could see the main range from Elie de Beaumont to Mount Ward—a peak in the Landsborough Valley; the Hooker Range from Mount Maunga to Mount Hooker. The whole of the Bismarck Range, Fox *névé*, and Balfour range were visible in the north; the offshoots of the Hooker range faded away in the dim distance to the south, and Mount Lyttle towered up, like a miniature Matterhorn, from the Stockje hut, across the valley of Architect Creek, to the bottom of which, 4,000 ft. below, we could roll the loose stones from the peak. To the west the low country, with its moraine hills, lakes and rivers, could be seen from the Wataroa River to Bruce Bay, and within six miles the waves of the blue ocean rolling lazily shorewards, always four in number, for as one disappeared another formed, and though they appeared to be ever silently moving towards the beach, yet the number never changing gave them the appearance of "still motion," if such a thing is possible. To the north the Paparoa Range by Greymouth was not only visible, but shows in the photograph I took from the peak a distance of 120 miles. The La Perouse Glacier swept down into Cook River almost at our feet, on the north, in graceful curves, and the course of the Balfour River was open to no further question, the view from here proving that our previous

conclusions respecting the Balfour and La Perouse Glacier were correct in every point.

After an hour or two on the peak basking in the sun and meditating on many things, we returned leisurely to our bivouac; and descending next morning to camp, we left our loads and went on to Scott's house. Here I stayed a few days with Douglas, and then returned to the camp to bring our things down. A severe gale blocked all the tracks, so I was delayed till after Easter, when I bid farewell to Douglas and rode up the coast for Hokitika, arriving there after four days' riding. This ride is usually dull and tiresome after so much work, but it was varied this time by a ducking in Saltwater Creek, where I took the horse out of his depth. Douglas, having recovered somewhat, went south to the Waiatoto River, where he has a hut, and lives a hermit-like existence, far from civilisation, amongst his beloved hills and surrounded by undisturbed nature.

The return to civilisation was pleasant after eight months away, of which only three weeks were spent in habitation, and for the remainder of which our mode of life is very well expressed in the following extract from an article by Professor Ludwig Büchner on "The Origin of Mankind":—"Now it is the shelter of a tree . . . now an overhanging rock, now a cave that affords primitive man a suitable sleeping-place; for during the day . . . he hardly, if at all, needs a regular dwelling. At times rough shelters are built of bark, or branches of trees, in bad weather. . . ." This describes our life during a great part of the season, with the exception that we had a piece of canvas always, generally a batwing—but never a tent. The batwing is really comfortable enough for all practical purposes, though I am perfectly aware very few would consider it fit shelter even for a week.

The hardest part of our life, as no doubt has been gathered from the foregoing pages, was the porterage of our provisions and other necessaries. This was very heavy work over such rough country, when enough stores for several weeks had to be carried by degrees up a river or glacier, together with instruments, field-books and cameras. It is a very different matter for a party out for a short holiday to go on small rations, sleep without any shelter, and so on, for they have an easy retreat to their starting-point, to which they can take a good camp on a packhorse. But let me ask any of those who have said, "Oh, *we* don't carry this or that," how they would care for a spell of seven or eight months with only one blanket, a fly and batwing, and, as a rule, only a spare shirt and socks by way of a change of clothes? And this in a part of the country where it rains about three days in a week, and where flooded rivers have to be considered.

I am sure a man requires *solid* food, and cannot rely on essences, extracts, and other such things entirely; and if this is true, then *ipso facto*, his loads must be heavy when going on prolonged expeditions over rough unknown country. I do not think that anyone after trying a few months with us would be inclined to take anything *off* our list of necessaries; they would soon come to a conclusion that several *additions* are needful to make the life endurable. We had not the means to afford an army of porters, nor did the authorities provide for any additional help; neither were we justified in rushing as fast as we could through the country and saying we had explored it.

The mountains, valleys, glaciers and rivers had to be properly examined and mapped, with the branches and tributaries—that is, as well as it could be done with prismatic compasses. This was a matter of time, as has been seen; hence a goodly amount of stores was necessary, and therefore, again, loads were heavy.

It is not intended to convey an impression that we thought the life hard, because we did not—both Douglas and I loved the work, and accepted its hardships as a matter of course. I have only put forward a few arguments to meet the remarks which have been made in the past, and may be again in the future, to the effect that we carried unnecessary loads and lived unnecessarily roughly. It must be admitted that had we been able to obtain any Kola biscuits, or any other food-saving invention, we could have avoided the spells of starvation up Cook River and in the Landsborough and Twain valleys. When first I took up the work I sent to England for Kola biscuits, and any essence or extract which might be serviceable—that was in 1893; again, while in civilisation during the winter of 1894, these things were sent for, but the orders were either never delivered, or not attended to. They could not be obtained in the colony so far as I could ascertain, therefore, though we made a mistake in not having them, it was our misfortune and not our fault.

Photography had to be done under great disadvantages. I carried no tripod; my plates had to be packed for 80 to 100 miles by the packhorse mail, and risked getting wet or broken; they were then left in some kindly digger's hut until required; they underwent very rough-and-tumble usage in the ranges; and after exposure were often deposited under a stone or some other shelter, until we returned and could pick them up. They were then probably again left in care of a digger or sent up by packhorse to Hokitika to be kept till I arrived and could develop them. Some of the valleys are so narrow and the mountains so high that many of the finest scenes—the Sierra, for instance—could not be photographed, unless by chance we made an ascent on the opposite side of the valley.

The exploration of the Twain and Karangarua completed the general exploration and mapping of the central portion of the Southern Alps. For all the glaciers and valleys on the eastern side of the Divide in this district had been explored by the end of the season 1889-90, and the map completed the next year.

So far as topographical knowledge is concerned, the information is very advanced. The Westland Survey Department has in its possession the trigonometrical heights and positions of every peak and *col* of the Dividing Range, from Elie de Beaumont to south of Mount Sefton, with all the chief peaks of the divergent ranges. These were obtained years ago by the Geodesical Surveyor to the Government, from stations on the sea-coast and lower hills. In addition to these observations, they have traverses by Douglas and myself of every river and all the principal glaciers in this part of the Alps—innumerable careful sketches—and some 300 of my photographs from sundry points of vantage on both sides of the Alps, from which alone a map could be made approximately correct with the compass, clinometer, and aneroid readings referring to them. Unfortunately, however, the Government do not consider it of sufficient importance to bring out a complete and accurate map, such as could be made from the above data. They have in the Geodesical Surveyor a careful worker, an enthusiast, and the very man to produce such a map, but for some time past he has been unable to devote his time and energies to a work which no one in New Zealand could do with equal success; consequently this wealth of information is lying *perdu* in the office safe, and we see very indifferent plans issued to travellers.

The Royal Geographical Society published the best existing map of this district* in January, 1893, to illustrate a paper by me on the Southern Alps. That was prior to the western valleys and glaciers being explored, and our last two seasons' work has greatly altered its appearance. There may be still considerable minor detail work to be done in the district, and a theodolite will have to be taken over the ground, of which Douglas and I have made reconnaissance surveys, but the whole country is now explored. Of peaks and passes there are hundreds to be climbed, and these will always add minor details to an almost complete map. The worst of it is that it will be difficult to say exactly what will be valuable as new information in the future, until the material in Hokitika is worked into shape.

Though some of our best peaks have been climbed, the topographical information derived from the climbs is of little value, for the object of the expeditions seemed to be merely the ascent of the peak. The fact is that all the main topographical features had been settled by those who climbed and explored prior to 1891,† and beyond the actual topping of peaks, little was left to be done on the eastern slopes of this district; and, excepting Von Lendenfeldt's ascent of

---

\* *The Geographical Journal*, vol. i., p. 32.
† See Appendix, Note VI.

the Hochstetter Dome, the complete ascents of the higher peaks were not made till after that date, namely, Cook, Tasman, Sefton, Haidinger, De la Bêche, Darwin, Malte Brun, the Silberhorn of Tasman (which is hardly a peak by itself), and Sealy.

The brunt of Alpine work was borne by a handful of men climbing before 1892, and this is often forgotten. It is not right to contrast our unsuccessful ascents before that date with subsequent work, because we were "learning the game," and those who came after us had the benefit of our experiences, and consequently saved a great deal of time and knew how to go to work. For men to attack such a difficult country without guides or experience is very different from following an experienced leader. Though peaks were not scaled then as they have been since, a great deal of necessarily hard work was done, and later comers do not always realise the benefits they derive from the gathered experience of the pioneers. The work of gathering topographical knowledge has to precede the ascent of peaks—the one may be called useful, the other ornamental.

## CHAPTER XIX.

### GLACIER OBSERVATION.

The Number and Area of the Chief Glaciers—Relation of *névé* to Trunk—Are the Glaciers Advancing or Retreating?—Rates of Motion—The Tasman compared with the Franz Josef—The Future of the Southern Alps.

WHEN it is considered that glacier exploration and observation have only been taken up seriously in New Zealand during the last few years, we have every reason to be pleased with the amount of information already collected; more especially as there have only been two or three persons devoting their attention to the subject, the majority having spent their time in climbing peaks only.

I assume that a glacier which descends from a *névé* to a point below the line of perpetual snow is of the "first order." On this basis there are, within a radius of seventeen miles from Mount Cook—or the central portion of the Southern Alps—thirty-one such glaciers, of which twenty-five are on the western and six on the eastern side of the Dividing Range.[*] Of these, twenty are of a respectable size—sixteen on the west and four on the east—while the remaining eleven are of minor importance, and only hanging glaciers sending a tongue of ice down a gully below the snow-line. Though fewer in number,

[*] Ice streams of the first order which are tributaries of large glaciers have been included with the main glacier as one.

the glaciers on the eastern side of the Alps are larger than those on the west—with two exceptions—because the valleys are fewer but longer. It is the number of offshoots and valleys on the west, descending to sea-level in so short a distance, that make that country so hard to explore.

In speaking of the eastern glaciers within the above radius I must rely on the figures given by Mr. T. N. Brodrick,* who has alone made any systematic observation on the four larger glaciers in the Tasman district, and who has most kindly placed his results at my disposal. All his work has been done with a theodolite, and therefore may be depended on as accurate. The following are his figures, showing the areas and dimensions of these ice-fields :—

| Name. | Area of Glacier in Acres. | Area on which the névé now lies. | Length. | | Average width. | | Greatest width. | |
|---|---|---|---|---|---|---|---|---|
| | | | miles. | chains. | miles. | chains. | miles. | chains. |
| Tasman | 13,664 | 25,000 | 18 | 0 | 1 | 15 | 2 | 14 |
| Murchison | 5,800 | 14,000 | 10 | 70 | 0 | 66·7 | 1 | 5 |
| Mueller | 3,200 | 7,740 | 8 | 0 | 0 | 50 | 0 | 61 |
| Hooker | 2,416 | 4,112 | 7 | 25 | 0 | 41·3 | 0 | 54 |

Of the many glaciers of Westland, only two are larger than the Mueller and Hooker, namely, the Fox and Franz Josef; there are several others, however, over four miles in length. As our work was only done with a prismatic compass, I cannot put the results forward as more than *approximate*, and have not attempted to ascertain the areas of supply and glacier ice. This being the case I shall not commit myself by quoting more than a few figures and results. The length of the Fox Glacier is

* "New Zealand Alpine Journal," vol. i., p. 307.

9¾ miles; the Franz Josef, 8½ miles; the Balfour, 6 miles; the McKerrow, 5 miles; the Strauchon, La Perouse, and Spencer, 4¾ miles; and the Victoria Glacier, 4¼ miles.

The Douglas Glacier has a trunk of 3 miles 70 chains, and a *névé*, running parallel to it, of 3 miles 20 chains in length, and therefore the whole glacier would exceed in area some of the above which have a greater length; the Horace Walker also, though only 3 miles 60 chains long, receives ice from a large *névé* for about 60 chains along its side, which would make it little less than the Spencer in area.

It would be interesting to make some comparison between the relative proportions between *névé* and trunk in the case of perfect glaciers and "disconnected" glaciers. One would imagine that, given the same general altitude of surrounding ranges, the trunk of a "disconnected" glacier would be smaller in proportion to its *névé* than in the case of one perfectly formed. If we examine the proportions on various glaciers of *névé* to trunk, we find it impossible to advance any rule as to the relation between the two areas. The Douglas Glacier has a *névé* approximately three times the size of its trunk, which is a larger proportion than that of all the other chief glaciers, excepting the Franz Josef and Fox Glaciers, which have *névés* approximately 5 and 3·5 times as large as their trunks. The supplies of the four glaciers in the Tasman district, based on the above table, are 1·8, 2·4, 2·4, and 1·7 times as large respectively as their trunks. The Douglas Glacier, therefore, shows an excess of *névé* such as would be expected. But when the area of the Balfour Glacier is examined, we find that its trunk *exceeds its névé*, and is three times as large in area (approximately). Of course, in this instance the precipitous nature of the surrounding ranges does not admit of a large snow-field; why, therefore, does the trunk of the Balfour attain such a size? It is larger than that of the Douglas, also both are shut in by precipices, and covered with moraine. The Douglas has a peak from which to draw supplies, 1,100 ft. lower than Mount Tasman, and probably has a smaller snow-fall to depend on, but it has a huge flat surface on which a large *névé* can find a resting-place; therefore it has better opportunities than the Balfour of receiving sufficient supplies to enable a larger trunk to form in the valley.

However, rapidity of descent in the valley bottom and many other facts have to be considered before a satisfactory answer can be given to the various questions which occur to anyone seeing these two glaciers. Everything favours a larger trunk glacier in the Douglas than in the Balfour; it is higher above sea-level, has a larger *névé*, and the relative positions of the two parts of the glacier are conducive to size. But in spite of these facts we find that the Douglas, with a *névé* about six times as large as the Balfour, has a trunk only two-thirds the size. I have assumed that the *névé* is that portion of the glacier well covered with snow at the end of the summer, so that the trunk is practically limited to the "dry ice."

Our observations on the glaciers are not of sufficient age yet to determine to what extent they are advancing or retreating. In the Tasman district reliable traverses, which can be re-plotted at any time, were made by Mr. Brodrick of the terminal faces of the Tasman Glacier in November, 1890, and the Mueller Glacier in March, 1889, and November, 1890. This is all that has been done here to determine advance or retreat, and no other observations have been made to compare the present positions of the terminals, nor can I ascertain that any cairns to estimate side shrinkage have been erected. Considering the number of climbers who have, during the last three years, been in this district, it is a pity that a day or two was not spared from the rush after new ascents for the purpose of putting up a few permanent marks. Personally I have only been in this locality during the few days mentioned with FitzGerald, since 1892, but, as far as I could estimate, there appeared to be a distinct advance on one side of the terminal face of the Tasman Glacier; owing, however, to the necessity of immediate return to my work on the West Coast, I had no time to make closer examination nor erect cairns. The Hooker River interferes to such an extent with the terminal of the Mueller Glacier that it will never be easy to determine whether alterations are due to retreat or not. In the absence of fixed marks, and owing to the shortness of time since observations were commenced, it can only be said generally, that to all appearances no change is taking place in any of the four large glaciers.

Owing to the terminal faces of the Fox and Franz Josef being so easy to reach, and being in a district overrun by diggers, we can to some extent estimate the change from hearsay or old photographs, and future retreat, or otherwise, can be measured from the cairns and marks which I have left in these two valleys.

The Franz Josef was, about the year 1867—according to an old photograph of the terminal face taken by Mr. Pringle—far in advance of its present position. The ice pushed its way * against the four *roches moutonnées*, and it was possible, so I hear from a digger, to touch it when on the top of the Sentinel

* See the map in Chapter XI.

Rock. The Park and Harper Rocks were covered, and apparently the Mueller and Strauchon were half enveloped by the ice. I estimate that the glacier at that date was 80 or 100 yards further in advance, and 10 yards wider on the east bank, on an average, than in September, 1894. There is evidence of this retreat on the rocky banks of the glacier on the east side, both at the terminal face and further up the valley. The rocks for some yards ahead of the ice, and for some feet above its present position, exhibit clean, newly rubbed surfaces, of a lighter colour than the rocks above. This at first misled me to expect a large winter advance, but it evidently testifies to a recent retreat "all along the line." The positions of the cairns which I have made for future reference can be seen in Appendix, Note VII.

The Fox Glacier, as already stated, is moraine-covered at the terminal face for a few chains back, and therefore the changes would not be so rapid. It is narrow and uninteresting at this point. During our visit in 1894 our scientific ardour was damped by excessive rain, and when I was alone on the glacier, my unlucky mishaps prevented extra work. We have, therefore, only two marks* at the terminal face for future reference. The moraine-covered ice here enabled many diggers to cross the river on the glacier, and we may gather to some extent the position of the "snout" in 1894, as compared with that of twenty-five years earlier. From these accounts I estimate that no change has taken place; a conclusion borne out by the fact that there are, here, no such marks of recently-dressed surfaces of rock like that noticed on the Franz Josef. At the terminal face there is a low "dead" moraine with some scrub

\* See Appendix, Note VII.

growing on it, and the ice practically touches that now, as it did twenty-five years ago. The surface moraine is evidently of great age, for there are several pieces of vegetation on it, some little distance from the actual " snout."

From hearsay evidence again, it is clear that some twenty years ago the Spencer Glacier in the Callery Valley descended into the river—the water washing against a face of ice, so the diggers say. In 1893, though not close enough to measure its exact distance from the river, I could see that it was at least a chain away. Thus retreat seems to be going on here, while from all accounts the Burton has not altered its position.

In summing up the results of my personal observation on the glaciers, it seems that while the Hooker, Mueller, Burton, and Fox Glaciers have undergone no change during the periods in which they have been known to us, the Spencer and Franz Josef are retreating, and the Tasman to a slight degree advancing. On the other chief glaciers, the McKerrow, Marchant, Horace Walker, Balfour, Strauchon, Fettes, Douglas, Victoria, and Murchison, I could see no marked signs of recent change of position. The conclusion, therefore, if we may presume to draw one after such short knowledge, seems to be that at present the New Zealand glaciers are not receding to any appreciable extent.

On the subject of glacier motion we have some interesting figures—those of Mr. Brodrick on the four glaciers of the Tasman district, and those of Douglas and myself on the Franz Josef. As Mr. Brodrick has been kind enough to place his at my disposal I shall quote them " in toto."

## Tasman Glacier.

Line I., near the Ball Glacier; rods set on the 5th of December, 1890, and reset on the 7th January, 1891.

| Station. | Total Movement. Feet. | Average Daily Rate. Inches. |
|---|---|---|
| 1 | 27·2 | 9·9 |
| 2 | 41·0 | 14·9 |
| 3 | 47·7 | 17·3 |
| 4 | 48·4 | 17·6 |
| 5 | 49·6 | 18·0 |
| 6 | 46·9 | 17·0 |
| 7 | 44·2 | 16·1 |
| 8 | 38·3 | 13·9 |

Line II., ranged from point of the Malte Brun spur; first set December 5th, 1890, and reset 7th January, 1891.

| Station. | Total Movement. Feet. | Daily Rate. Inches. |
|---|---|---|
| 2 | 6·5 | 2·4 |
| 3 | 25·9 | 9·4 |
| 4 | 28·7 | 10·4 |
| 5 | 32·7 | 11·8 |
| 6 | 36·6 | 13·3 |
| 7 | 33·7 | 12·2 |
| 8 | 34·4 | 12·5 |
| 9 | 29·0 | 10·5 |
| 10 | 25·4 | 9·2 |
| 11 | 13·9 | 5·0 |

## Murchison.

Line ranged from point above Dixon Glacier; set on December 29th, 1890; reset forty-eight hours later.

| Station. | Total Movement. Feet. Inches. | Daily Rate. Inches. |
|---|---|---|
| 78 | 0  1 | 0·5 |
| 79 | 0  7 | 3·5 |
| 80 | 1  4 | 8·0 |
| 81 | 1  5½ | 8·7 |
| 82 | 1  2 | 7·0 |
| 83 | 0  9 | 4·5 |
| 92 | 0  9·2 | 4·6 |
| 93 | 0  5·2 | 2·6 |

## HOOKER.

Line ranged at a point ¾ mile from terminal face, set at noon on April 4, 1889; and reset April 7th, 1889, at 8 A.M.

| Station. | Total Movement. Inches. | Daily Rate. Inches. |
|---|---|---|
| 1 | 3·3 | 1·1 |
| 2 | 8·2 | 2·9 |
| 3 | 12·0 | 4·2 |
| 4 | 15·4 | 5·4 |
| 5 | 12·8 | 4·5 |

## MUELLER.

Various marked stones first observed on the 29th March, 1889, and again on the 14th November, 1890, and 3rd December, 1893.

| Station. | 1889 to 1890. | | 1890 to 1893. | |
|---|---|---|---|---|
| | Total Movement. | Daily Rate. | Total Movement. | Daily Rate. |
| | Feet. | Inches. | Feet. | Inches. |
| 1 | 239·3 | 4·8 | 392·7 | 4·2 |
| 2 | 271·7 | 5·5 | 371·4 | 4·1 |
| 3 | | | 406·3 | 4·4 |
| 4 | 262·6 | 5·3 | 424·8 | 4·5 |
| 5 | 359·6 | 7·3 | 436·4 | 4·7 |
| 6 | 398·0 | 8·0 | | |
| 7 | 611·0 | 12·3 | | |
| 8 | 506·0 | 10·2 | 889·2 | 9·6 |
| 9 | 409·0 | 8·2 | 577·5 | 6·2 |
| 10 | 388·1 | 7·8 | | |
| 11 | 146·1 | 2·9 | | |

On the Tasman, Murchison, and Hooker, rods were carefully set and reset in lines across the glaciers; the instrument used was a five-inch theodolite. "A different method was adopted on the Mueller, in order to show the direction as well as the velocity. Four trigonometrical stations were placed on the huge lateral moraines near the lower end of the glacier ... and they were then used as bases for determining trigonometrically the positions of the stones on the ice. ... Each stone had a number painted on it, and every care taken in observing. ... The great steadiness of the ice motion is a noticeable feature. The stones ... have retained the same upright positions for nearly five years, and the rods supported on them by piles of stones in 1889 were found there in 1893."

The original positions of the stones on the Mueller Glacier must be stated, in order to draw any conclusions from their rate of motion:—

No. 1 is in the centre of the glacier 63 chains from the terminal.
,, 2    ,,    ,, 53  ,,  ,,  ,,
,, 3    ,,    ,, 61  ,,  ,,  ,,
,, 4    ,,    ,, 77  ,,  ,,  ,,
,, 5    ,,    ,, 89  ,,  ,,  ,,
,, 6    ,,    ,, 107 ,,  ,,  ,,
,, 7    ,,    ,, 122 ,,  ,,  ,,
,, 8    ,,    ,, 145 ,,  ,,  ,,
,, 9 is 10 chains from south side and 122 ,,  ,,  ,,
,, 10 ,, 2 ,,    ,,     111 ,,  ,,  ,,
,, 11 ,, 11 ,,   ,,      48 ,,  ,,  ,,

From these figures we see that the rate of motion is not constant, for the stones had not travelled so far towards the terminal face as to account for the decreased motion in 1893. It is also evident that the winter flow must be very sluggish, for the Mueller Glacier has a greater fall per mile than the Tasman, and, therefore, at least as great a rate of motion would be expected. It is evident that the lower average rate is due to the observations extending over winter as well as summer; all the other measurements record summer motion only.

The only glacier measured on the West Coast is the Franz Josef, the motion of which Douglas and I endeavoured to estimate in 1893. I put forward our results with some misgivings, for they are very startling. We placed a row of stakes along the ice, and reset the line again after the intervals mentioned in the table below, but though every care was used, the results can only be quoted as *approximate*, for a prismatic compass is not sufficiently accurate, and may be responsible for a considerable error in such observations. The figures, however, are just as likely to be under, as over, the mark, for it is impossible to say on which side the error would be. When it is considered that we could see with the naked eye the change in position of a mark on the ice after an interval of twenty-four hours, it is evident that the daily summer motion is very considerable. The side motion in the following table is accurate, for we had marks on ice and rock to check our results.

FRANZ JOSEF.

| Station. | Number of days. | Total movement. | Daily Rate. | Direction (magnetic). | Remarks. |
|---|---|---|---|---|---|
| | | Inches. | Inches. | | |
| Line I.—1 | 7 | 35 | 5 | 320 | 15 yards from north side. |
| ,, 2 | 20 | 600 | 30 | 335·30 | About 5 chains north side. |
| ,, 3 | 4 | 531 | 132·75 | 300 | |
| ,, 4 | 4 | 408 | 102 | 352 | |
| ,, 5 | 4 | 212 | 53 | 314 | |
| ,, 6 | 4 | — | — | — | No return. |
| Line II.—1 | 3 | 460 | 153·3 | 286 | 8 chains from north side. |
| ,, 2 | 3 | 474 | 158 | 308 | |
| ,, 3 | 3 | 600 | 200 | 285·30 | |
| ,, 4 | 3 | 621 | 207 | 260·30 | |
| ,, 5 | 3 | — | — | — | Crevasse opened—peg lost. |
| ,, 6 | 3 | 71 | 23·6 | 242·30 | 6 chains from south side. |
| Side motion by Arch Creek. | 7 | 57 | 7·28 | 335 | 8 feet from north side. |

Line I. was just above a small ice-fall 90 chains from the terminal face, and was set on the 22nd November, 1893.

Line II. was above another steep fall in the glacier, and at the foot of the great ice-fall, 190 chains from the terminal face. Peg No. 6 shows that the motion is considerably checked by Cape Defiance, and that the ice is taking a direction towards Harper's Creek. The very rotten nature of the ice at the margin of the glacier prevented a nearer approach to either bank here. This line was set on November 23rd, 1893.

The last station, by Arch Creek, was set on November 13th, 1893, and checked by marks on the rocks. It was 43 chains from the terminal face.

The above tables fully bear out the fact that a glacier moves faster in the centre than at the sides, and also that the rate of motion decreases as the terminal face is approached.

The actual influence of the tributary streams of ice on the motion of the main glacier cannot be decided from our observations. It would be interesting to set on foot a system of measurements, from which to arrive at some comparison between the rate of flow of tributaries and that of the main glacier, and, if possible, follow the movement of the ice of the various streams after they have joined forces—for I presume that, though to all appearances these streams unite, yet they do not *mingle*, nor do they lose their individuality altogether. If this is true, it would add to our general knowledge on the subject to try and follow the individual streams after they meet.

To draw satisfactory conclusions with regard to the rapidity with which a glacier flows at different angles of descent would be impossible from the above tables. Before any law can be laid down on the subject, much more complete measurements are necessary. The lines of pegs would have to be arranged at relative distances from the respective terminals. In the tables quoted, the rates of motion have been taken promiscuously, and only in two instances do the lines lie in at all similar positions as regards the terminal face. Reducing each glacier to 100 chains in length, we find by reducing the other figures that the lines of measurement were placed as follows:—

|  |  |
|---|---|
| Tasman, Line I. | 36·1 chains from terminal. |
| ,, ,, II. | 26·3 ,, ,, |
| Hooker | 10·2 ,, ,, |
| Franz Josef, Line I. | 13 ,, ,, |
| ,, ,, II. | 27·5 ,, ,, |

This gives us two cases in which the rates of motion can be in any degree compared, namely Line II. on the Tasman and Line II. on the Franz Josef.

Assuming that the figures returned for the latter glacier are correct, we find that its maximum rate is rather more than fourteen times as great as that of the former. This is a very startling difference until we examine the respective falls per mile of these two ice-streams, which are as follows:—

Tasman . Total fall 313·3 ft. per mile. From *névé* to terminal 187·7 ft. per mile.
Franz Josef ,, 941·1 ,, ,, ,, ,, 1064 ,,

The latter glacier, therefore, has three times as great a total fall, and nearly six times as great a fall per mile below the *névé* as the former. A series of careful observations, which would give us the motion of the tributary streams and their influence in retarding or helping the flow of the whole mass—together with systematic measurements in similar relative positions—combined with the average fall per mile, should give us considerable help in deciding the laws relating to glacier motion, the effect of obstructions in the valleys, and various other results which we cannot compute from our present observations. I have in the case of the Tasman and Franz Josef merely set down the particulars, for they are the only two that can be compared from observations already taken. Some one may, perhaps, be able to draw satisfactory conclusions from the figures, which I fear I am unable to do.

All these points of scientific interest can be determined in Europe with as great exactness as in the New Zealand Alps; but the great attraction of the latter is, that besides being able to make satisfactory observations, the observer has the pleasure of several virgin peaks to ascend, and also can observe the effects of a low snow and ice line in a warm climate. There is far greater *activity* in the Southern Alps than in the European, and therefore the effects of snow and ice are more marked, and more easily recorded. The avalanches are more frequent—falling night and day—than in Europe; the glaciers descend to a lower level, and the country is more shattered. Consequently the action of snow and ice in altering the conformation of the country is going on to a greater and more noticeable extent. I do not know the Caucasus, but am well acquainted with Switzerland, and know Norway more or less; my comparison, therefore, only applies to the two latter countries.

To a traveller seeking fine scenery the Southern Alps, especially the western side, offers a splendid field. I used to say that, below the snow line, New Zealand could not be compared with Switzerland—that was before I had been into the then unknown Western Ranges. I now say, without hesitation, that the Southern Alps can not only be compared to, but in many cases exceed in grandeur, the scenery of Switzerland. The only thing lacking is the presence of human interest, for there are no picturesque peasants and *châlets* to give an added charm to the wild and glorious scenes met with at every turn.

I often picture to myself a flood of tourists overrunning New Zealand, as they overrun Switzerland and Norway, and imagine future developments resulting from such an influx. We should see perhaps a fine hotel or two on Welcome Flat, others on Cassell's Flat, or at the head of the Twain; all of which localities far surpass many popular resorts in Europe in their attractions. However, may the day be far distant when hotels shall spring up like mushrooms in the glorious valleys of Westland, and the crack of the whip and clatter of the wheels of Cobb and Co.'s Royal Mail coaches disturb their solitudes, and awake protesting echoes from their awe-inspiring cliffs and precipices! I do not wish these glories of nature to be hidden from travellers—far from it—but should like to see a far-seeing Government constructing a few horse-tracks and huts in some localities, which Douglas or I can mention. A few hundred pounds a year less spent on experimental legislation would enable such tracks to be gradually made, and the localities thus rendered accessible would attract travellers, who would benefit the colony far more than Acts of Parliament.

Travellers, however, must not expect to view magnificent scenery without some trouble and a little discomfort in a young colony; but for all that they should not be debarred from seeing the finest sights for want of a few tracks. If the foregoing pages induce any persons to make an attempt to visit the Southern Alps for pleasure, or in pursuit of science or adventure, and if they cause the authorities to value properly one of the finest assets in the wealth of the colony, I shall feel that my work has produced some tangible result.

# APPENDIX.

## NOTE I.

### METEOROLOGICAL CONDITIONS OF THE SOUTHERN ALPS.

OWING probably to the low altitude of the Fox and Franz Josef Glaciers, together with their bulk and rapid motion, it has been assumed that a great difference exists between the east and west sides of the Southern Alps in the matter of glaciation. Various theories have been put forward, and the meteorological conditions have been called in to account for this peculiarity. The average rainfall at Hokitika is 126 inches a year and at Christchurch only 25 inches. There is apparently a great difference between the insolation and radiation, and also the degree of moisture, on the one side and the other of the island, *on the sea-board*. I do not pretend to be an authority on, or even to have attempted to study meteorology, and do not put forward my opinions on the subject from that point of view. At the same time I should like to point out a few facts regarding the rainfall and the glaciation of the Southern Alps, concerning both of which I am in as good a position as anyone to speak, for at present I have the honour to be the only person intimately acquainted with *both* sides of the High Alps.

In the first place—until recorded observations prove that I am wrong—I believe that the rainfall in Alpine districts near the Dividing Range is very little greater on the western slopes than on the eastern. My experience has been that the north-west wind—which brings the heaviest rain—is very nearly as wet for four, or possibly five, miles on the east as on the west. This region includes the greater proportion of the eastern glaciers, and it is within this area that the heaviest snowfall is found. Consequently, if I am correct in my premises, it follows that there is no reason why there should be a heavier snowfall, or greater glaciation, on the one side than on the other.

Now comes the second point, namely: *Is there more snow and ice on the West Coast than on the East?* I submit that there is not. True, there are a greater number of separate glaciers, but they do not compare with the eastern glaciers in size. They are due, not to a greater snowfall, *but to a larger number of valleys*. On the East Coast we find the Great Tasman Glacier flowing for nearly twelve miles *at the foot of* the Divide, and receiving many tributaries. Supposing that, instead of flowing in this direction, there were spurs and divergent ranges jutting out at right angles to the main range, from Elie de Beaumont to Mount Dampier, what would be the result? Assume, for sake of argument, that long spurs ran off at right angles from the former Peak, De la Bêche, Conway, Haast, and Dampier. I contend that if the valleys enclosed by these spurs narrowed and descended rapidly, we should have a second Franz Josef in the first-named valley; the Rudolph would equal the Balfour, if not exceed it; the Haast valley would contain a glacier little less in area than the Franz Josef Glacier, and the Hochstetter ice would exceed the La Perouse Glacier.

Examine other districts. The ice at the head of the Godley River far exceeds that on the western side; at the head of the Rakaia, the glaciers equal if not exceed those in the Wanganui River; on the Malte Brun and Hooker Ranges the chief glaciers lie on the *eastern*, not the *western* slopes.

It may therefore be said that—*even allowing the excess of rainfall on the western side of the Southern Alps to be as great as has been assumed* by those who have written on the subject—the difference in the matter of glaciation between the eastern and the western sides of the Dividing Range is not great, and the preponderance of snow and ice does not lie on the West Coast.

I have stated above that I believe the rainfall, for five miles on each side of the Dividing chain, is almost as great on the east as on the west. But beyond this limit we find a great excess on the latter side—probably $4\frac{1}{2}$ *times as great*. Consequently those glaciers which extend beyond that limit on the east reach the dry district, and those on the west are still within the wet region. Therefore, even if the glaciers on the former slopes descended in steep rock-bound valleys, their descent would not be quite so low or so rapid as those on the latter side; because they would not have the assistance which a very warm and frequent rainfall on their trunks must give. But so far from the former descending in steep narrow valleys, they flow down over comparatively easy slopes, and yet reach a low altitude.

To account, therefore, for the extraordinarily low position of the *only two* glaciers which descend to very low altitudes on the West Coast, we need not turn to meteorological conditions for a solution of the difficulty, but only need examine the formation of the country. *For even allowing everything—steep valleys, and climate—to aid them to reach a low altitude,* we find that, with the exception of the Fox and Franz Josef Glaciers, *the ice-fields of the West Coast do not reach such a low general altitude as those on the East.* And the reason that these two are so very exceptional is that they have such *large névés in proportion to their trunks,* combined with the narrow and steep valleys.

I have not intended to imply that meteorological conditions do not affect the glaciation of the Southern Alps, but merely wish to point out :—

(*a*) That *within the area of glaciation* the difference between the meteorological conditions is not nearly so great as supposed.

(*b*) That the glaciation of the West Coast is not greater than that of the East.

(*c*) That the altitude of the glaciers on the east is, as a whole, as low as, if not lower than, on the west.

(*d*) That it is not necessary to turn to meteorological conditions to account for the difference in glaciation, if any, for that can be accounted for entirely by the conformation of the country.

## NOTE II.

### ALTITUDES.

IN semi-official guide-books to New Zealand there are so many reckless statements with regard to the heights of the various peaks of the Southern Alps that it would be, perhaps, useful to give a list of the chief mountains. On p. 123 of "Brett's Handy Guide" we find Mount Aspiring given as "the highest after Aorangi (Mount Cook)," whereas it comes twentieth on the list; in another place the Hochstetter Dome is put down at 11,500 ft., and so on. Persons who take an interest in Alpine matters, and make annual excursions into the glacier districts, ought to be free from such mistakes, but some are just as reckless. To give only two examples: I have seen an account of the ascent of Mount Earnslaw in which it is called "one of New Zealand's three great peaks"—its place on the list is thirty-fifth. In a description of an attempt to ascend Mount De la Bêche, the narrator was within 1,000 ft. of the summit, and could see the upper part of the Tasman Glacier 7,000 ft. below him. This peak is only 9,815 ft. above sea-level, and the upper portion of the Tasman Glacier is at this point upwards of 5,000 ft. in height above the sea. A mistake, therefore, of over 3,000 ft. was here made! These errors are often made by persons who should know, at least, the approximate heights. The omission of units, tens and hundreds would not matter, but there is little reason to quote such exceedingly round figures when naming the thousands. I could give many other instances.

To avoid, if possible, the repetition of such mistakes in the future, the following list of the peaks over 9,000 ft. is given, with a few additional points of interest. Most of the figures are *exact*, and the rest are subject to very trifling alteration when new values are worked out from recent completed observations. I have confined myself to the central district, only giving one or two peaks outside —these are marked * :—

|  | Feet. |  | Feet. |
|---|---|---|---|
| Mount Cook (1) | 12,349 | Haidinger | 10,107 |
| ,, (2) | 12,173 | Stokes (La Perouse) | 10,101 |
| ,, (3) | 11,844 | The Horn | 10,063 |
| Tasman | 11,475 | The Minarets | 10,058 |
| Dampier (Hector) | 11,323 | Stokes, lower peak | 10,034 |
| Lendenfeldt | 10,551 | The Minarets, lower peak | 10,022 |
| Silberhorn | 10,500 | Glacier Peak | 10,017 |
| Malte Brun | 10,421 | Wilczek Peak | 9,968 |
| Hicks (David's Dome) | 10,410 | *Aspiring | 9,960 |
| Sefton | 10,359 | Hackel Peak | 9,949 |
| Elie de Beaumont | 10,200 | Hamilton | 9,915 |

APPENDIX. 321

|  | Feet. |  | Feet. |
|---|---|---|---|
| Haast | 9,835 | Baker's Saddle | 6,300 |
| De la Bêche | 9,815 | Ball Pass | 7,426 |
| Cook (4th peak) | 9,716 | Ball Hut (approx.) | 3,700 |
| Darwin | 9,715 | De la Bêche Bivouac | 4,782 |
| (Peak near Darwin) | 9,607 | Green's Bivouac (approx.) | 6,780 |
| Conway's Peak | 9,511 | Terminal Face Murchison | 3,452 |
| Green | 9,325 | ,, ,, Tasman | 2,354 |
| Hutton | 9,297 | ,, ,, Hooker | 2,852 |
| Hochstetter Dome | 9,258 | ,, ,, Mueller | 2,516 |
| ,, lower peak | 9,179 | ,, ,, Fox (aneroid) | 670 |
| *Arrowsmith | 9,171 | ,, ,, Franz Josef | 692 |
| Spencer | 9,167 | ,, ,, Victoria (aneroid) | 3,685 |
| *Earnslaw | 9,165 | ,, ,, Balfour ,, | 2,300 |
| (Peak near Darwin) | 9,144 | ,, ,, Douglas ,, | 3,663 |
| Footstool | 9,079 | ,, ,, { Horace Walker } ,, | 3,511 |
| Kron Prinz Rudolf Peak | 9,039 | | |
| Dwarf | 9,025 | ,, ,, McKerrow ,, | 4,006 |
| Graham's Saddle | 8,739 | ,, ,, Fettes ,, | 2,950 |
| Minaret's Saddle | 9,620 | Karangarua Pass | 5,641 |
| Lendenfeldt Saddle | 7,991 | Douglas Pass ,, | 6,115 |
| Harper's Saddle | 8,580 | | |

In addition to the above peaks, there are one or two more on the main chain outside this district—Tapuanuka in the Kaikoura Ranges, and Ruapehu, an extinct volcano, in the North Island—above 9,000 ft., besides hundreds of fine peaks of over 8,000 ft. in the Southern Alps.

## NOTE III.

### BLACK SWANS.

THESE birds are natives of the Australian continent, and were introduced, many years ago, into New Zealand by private individuals. They have since then increased enormously, and are to be found in thousands on our lakes and lagoons. I am not sure whether they were brought over to the West Coast, or found their way unaided,

Y

but it was not until the early seventies that they first became established on this side of the South Island.

Three or four pairs settled themselves on the large lagoon at Okarito, and, unaccustomed to the heavy and frequent floods which occur in the spring, they built their nests too near the water, and for two or three consecutive seasons were flooded out, and lost their eggs. After having shown no signs of increase for three years, they apparently decided to change their usual mode of procedure. Instead of building their nests out of reach of high floods, they still remained close to the water's edge, but got over the difficulty by erecting huge heaps of rushes and dry sticks, so constructed that when the floods came they floated on the surface of the water. Consequently the female birds could remain sitting on the eggs in spite of a general rise in the level of the lagoon, and on the flood subsiding they were again safely stranded on dry land.

Since this method was adopted, it has become the general practice of all black swans on the West Coast to construct floating nests, and they now never lose their eggs in floods. Whether the swans in other parts of the colony follow this rule or not, I do not know; but it certainly took them three years to discover this mode of avoiding floods on the West Coast. I was told of it by a man who is a keen naturalist, and who observed the whole proceeding from their first appearance to their adoption of the new plan.

## NOTE IV.

### MOUNT EGMONT.

IN company with Mr. C. Wiggins and my brother, R. T. Harper, I made the ascent of Mount Egmont in December, 1895, and was interested to find so much similarity between the vegetation on the peak and that on the Southern Alps. Egmont—Taranaki, as the Maoris call it—is an extinct volcano of 8,260 ft. in the North Island, and rises from a practically level plain of 200 ft. above sea-level—it is the most perfect cone that it is possible to conceive. Egmont has been said, by persons who have seen both, to rival Fusi-yama of Japan. From a mountaineering point of view, it is only a very steep walk, no hand-and-foot climbing being necessary, and there are in the summer well-beaten tracks to the summit. When we went up, it was coated with snow from 6,300 ft. to the top, and consequently we had a much less tedious walk than it would have been when the loose scoria is uncovered. However, curiously enough, an ascent with much snow on the peak is rarely, if ever, made; nearly all expeditions are postponed till the peak has put off his winter garb. In spite of the height above sea-level, there was no sign of glacier ice, and though in accounts of climbs, which are constantly appearing, we see mention of glaciers—notably the "Chadwick Glacier"—it is erroneous to suppose that glacier ice exists. There are several hard snow patches all through the summer, but no more. When snow is on the peak there is necessarily a certain amount of ice, or frozen snow, in which a step or two have to be cut, and this has given rise probably to the idea concerning glaciers.

The interesting feature to me in the climb was that from 4,000 ft. a low dense Alpine scrub was found extending up to about 5,000 ft. above sea-level. This grew to 15 ft. in height at the lower limit, and gradually became dwarfed to 2 ft. at the upper level. In nearly every respect it is the same as that found on the Southern Alps. With the exception of the Nei-nei, I saw all the other chief shrubs. Above this the grass and Alpine flowers were found—very poor in variety and size; however, the few varieties seen were also to be found on the Southern Alps. The transplanting of the *Ranunculus Lyalli*, *Calmisias*, and *Edelweiss*, would no doubt be simple and meet with success.

The reason why I was surprised at the presence of this vegetation is, that Egmont is isolated. The nearest mountain which attains an altitude sufficiently high to carry sub-alpine vegetation is Ruapehu (9,167 ft.), and it is eighty miles away "as the crow flies," and—with Mounts Tongariro and Ngaruhoe—is probably the only peak besides Egmont, on which such vegetation could be found in the North Island; in any case it is the nearest mountain to Egmont of sufficient altitude.

Ngaruhoe (7,376 ft.) is still an active volcano, but Tongariro

(6,500 ft.) and Ruapehu are extinct. The latter has a hot crater lake surrounded by perpetual ice, which by its melting feeds the lake. Accounts of this peak are to be found in the "Proceedings of the Royal Geographical Society, 1885," p. 272; also "New Zealand Lands and Survey Reports of the years 1893-4 and 1894-5."

## NOTE V.

### FITZGERALD'S PASS AND C. E. DOUGLAS.

IT is a remarkable instance of the truth of the old proverb—"a prophet is not without honour save in his own country," that when Mr. FitzGerald and Zurbriggen went over the Range from the Hermitage to the West Coast, the Christchurch and other newspapers wrote articles on the "discovery," stating that it was a notable fact that Mr. Douglas had been for some years looking for a pass to the Hermitage, and had been unsuccessful, though he had actually been up this very river—the Copland; and that Mr. FitzGerald, who had only been in the colony for a few weeks, had been able to do that which had beaten the Government explorer. The latter stated in the *Alpine Journal* of August, 1895, that parties had tried to find a pass but had been unsuccessful, and therefore he himself decided to undertake the task. Both these observations are most unjust, because the instructions Douglas had were to find some saddle "*free of snow and ice for three months every year,*" in order to allow a track to be taken to the Hermitage from the West Coast. There had been numbers of passes made since 1857 from coast to coast, but they were either not in the Hermitage district, or did not fulfil this condition. FitzGerald's Pass itself does not fulfil the requirements of the Government, and should never have been noticed as valuable in *that* respect, though it is so in others. No doubt a track could be taken over it, and it will have to be accepted as the best and only route in course of time.

Douglas stated in his report which he made, with a map, in 1892 —*a map used by both FitzGerald and myself in our journeys down the Copland*—that he found a high saddle fairly free of snow, but *as it would not be free for the period required* by Government, he did not ascend or cross it. The observation, therefore, was made recklessly, and without any inquiry into the real instructions or requirements of the Government. To anyone who knows Douglas and his work in the past, the idea that he could not force a way over a pass of this kind is absurd, for no one has done such good work as he has in the New Zealand Alps. To give more than a bare record of his explorations would be impossible, for he began traversing and exploring the rivers of South Westland in 1874 and continued, with few interruptions, until November, 1895—when he had to leave me in the Karangarua River. The full records of his work are in the Survey Office at Hokitika, and as space will not allow me to enter into details, it will be sufficient to enumerate shortly the actual rivers explored by him, taking them in their order of position, not of date.

In 1884, Douglas explored the Arawata River, at the head of which is the grand Alpine district of the Aspiring group, several fine summits rising between 8,000 and 10,000 ft. above sea-level. From an Alpine point of view they are untouched, for Douglas did not go above the snow-line, except in the case of the Bonar, a fine "disconnected" glacier, similar though far smaller than the Douglas up the Twain River. The Waipara River drains the ice-field and flows into the Arawata.

The Waiatoto River, coming from the ranges near Castor and Pollux, two fine peaks of nearly 9,000 ft., he has traversed to its head. It drains the Therma and Pickel-haube glaciers, the former of which he went up. He describes it as being walled in like the Balfour by wonderful terraces and cliffs of rock rising sheer for 2,000 ft.—one of the most striking scenes he has witnessed. The "ice lines" are, in this valley, most marked, and the rocks polished and grooved in a very noticeable manner. In fact Douglas constantly refers to the head of these two rivers as containing some of the grandest and most magnificent scenery he knows, and it is not very difficult to reach. If it exceeds in grandeur the country he and I have seen together, I can only say it must be very wonderful. He twice reached the summit of the Dividing Range here, low saddles to Otago being the rule.

The Okura River is another draining the Divide, and was explored by Douglas. It has a low pass at the head which he crossed —the Actor Pass—and which is accessible for a horse on the eastern side.

The Landsborough River, the longest on the West Coast, was first explored and traversed by a party led by Douglas. Particulars of this river can be seen in a previous chapter. Going further north, we come to the Poringa River, with its tributary the Otoko, and the Copland River which with the Turnbull, Cascade, and Maitahi Rivers, were all explored, mapped, and reported on by him. The Turnbull and Cascade should have been mentioned earlier, as they lie "away south."

His work in conjunction with me has already been chronicled, and had the above explorations been recorded as fully, we should have at least three volumes of the same size as this. His reports are voluminous and most interesting. He has a quaint, amusing style of describing the natural features of the country, which are, however, most faithfully recorded, and the theories advanced are valuable. Unfortunately, I cannot persuade him to write an account of his work; it is no use to tell him he ought not to keep such interesting matter to himself. Had I time to look over his diaries and reports I could, with help, produce a very thorough and valuable record of this southern country—but I am not a man of leisure, and the diaries are in the safe of a Government Department.

As a naturalist and explorer, Douglas has had few equals in New Zealand; no amount of hardship or difficulty deterred him from his purpose; he was painstaking and accurate in his reports; he has explored chiefly from love of such work, and only recently received aid from the Government; he never exaggerated his difficulties or the results of the expedition; he never attempted to take credit for a single thing which he had not done; he always allowed his companion, when he had one, a full share in the honour of the exploration, and never tried to add to his own credit by depreciating the work of others. In fact he is, in my opinion, an ideal explorer. A vast deal of his travelling was done alone, with only a dog for company. He carried little, until the gradual disappearance of birds compelled him to increase his loads.

Douglas says he does not believe in a man unless he has a petty vice, and that is the reason, I suppose, why he allows the virtue of modesty to become almost a vice! These notes concerning him are written without his knowledge, for I feared to risk a refusal if I asked his leave. I have taken the responsibility because I feel that a man who has done what he has in the past, and who is too worn out to do much more, ought not to be allowed to hide his light under a bushel. It is of public interest, to New Zealanders at any rate, that he should be known as a great explorer. Many who have done work of a hundred times less importance are well known in the colony—and some who have done far less in other parts of the world, with all the advantages of porters, guides, and other luxuries, are of world-wide renown, while for want of a few words, Douglas remains unknown, save to a small circle—even in New Zealand. Had he written, or lectured, on his work, he would have ere now received honours from learned societies as a naturalist and explorer. I trust he will forgive me for dragging him before the public from his remote corner of Westland; and hope he will look upon my action in so doing as evidence of the great admiration I have for his past work.

## NOTE VI.

### EARLY EXPLORATIONS.

The names of those whose work has materially advanced our knowledge of the topographical features of the central portion of the Southern Alps should be recorded.

On the East Coast, in 1862, Sir Julius Von Haast made the first recorded expedition into the Tasman district.

In 1867 and 1870 Mr. E. P. Sealy photographed and explored the Tasman, Hooker, and Mueller to their upper basins, also the Godley and Classen Glaciers at the head of the Tekapo River.

In 1882 the Rev. W. S. Green practically ascended Mount Cook, and his climb should be considered the real first ascent. Beyond information respecting the eastern slopes of that peak, his climb was not of topographical importance.

In 1883 Dr. Von Lendenfeldt made a survey—with some rather bad errors, owing to a faulty theodolite—of the Tasman Glacier.

In 1889, '90, '91, Mr. T. N. Brodrick completed the survey of the Eastern Glaciers, including the Godley and Classen on the Tekapo River.

In 1890 Messrs. G. E. Mannering, M. Hamilton, and I made the first exploration of the Murchison Glacier and valley as already related.

In the same year Messrs. G. E. Mannering and M. Dixon on Mount Cook, and R. Blakiston and I on Harper's Saddle, confirmed the fact that Mount Cook did not lie on the Dividing Range.

On the West Coast, in the seventies, the Geodesical Surveyor carried a triangulation down the coast, fixing all the high peaks; and between 1892 and 1895, Douglas and I explored, as related in the foregoing pages, all the valleys and glaciers of Westland in this district.

Thus, with the one exception of the Tasman Glacier, the exploration of this district, both east and west, has been carried out by the enterprise of New Zealanders. It remains to be seen when and by whom the Alpine exploration of other districts, named in Chapter I., will be completed. Let us hope that New Zealanders will not allow the credit of that work to be taken from them by visitors from other countries, and that they will hold their own in the matter of climbing peaks as well.

## NOTE VII.

### MEASUREMENT CAIRNS AND PHOTOGRAPHS FOR REFERENCE.

WHILE on the Franz Josef I placed some cairns on the eastern bank of the glacier, and for sake of reference while there, distinguished them with letters of the alphabet, with the letter M prefixed, to avoid confusion with other survey stations. These are in brackets in the following table, and the cairns are numbered from the terminal face upwards—*i.e.* southwards.

| Cairn. | Distance from nearest ice. | Height above the edge of glacier. | Date. |
|---|---|---|---|
| I. (M.F.) | 39 feet | 25 feet | Sept. 19th, 1894. |
| II. (M.E.) | 48 ,, | 20 ,, | ,, ,, |
| III. (M.D.) | Photograph cairn | (see below) | ,, ,, |
| IV. (M.) | 198 feet | 70 feet | Sept. 16th, 1894. |
| V. (M.A.) | 23 ,, | 15 ,, | ,, ,, |
| VI. (M.B.) | 111 ,, | 40 ,, | ,, ,, |
| VII. (M.C.) | 30 ,, | 20 ,, | ,, ,, |

The two first are on the south and north banks of Arch and Rope Creeks respectively. No. III. is on the north bank of a small creek reached after passing Rope Creek. No. IV. is some 18 chains south of No. II. on the line of stones forming a remnant of lateral moraine. No. V. is on the south bank of a deep gorge, about 30 chains south of Rope Creek, on a large hummock of rock. No. VI. is about 4 chains south and 50 ft. below a large erratic block on the lateral line of stones just before reaching the Rocky Cape (E on the map); and No. VII. is on a knob of rock south of the last small creek immediately below the said point E. In December, 1893, No. IV. was the only cairn erected, and was 209 ft. away from the ice, according to a note I have by Douglas. There is some error in this figure, because the ice had noticeably retreated—and *not advanced*—in September, 1894.

For future visitors I may mention that Arch Creek is the deep gorge at the mouth of which an isolated *roche moutonnée* stands, and Rope Creek is a large stream flowing in a shallower gorge some 20 chains south of the former. The edge of the glacier mentioned in the third column is the point at which *the ice meets the rock.*

The cairns are heaps of stones of two and three feet high, on the bare ice-worn bank, and easily seen. The only other mark we have is a + on the back of the Sentinel Rock, about 4 ft. from the ground and 2 chains from the western end; but I fear it will be not easily found, except by us, for it has weathered a great deal. The paint, which should have been sent to the Franz Josef, went on to Gillespies and we were unable to use it. This + I have already mentioned in Chapter XI., also the general retreat visible on my second visit. Photographs from the Sentinel Rock, looking east;

from the Barron Rock, showing the contact of ice and rock at the outlet on the eastern bank; from the point at which the horse-track descends on to the gravel flat, showing the whole terminal face; from Cairn No. III., in the above table, looking south, to show the encroachment of the ice on the rock bank; and from Cairn VI., looking towards point E, can be compared with similar photographs taken by me, and in possession of the Alpine Club Glacier Committee. Unfortunately a dozen or more taken in September, 1894, especially for the purpose of comparison, were lost when my load went out to sea on the way to Gillespies.

On the Fox Glacier, owing to mishaps and general bad luck, we only built two cairns. One of these is on a small terminal moraine, between the fringe of scrub and the ice, right at the terminal face. This was on April 4th, 1894, distant 43 yards from the ice, in a direction of 96° 30′ (magnetic); and lines drawn at 150° 30′ to the south, and 25° 30′ to the north, touch the furthest advance of ice on each side. On the north side of the terminal face the ice touches the rocky hillside until within 8 chains of the actual terminal, and then it leaves the rock and continues to the snout at a distance of 10 to 30 yards from the hillside. On the southern side we erected a cairn on a ledge at the foot of the Cone Rock, which ought easily to be found. On April 25th, 1894, at a bearing of 355 (magnetic), the ice was 37 yards distant.

Photographs should be taken from a stone in the large creek which joins the river here, about 1 chain from its inflow into the river, looking north to show the terminal, and east to show the encroachment of the ice on the side of the Cone Rock. Photographs also showing the position of the ice on the various rocky capes on the north side of the valley can be compared with those I have taken.

The only other Westland glacier which has any special interest for future observation is the Douglas. I think a series of photographs of the *névé* would be valuable to show whether it is gaining, losing, or stationary. A picture taken from Douglas Pass, or the lateral moraine just below the northern end of the gravel flat, would show any alteration, if compared with those I have taken. Unfortunately I had too much to do when in the Twain valley to spend time over erecting cairns; for the work done there occupied about twelve hours each day, and as I was working alone it was quite enough to do, without even an additional hour or two to fix cairns. It would, however, be a most interesting thing to compare the rate of increase or decrease of the trunk with that of the névé. For there must be some law of relation between the bulk of the supply and the glacier ice, and this may help, a little at least, towards its discovery.

These marks, and suggestions as to photographs, have here been recorded in hopes that someone, in the future, may make fresh measurements for comparison. The two first-named glaciers may expect many visitors, for they are easily reached, but the Douglas is too remote to have much attention paid it for many years. The Franz Josef, however, is the most likely of the three to attract visitors, for it has a horse-track to its terminal. I therefore made a point of placing the various cairns along its side. In the interests of glacier science, it is to be hoped that some visitor will check the position of the ice, and send the results, with photographs, to the Alpine Club, London. Everyone should remember that *any measurement or photograph, however insignificant, is of value, which shows the position of the ice with regard to some conspicuous object.* We may not realise the value of such ourselves, but those investigating the laws of glacier motion and action, in the Alpine Club Committee, can put forward *theories* if we send them the *facts*. Surely it is worth while to devote a day to such useful work, instead of spending the whole time in scaling peaks, and bringing back no information of value.

# INDEX.

## A.

ACCIDENTS, 102, 103, 184, 207, 243
Actor Pass, 326
Almer Glacier, 61, 67
Alpine Club, 279
Alpine vegetation, 265
Altitudes, note ii., 320
Aorangi, 11, 12
    Maori meaning of, 13
Arawata River, 325
Ark, the, 7
Arrowsmith, Mount, 3, 320
Arthur's Pass, 2
Aspiring, Mount, 7, 320
Avalanches, 146, 230, 248

## B.

Baker's Saddle, 24, 263, 320
Balfour Glacier, 5, 85, 153, 320
Balfour River, 85
Ball Hut, 15, 320
Ball Pass, 19, 320
Beach travelling, 81
Birds, 35-52
    decrease of, 43, 150, 219, 220, 292
Bismarck Range, 71
Bivouacs, 137, 247
    De la Bêche, 27, 320
    Green's, 18, 320
Black butterfly, 266
Black swans, 321, Note iii.
Black weta, 266
Blakiston R., 23
Blazing tracks, 64, 132
Blow-fly, 266
Brodrick, T. N., 23, 179, 224, 307, 328
Brodrick's Pass, 188, 225, 226
Boulders, 91, 128, 133, 142, 258, 261
Bush or Forest, 32
Burster Ridge, 76
Burton Glacier, 5, 76, 77

## C.

Callery Gorge, 49
Callery River, 10, 49
Camping, 34
Camps, 42, 50, 90
    burnt, 114
Canaries, 39
Cape Defiance, 54
Cascade Moraine, 155, 177
Cassell's Flat, 186
Castle Rock, 130
Castor and Pollux, 7
Cats, wild, 43
Cave camp, 138
Chadwick Glacier, 323
Chancellor Ridge, 71, 102
Check-shirt bird, 147
Christmas Day, 208
Christmas Flat, 208
Classen Glacier, 4
Climatic conditions, 8
Cock-a-bullies, 202
Coleridge Creek, 206
Cone Rock, 100
Conway Peak, 66, 320
Cook, Mount, 6, 11, 13, 23, 25, 48, 84, 290, 320
    Ascents of, 18, 19, 26
Cook River, 5, 80, 84, 126
Cook River Flats, 80
Copland River, 6, 28
Craig's Peak, 87
Crows, 39
Crystals, 87

## D.

Daisies, 265
Dampier Mount, 25, 320
Dan Koeti, 273
Darwin Mount, 19, 320
Dechen Mount, 220, 226
De la Bêche Mount, 26, 27, 320

Diggers, 158
Digging gold, 30, 31, 157
Dividing Range, 151, 163, 180, 232, 317
Dixon Glacier, 308
Dixon, M., 19. 328
Douglas, C. E., 29, 45, 63, 75, 103, 179, 183, 200, 205, 253, 292. Note v., 324
Douglas Pass, 234, 320
Douglas Glacier, 6, 235, 320
Doughboys, 139
Dovetail Gorge, 203, 206, 257
Dry Camp, 65
Ducks, 40
   Blue, 42
   Paradise, 42, 204
Dug-out Canoe, 45

E.

Earnslaw, Mount, 7, 320
Edelweiss, 58, 266
Edible plants, 33
Egg-cup Rock, 133
Egmont, Mount, 322
Elie de Beaumont, Mount. 14, 76, 320
Erratic blocks, 81, 101, 107, 122, 130, 142, 258, 262
Expeditions, First, 18, 19, 20, 23, 26, 27, 327
Exploration, 9, 16
Exploration, First, 211

F.

Fettes Peak, 208, 227
Fettes Glacier, 229, 320
Fire in camp, 114
Fitzgerald, E. A., 27, 108, 124, 235, 270 et seq., 324, Note v.
Fitzgerald Glacier, 6, 212-235
Fitzgerald Pass, 280, 329
Five navigators, 89
Floods, 77, 134, 184, 194
Fog, a race with, 92
Footstool, the, 320
Forks, the. 76
Fox Glacier, 5, 71, 98, 106, 120, 320
   Terminal face, 122, 305, 320
Franz Josef, 5, 47, 311, 320
   Névé, 61, 163, 275
   Rocks, 52
   Terminal face, 8, 51, 305, 320
   Waves, 52
Fritz Glacier, 71

Futtah, 181
Fyfe, 26, 28, 201
Fyfe Glacier, 212

G.

Gabardine, 65, 150
Gales, 72, 73
Geology, 231
Geodesical survey, 297, 298
Gillespies, 82
Glaciers, altitude of, 7, 8, 320
   Advance of, 123
   Ancient, 87, 108, 154, 155, 156, 256, 263
   Comparison of, 303, 305
   Disconnected, 153, 236, 303
   Retreat of, 156, 172, 176
   Side motion, 311
   Summer motion, 165, 311
   Winter motion, 123, 175, 310
Glacier Dome, 18
Glacier Peak, 320
Glorious, Mount, 245
Godley Glacier, 4
Government Preserves, 43
Graham's Saddle, 162, 275, 320
Grasshoppers, 267
Green, W. S., 11, 327
Green's Bivouac, 18
Green's Fifth Camp, 17
Green, Mount, 77

H.

Haast, J. von, 327
Haast Pass, 7, 221
Haast River, 6, 221
Haidinger, Mount, 124, 320
Harper Saddle, 23, 320
Hermitage, 14, 15, 279
Hicks, Mount, 25, 320
Hochstetter Dome, 14, 320
Hokitika, 5
Hooker Glacier, 4, 14, 23, 309, 320
Horace Walker Glacier, 6, 212, 238, 244, 320
Horn, The, 124, 320
Hot Springs, 50, 55, 56, 120
Howitt, Mount, 211

I.

Ianthe Lake, 45
Ice Cave, 78

# INDEX.

Ice Insects, 268
Ice Lamination, 121
Ice Lines, 170, 177, 261
Incense Plant, 218, 264

## K.

Kakas, 40
Kakapos, 40, 41
Karangarua Gorge, 178
Karangarua River, 5
Keas, 40, 109, 110, 111
Kiwis, 39, 68, 144, 188
Kron Prinz Rudolf, 26

## L.

Lame Duck Flat, 204
Landsborough River, 6, 214-233
Landsborough Valley, 214
La Perouse, 5, 25, 89
Liebig Range, 14
Lindt Glacier, 18, 25
Lizards, 267
Lydia, Mount, 7

## M.

Maimai, 51
Malti Brun, Mount, 14, 21, 26, 320
Mannering, G. E., 11, 16, 19, 210, 328
Maori Companion, 210, 216, 229, 245, 250
Maori Tradition, 13, 78, 273, 288
Map-making. *See* preface and 297-298
Maporika Lake, 48
Marchant Glacier, 6, 289
Maunga Mount, 235
McKerrow Glacier, 237, 320
McKenna Creek, 91
Memorable Meeting, A., 279
Minarets, The, 26, 320
Moltke, Mount, 71
Moraines, Ancient, 80, 120, 155, 168, 171
Moraines, 20, 54, 91, 122, 152, 157, 171, 233, 289
Moraine Spider, 267
Morse Glacier, 212
Moulins, 121
Mountain Lily, 265
Mountain Wren, 39, 268
Mueller, G., 214, 215
Mueller Glacier, 4, 309, 320
Mueller Rock, 52
Murchison Glacier, 4, 19, 20, 308, 320
Musk Camp, 215

## N.

Nei-nei, 58, 69
Névé, 61, 88, 163
Ngaruhoe, 323

## O.

Owl, 268

## P.

Pass to Tasman, 108
Photographing, difficulties of, 92, 93, 143, 297
Pigeons, 40
Pikipiki, 33
Pilkington Glacier, 212
Pioneer Peak, 312
Pioneer work, 300
Plants, edible, 24, 33
Poison camp, 183
Pukaki, 4

## Q.

Queen's Knoll, 187
Queen's Rock, 131

## R.

Rabbits, 225
Rainfall, 8, 318
Rakaia, 3, 10
Rangitata, 3, 10
Ranunculus Lyalli, 2, 265
Rata-trees, 101, 130, 166
Regina Creek, 193
Road Party Camp, 222
Roberts, G. J., 3, 25
Robins, 38
Roches Moutonnées, 52
Roon Mount, 69
Ruareka Peak, 288
Ryan's Peak, 85

## S.

Scenery, Description of, 48, 57, 88, 111, 146, 199, 212, 227, 287
Sealey, E. P., 327
Sealey's Pass, 5
Sealey, Mount, 26
Sefton, Mount, 7, 25, 320
Sentinel Rock, 52, 174
Sierras, 287, 298
Silberhorn, 320

Snow Line, 7, 8
Spencer Mount, 5, 10, 66, 76, 77
Spiders, 267
Spike, The, 292
Starvation Saddle, 22
Stewart's Station, 221
Stokes Mount (La Perouse), 24, 25, 320
Strauchon Glacier, 6
Sub-Alpine Flora, 266

### T.

Taipo, 248
Tasman Glacier, 4, 5, 11, 14, 308
Tekapo Lake, 4
Thunderstorms, 199, 248
Tony's Rock, 141
Topography, 9, 25, 151, 298
Topsy, 95
Totara River, 49
Trees, Reasoning Powers of, 130
Troyte River, 204
Tuckett, F. F., 279
Twain River, 6, 190
   Gorge, 190
Tyndall, Mount, 4

### U.

Unser Fritz Falls, 61, 161

### V.

Vegetation, 31, 33, 35, 64, 70, 189, 264
Victoria Glacier, 71, 102, 107, 320
Von Lendenfeldt, 11, 300, 328

### W.

Waiho River, 5, 49
Waimakariri River, 5
Waitaki River, 4
Wanganui River, 3, 5, 10
Wataroa River, 5, 10
Weasels, 43, 219
Wekas, 36, 66, 117, 160
Welcome Flat, 283, 288
Westland or West Coast, 29
Wicks Glacier, 212

### Z.

Zurbriggen, 28, 235-270, *et seq.*

THE END.

PRINTED BY J. S. VIRTUE AND CO., LIMITED, CITY ROAD, LONDON.

www.ingramcontent.com/pod-product-compliance
Lightning Source LLC
Chambersburg PA
CBHW051737300426
44115CB00007B/599